Letters and news from
THE TRENCHES
and the home front

Letters and news from
THE TRENCHES
and the home front

Edited by Robert Hamilton
Photographs and Facsimiles from the Daily Mail

ATLANTIC PUBLISHING

A UNIQUE WINDOW ON THE GREAT WAR

The course of the First World War, the great offensives and epic battles that preceded the defeat of Germany and her allies, is well documented. Historians provide polished analysis of the what, where and when. But how did the humble Tommy doing his bit see things? Or those keeping the home fires burning? Amid the geopolitics and grand military strategies of the Great War lay myriad human dramas; lives hanging in the balance, forever altered if not lost; families torn asunder with reunion down to chance or Fate. The flow of correspondence between front and home puts flesh on the bones of the struggle. Personal letters lend an immediacy and intimacy to the conflict that sweeping overviews cannot hope to achieve. It is only from contemporaneous accounts and reports that we can see a war being played out in real time; that we can become the privileged witness to thoughts, opinions and deeds set down at a time of immense dislocation and stress. To delve into the wide-ranging correspondence and articles that make up this volume is to study the conflict from a worm's-eye view rather than bird's-eye perspective; the feel of a ground-level, live struggle rather than a distant historical event.

Frontline experience, naturally, is well represented. One soldier describes reaching the German line to find it strewn with fallen enemy, but his work was not done. "On, on, over the bodies. The Germans were in a second trench line, a hundred yards or so behind the first. A yell and a dash and out jumped the Germans in swarms, as keen for a fight as our own men. They went for each other with rifles and bayonets – bang, stab, scuffle. One shot at close quarters, then the cold steel. You can't miss. You may fall. You don't bother about that – there is no time. The thing is, bowl over as many of the enemy as you can and recover your bayonet quick." In the fog of war, such acts of heroism routinely went unsung. The psychological toll of physical engagement is also evident. A doctor discourses on how a shell whistling close by can incapacitate every bit as much as a direct hit, reflections that show science struggling to comprehend what we now term PTSD.

Even during lulls in the fighting, there is the misery of vermin-infested trenches to contend with. "Alas, they never go short of food," says one soldier of the rats that were constant companions. "One thinks with a shudder of their loathsome feasts and impish gambols among the unburied dead of No Man's Land." Another describes attempts to snatch precious sleep by resting his head on a rum jar or petrol tin, trodden on by each passer-by. Better not to look too far ahead in such

circumstances. "You get into the habit," as one puts it, "of living each day as a separate little life of its own."

On the home front, there are different preoccupations. One correspondent testifies to the tastiness of perch as an answer to food shortages; another that dispensing with afternoon tea would aid the war effort. Women's entry into the labour market in erstwhile men's occupations prompts the assertion that it is "changing their looks, their manner and their character". Young women engaged in dispatching chickens appeared to have undergone a change in attitude, at least, according to another contributor, who avers: "Either their natural sensitiveness had become dulled, or they were holding it strongly in check." The "frightfulness" of the Zeppelin raids sparks much debate, raising the question of whether we should repay the enemy in kind and bomb civilian targets. Recruitment also generates plentiful comment. One veteran writes that more effort should be made to get 20-year-olds into uniform. Weigh that against a poignant letter from beyond the grave – written by one such 20 year-old - to be given to his parents in the event of his death; a missive that had to be delivered. Two other bereaved parents find a girl's picture in their son's effects and search for the sweetheart of whom they had no knowledge and who might have become their daughter-in-law. Then there is the mother who has lost four sons, gratefully spared a dreaded fifth telegram when the boy next in line is granted exemption from service. Some take a firmer view on the defence of the realm, such as the correspondent advocating withdrawing pension rights from "conscientious shirkers".

Luminaries of the literary world also take up cudgels. For John Galsworthy the cause is horses wounded at the front, draught animals who "know none of the sustaining sentiments of heroism; feel no satisfaction in duty done". Thomas Hardy bemoans the "mutilation" of Rheims Cathedral, while Sir Arthur Conan Doyle's sharpens his pen to warn of the submarine threat. Household names and household heroes juxtaposed in print, with contributions from far beyond the native shores.

This book gives a unique window on the wartime experience of those who served, both in khaki and on the home front. It is a powerfully evocative, viscerally raw and often haunting record of an imperilled people airing their views on a host of war-related issues; a record that vividly captures the mood of the country at a crossroads in world history.

THE BRITISH ARMY IN FRANCE

The British Expeditionary Force is in France. This news, officially promulgated to-day, discloses the great secret. The military authorities have accomplished a thrilling feat. With perfect secrecy they have mobilised, assembled in British ports, and moved to France the largest army that ever left British shores. We may justly congratulate them on their energy and organisation. They have worked in silence with admirable efficiency.

This is not the first time that a British army has gathered on French soil. But it is the first time that British troops have entered France to aid her. The cause for which that gallant army marches today is the same as that for which its forefathers fought in 1814 and 1815. It has gone forth to defend the right, to protect the weak against lawless attack, to uphold the great cause of human freedom against the onslaught of military despotism. It stands, as the England of 1814 stood, for liberty against tyranny. And in that fight, however protracted, however terrible, it will not quail. He was a wise French soldier who said that England, when she had once taken hold, never let go. Through whatever suffering and sacrifices this army which she has sent forth with all her love and faith will carry her standard to victory.

18 August 1914

Letter from Lieutenant—, of the 26th Regiment of Field Artillery.

For the last five weeks we have undergone colossal fatigue, lack of sleep, and desperate combats. The 10th Corps has been constantly on the move since the first day of the campaign. My battery is especially always with the advance guard. Our horses are for the most part worn out; we are now using Belgian and French horses. There are moments when they simply cannot go on; then they just lie down—add to that the numerous wounds which they receive. From five in the morning to eight at night we are under the enemy's fire without being able to eat or drink. I was so tired I could not keep on my horse even at a walk.

Towards midday our battery was literally plastered with the enemy's shrapnel and shells. We could not make the least movement behind our guns without running the risk of being shelled.

There was a murderous battle which lasted from Sunday, the 6th, to Wednesday, 9th September. The 10th and Guard Corps were the chief sufferers. Let us hope that we shall soon have a decisive battle and so end these masses of carnage—even in bivouac at night the troops are not safe.

An airman dropped four bombs. Three of these were effective, with the result that 20 horses were killed, 10 wounded, 4 men killed, 8 wounded. We no longer get any letters; the post office motor-car of the 10th Corps has been burnt.

14 November 1914

TREMENDOUS GERMAN LOSSES.

(A staff officer writes to his wife.)

The war is absolutely different from what I expected it to be. There is no what I call glamour about it or any kind of chivalry.

The Germans now are always attacking, and must be losing a tremendous number of men. I was up in the roof of a farmhouse yesterday when the Germans were making a fierce attack against this brigade, watching the guns bursting shells on the Germans as they were lying in a long line in the open. The shrapnel simply mowed the Germans down and left a great many dead on the field. This morning at two o'clock the Germans made a big attack on our right, and the noise of rifle and shellfire was just like a heavy thunderstorm.

Our headquarters to-day are in a large farmhouse, where we have all the telephone and field telegraph wires joining up. We have a good strong cellar to go into if they start dropping high explosive shells on us, and also a pit dug in a ditch behind the house.

We have our breakfast every morning now at five o'clock before dawn, but if there is no fighting on we have it at 8.O. or 7.O. We are usually, or when possible, asleep by 9p.m. I have not had my clothes off for five nights now.

2 November 1914

BELGIANS' RUSE AFTER ANTWERP.

(Letter to a friend in Manchester by a Belgian soldier in Holland after the evacuation of Antwerp.)

Many of us and our English comrades by surprise crossed the Dutch frontier, which we only realised when Dutch infantry disarmed us. This happened at eleven o'clock in the night at Clinge, on the Dutch border. The number of Dutch soldiers there was quite insufficient for severe control. Seven of us, knowing that being in Holland meant for us forced rest, held a secret council, and a plan to escape that fate was soon made. We must regain Belgian territory, find some civilian clothes, and come again into Holland as refugees. Then we might be able to join our Army somehow.

The darkness of the night was favourable to our scheme and without much difficulty we found ourselves soon in Belgium again. No sign of the enemy, but a red sky westwards; the village of Kemscke had been set on fire.

After two hours' dragging through woods we found the ruined village empty. The houses saved from the fire were open, not a soul was there. We found some peasants' clothes and left our uniforms. Soon we were in Holland again. The dawn was breaking; it was Sunday.

We followed the crowd of refugees, and, partly on foot, partly in train, we reached Rotterdam.

Our case is so general that the neutral Government of Holland has given orders that no help may be given to soldiers in civil dress to cross to England. But that's all; we are free to go, and ask not better than to go as soon as possible. The fare will be a matter of only a few days, and once in England we will soon be able to reach the front.

2 November 1914

NAVY

A survivor from HMS Pathfinder:
My twenty-eighth birthday, and I reckon I have had a good birthday present by having my skin save whole, and am glad to say I can still put the following words "I am still alive and well."

I got off scot-free bar a few scratches on my legs. All the ship's company were in the fore part having their tea; in fact, your humble was just going to get his. I saw a flash and the ship seemed to lift right out of the water, down went the mast and forward funnel and fore part of the ship, and all the men there must have been blown to atoms.

I bobbed down for a few seconds for fear of being hit by debris (some of it weighed nearly 112lbs) which was blown sky-high. I scrambled to the quarterdeck, which was littered with mangled corpses, and looked about for something to cling to. The captain shouted, "To the boats!" but there were only two, and they were smashed. The other boats and practically all woodwork had been left on shore. We fired a gun for a distress signal. By this time the ships was practically covered with water.

"Every man for himself," and I at once pulled off my boots, coat, and trousers and over I went. I think I broke all swimming records trying to put as much space between me and the ship, being afraid of suction.

Turning round the last I saw of the ship about fifty yards away, the after end was sticking upright in the air about a hundred feet. She then gradually heeled over towards me and sank. Then I swam again to get out of its way, thinking it might hit me as it came down, but it cleared me all right. It was all over in about five minutes from the start. When she sank something blew up and on came the water, and round and round I went like a cork. A reindeer buoy came speeding by me, and I grabbed it, and that was what kept me afloat.

14 September 1914

Above: **Lord Kitchener was selected as Secretary of State for War the day after the conflict was declared. Kitchener had been the hero of the campaign to win back the Sudan in 1898, after which he commanded troops in the Boer War. He then became Commander-in-Chief in India, reorganising the Indian Army.**

Above left: **HMS Pathfinder was the first ship sunk by a torpedo fired from a submarine. She was just off St. Abbs Head, Berwickshire, Scotland, on 5 September 1914 when she was hit by the German U-21. There were only eighteen survivors out of an estimated crew of 270.**

Below: **The Canadian Infantry march to the front line in October 1916.**

Opposite: **Tommies on their way to the trenches. They smile broadly at the camera knowing the photograph will be sent back to England.**

MR. ASQUITH'S PROMISE TO THE NATIONS.

We shall never sheathe the sword, which we have not lightly drawn—

Until Belgium recovers in full measure all and more than all that she has sacrificed;

Until France is adequately secured against the menace of aggression;

Until the rights of the smaller nationalities of Europe are placed upon an unassailable foundation.

Until the military domination of Prussia is wholly and finally destroyed.

—Mr. ASQUITH at the Guildhall.

11 November 1914

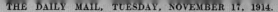

FIRST VICTORIA CROSSES OF THE WAR.

GLORIOUS DEEDS REWARDED.

NATIONAL MONUMENT TO LORD ROBERTS.

PRINCE OF WALES AT THE FRONT.

MORE FLOODS TO STOP THE ENEMY.

KAISER'S PUZZLE IN RUSSIA.

NOT ENOUGH GERMANS TO GO ROUND.

RUSSIAN CHECK AND AN ADVANCE.

MILLION A D. WAR.

MORE MONEY & MO TROOPS.

NINE TALES OF IMI

SAVING THE G
INFERNO

LIES REGAIN IMPORTANT
LO

ISH OR

VOTE OF £225,000,

MR. ASQUITH'S STATEMENT.

INCREASED PAY F OFFICERS.

ATTACK ON CENSOR

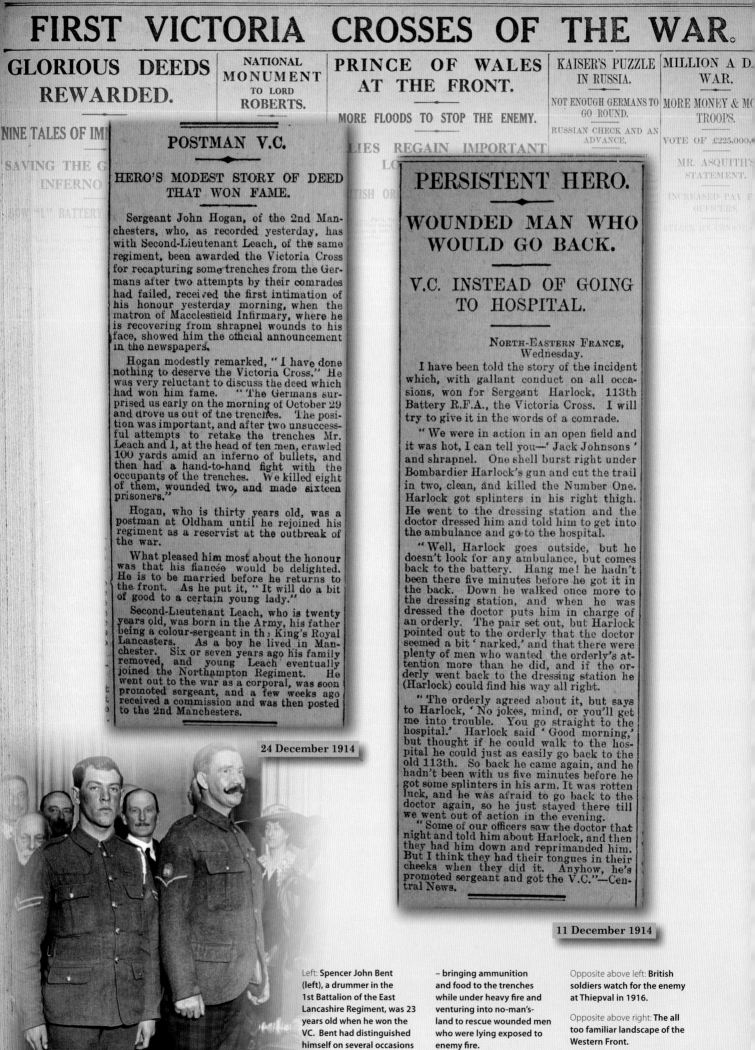

POSTMAN V.C.

HERO'S MODEST STORY OF DEED THAT WON FAME.

Sergeant John Hogan, of the 2nd Manchesters, who, as recorded yesterday, has with Second-Lieutenant Leach, of the same regiment, been awarded the Victoria Cross for recapturing some trenches from the Germans after two attempts by their comrades had failed, received the first intimation of his honour yesterday morning, when the matron of Macclesfield Infirmary, where he is recovering from shrapnel wounds to his face, showed him the official announcement in the newspapers.

Hogan modestly remarked, "I have done nothing to deserve the Victoria Cross." He was very reluctant to discuss the deed which had won him fame. "The Germans surprised us early on the morning of October 29 and drove us out of the trenches. The position was important, and after two unsuccessful attempts to retake the trenches Mr. Leach and I, at the head of ten men, crawled 100 yards amid an inferno of bullets, and then had a hand-to-hand fight with the occupants of the trenches. We killed eight of them, wounded two, and made sixteen prisoners."

Hogan, who is thirty years old, was a postman at Oldham until he rejoined his regiment as a reservist at the outbreak of the war.

What pleased him most about the honour was that his fiancée would be delighted. He is to be married before he returns to the front. As he put it, "It will do a bit of good to a certain young lady."

Second-Lieutenant Leach, who is twenty years old, was born in the Army, his father being a colour-sergeant in the King's Royal Lancasters. As a boy he lived in Manchester. Six or seven years ago his family removed, and young Leach eventually joined the Northampton Regiment. He went out to the war as a corporal, was soon promoted sergeant, and a few weeks ago received a commission and was then posted to the 2nd Manchesters.

24 December 1914

PERSISTENT HERO.

WOUNDED MAN WHO WOULD GO BACK.

V.C. INSTEAD OF GOING TO HOSPITAL.

NORTH-EASTERN FRANCE,
Wednesday.

I have been told the story of the incident which, with gallant conduct on all occasions, won for Sergeant Harlock, 113th Battery R.F.A., the Victoria Cross. I will try to give it in the words of a comrade.

"We were in action in an open field and it was hot, I can tell you—'Jack Johnsons' and shrapnel. One shell burst right under Bombardier Harlock's gun and cut the trail in two, clean, and killed the Number One. Harlock got splinters in his right thigh. He went to the dressing station and the doctor dressed him and told him to get into the ambulance and go to the hospital.

"Well, Harlock goes outside, but he doesn't look for any ambulance, but comes back to the battery. Hang me! he hadn't been there five minutes before he got it in the back. Down he walked once more to the dressing station, and when he was dressed the doctor puts him in charge of an orderly. The pair set out, but Harlock pointed out to the orderly that the doctor seemed a bit 'narked,' and that there were plenty of men who wanted the orderly's attention more than he did, and if the orderly went back to the dressing station he (Harlock) could find his way all right.

"The orderly agreed about it, but says to Harlock, 'No jokes, mind, or you'll get me into trouble. You go straight to the hospital.' Harlock said 'Good morning,' but thought if he could walk to the hospital he could just as easily go back to the old 113th. So back he came again, and he hadn't been with us five minutes before he got some splinters in his arm. It was rotten luck, and he was afraid to go back to the doctor again, so he just stayed there till we went out of action in the evening.

"Some of our officers saw the doctor that night and told him about Harlock, and then they had him down and reprimanded him. But I think they had their tongues in their cheeks when they did it. Anyhow, he's promoted sergeant and got the V.C."—Central News.

11 December 1914

Left: **Spencer John Bent** (left), a drummer in the 1st Battalion of the East Lancashire Regiment, was 23 years old when he won the VC. Bent had distinguished himself on several occasions – bringing ammunition and food to the trenches while under heavy fire and venturing into no-man's-land to rescue wounded men who were lying exposed to enemy fire.

Opposite above left: **British soldiers watch for the enemy at Thiepval in 1916.**

Opposite above right: **The all too familiar landscape of the Western Front.**

ALONE IN A TRENCH.

(Private Albert J. Woollard, formerly an Essex constable stationed at Brentwood, now serving with the Grenadier Guards, writes.)

I am resting now and need it badly, but I hear that the French are doing some splendid work where they relieved us. They tell us that they found hundreds of German dead where we had been at work, but we had a warm time.

That was where the famous Prussian Guard made their attack. But what a sad reverse they got! We stood in our trenches, took a good aim, and mowed them down in scores. Then the Field Artillery did the rest. We could see them running backwards and forwards in a wood, not knowing which way to go. Two days later I had a terrible experience. We were guarding some trenches near——. The German attack was on the right causing the —— to retire a few yards. I was in the trench nearest to the —— with one chum when this happened and I knew we two were in for a warm time.

My chum was wounded then, and I bandaged him up while the Germans were coming on. Then my chum said, "Look, there are two Germans firing down the trench at us!" I said we must make a run for it, and told him to go for the wood while I got to another trench. I don't know whether my chum reached the wood. I found the next trench unoccupied and my company had retired and we two in the end trench had not received the message. There was nothing to do then but run for my life and join my company. A machine gun was firing at me the whole way, besides rifle fire and shclls bursting over my head. I had my kit-bag in one hand, rifle in the other, and was wearing my great-coat, but I did hop it. I passed several dead comrades, killed by shell fire.

How I got through is a marvel. We were sleeping as we stood upright in the trenches. I had not washed for a fortnight and was a regular nut. A merry Christmas to the boys of the Brentwood division.

24 December 1914

SHELL HOLE LIFE.

With the passing of elaborate trench systems the shell hole comes into its own as a field work. At one time, before artillery was so numerous, infantry had to dig themselves in with entrenching tools—an unenviable task under fire—but now the frequent shell holes provide ready made rifle pits.

The number of shell holes is a protection in itself. Only some are garrisoned, and if the garrisons have taken cover skilfully and refrained from making themselves conspicuous the Hun is in a quandary as to which holes are occupied and which are not.

Barraging No Man's Land is not always effective. A trench has been in the same position for months, and even years, and the artillery have the correct range of every traverse and firing bay, but to barrage shell holes many of which have been made within only a few hours is another matter. It can be done, but not always effectively.

Garrisoning a shell hole is a task demanding the greatest endurance. The greater self-reliance of the Briton renders him better at this work than the Hun. In small groups the Hun has a tendency to surrender—hence the German authorities prefer to have their men under the direct supervision of officers in elaborate trench systems, such as the Hindenburg line.

In a shell hole movement is possible only at night, and only those who have experienced it can appreciate the discomfort of squatting on one's haunches all day, unable to move about, and conscious that any indulgence of the craving to stand erect and stretch oneself will ensure a bullet through the head or the betrayal of the position.

Away back in the trenches if a man is hit there is an aid-post available, and if a "strafe" begins there is a dug-out handy. In a shell hole, if a soldier is hit at dawn he must wait until darkness before he can be removed, while overhead there is no protection against either weather or shells. In a trench, if anything goes amiss there is communication with officers and headquarters; in a shell hole the garrison is limited very often to fewer than a dozen men under the command of an N.C.O. Everything depends on him.

That he is "up to his job" is proved by such men as Corporal David Hunter, of the Highland Light Infantry.

SIDNEY HOWARD.

2 October 1918

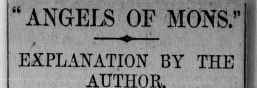

"ANGELS OF MONS."

EXPLANATION BY THE AUTHOR.

THE BOWMEN: AND OTHER LEGENDS OF THE WAR. By ARTHUR MACHEN, with an Introduction by the Author. Simpkin, Marshall, and Co., Ltd. 1s.

PUBLISHED TO-DAY.

The legend of the Bowmen will pass into history and be remembered with the wonderful Retreat from Mons itself.

The story, brilliantly drawn by Mr. Arthur Machen, was published in the London *Evening News* on September 29 last. From the point of view of artistry it deserved to be widely read and discussed, but its author cannot have foreseen that after ten months the public should be clamouring for the story again in volume form.

Mr. Machen has written an admirable introduction in which he explains how the legend of the Bowmen came to be conceived by him and how its origins were composite. "First of all," he says, "all ages and nations have cherished the thought that spiritual hosts may come to the help of earthly arms, that gods and heroes and saints have descended from their high immortal places to fight for their worshippers and clients. Then Kipling's story of the ghostly Indian regiment got in my head and got mixed up with the mediævalism that is always there; and so 'The Bowmen' was written."

In every direction it was read as the story of a vision not invented but only framed and set in order by a craftsman. Mr. Machen repeatedly denied its truth, yet parish magazines reprinted it, sermons were founded upon its vivid revelation of the supernatural, "confirmation" of its truth came in a great flood from the trenches and the hospitals. According to the introduction, "the snowball of rumour that was then set rolling has been rolling ever since, growing bigger and bigger, till it is now swollen to a monstrous size."

THE LINK.

Mr. Machen shows how "The Bowmen" became the story of the Angels of Mons. "In 'The Bowmen' my imagined soldier saw 'a long line of shapes with a shining about them.' And Mr. A. P. Sinnett, writing in the May issue of the *Occult Review*, states that those who could see said they saw a row of shining beings between the two armies. Now I conjecture that the word 'shining' is the link between my tale and the derivative from it. In the popular view, shining and benevolent supernatural beings are angels and nothing else, and must be angels, and so I believe the Bowmen of my story became the Angels of Mons. In this shape they have been received with respect and credence everywhere or almost everywhere.

"And here I conjecture we have the key to the large popularity of the delusion—as I think it. We have long ceased in England to take much interest in saints, and in the recent revival of the cultus of St. George the saint is little more than a patriotic figurehead. . . . The appeal to the saints to succour us is certainly not a common English practice . . . but angels, with certain reservations, have retained their popularity, and so when it was settled that the English Army in its dire peril was delivered by angelic aid the way was clear for general belief and for the enthusiasms of the religion of the man in the street."

The introduction is scarcely less arresting than the legends themselves.

10 August 1915

MONS ANGELS: TWO VIEWS.

The Rev. John Hilton, of St. Matthew's Church, Essex-road, Canonbury, London, preaching yesterday on "The Angels of Mons," said:

"I find no difficulty in believing that God did actually raise the veil between the seen and the unseen and that He allowed some of those tired, weary, worn-out defenders of right, honour, purity, and truth to see that there was a wall of protection between themselves and the Germans, and that that wall of protection was a body of His own ministers, whom we call angels."

The Rev. Father Ross, at St. Joseph's, Aldershot, said:

"The men were probably overcome by marching and the heat of battle, and this is the view which thoughtful Catholics take of the story of Mons. Yet God did at times so manifest His divine will and intervene in the affairs of man."

1 August 1915

The first British battle against the Germans at Mons on 22 August 1914 resulted in heavy casualties for the Allies who were then forced to retreat. Welsh writer Arthur Machen penned a short story entitled 'The Bowmen', which was subsequently published in The Evening News the following month. Set during the Mons withdrawal it featured phantom bowmen from the Battle of Agincourt. Despite his insistence that it was a fictionary tale, readers preferred to believe it was real, with the archers saving the British Army. This was further reinforced by soldiers giving eye-witness accounts of visions of heavenly archers coming to help them.

Top: **Allied troops in France. The German Army came tantalisingly close to taking Paris in August 1914. Many fled the capital, fearing that its fall was imminent.**

Above left: **The first German trenches along the bank of the River Aisne where the Kaiser's army were on the defensive.**

Below: **British troops outside Mons. The training received by the British Expeditionary Force put an emphasis on rapid marksmanship, with the soldiers able to fire accurately at a target fifteen times per minute. This skill was to prove very effective in later battles.**

Opposite: **Soldiers, laden with equipment, make their way to the front-line.**

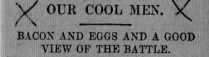

GERMANS AFRAID TO CHARGE.

THE SATISFACTION OF FIRING BACK.

From a Manchester Soldier:
What do you think of our Army now? I wonder what the Kaiser thinks about it. His famous crushing machine turns out to be an easily demoralised crowd of automatic, soulless clods, who don't know the meaning of individual effort and efficiency. Take away their driving power (the fear of their brutal officers) and they stand a useless mass of brainless, bewildered men (they have a certain amount of pluck, but they don't know how to put it to account).

Three times on the run they came up to within 100 yards of our lines, when a determined charge, with their superior numbers, must have wiped us out; but, no, as soon as they spotted us preparing with steel to meet them about-turn they went helter-skelter for their very lives. No wonder our infantry hold them in contempt. Their cavalry are very daring "until they spot ours"; then the same things happen again.

Their artillery is grand; their shooting deadly accurate, as we found out to our cost. Their guns throw a far heavier shell than ours; it explodes with a deafening crash. At Cambrai and Mons the air was simply alive with them, and how any man lived through it was a marvel. One thing I noticed—a lot of their high explosive shells never burst. Several fell just behind me, splashing me with great clods of earth. I fully expected, as each one screamed over my head, to be blown to atoms, but there must have been a good angel keeping watch and ward over me, for not one exploded that came over me. I am afraid that if we were not granted the satisfaction of firing back there would have been a kind of panic; for what with the terrific explosion of the shells and the perpetual hiss and whistle of bullets, the place was a hell on earth. Only the excitement of firing, I think, kept our men so cool. There seemed to be a grim determination to slay, and slay as many as possible,

and the cool yet rapid shooting of our fellows proved too much for even the vast crowd that never seemed to thin out. They staggered and reeled back like drunken men, then ran for cover, lashed by our gunners, who are superb.

GRAND OFFICERS.

So are our cavalry; they simply don't care a cuss for anything or anybody, and when our fellows get going with the bayonet, as they did at Cambrai later in the day, they are perfect devils; they repeatedly drove twice and three times their number back and back again; the trouble is to keep them from charging. Our officers are grand and they cheer our men by their laughter and jokes in the trenches. They are gluttons for work and are always in the thick of it, always cheerful, cool, and quick to see and seize any chance of delivering a punishing blow at any part of the enemy's lines.

I watched a duel between our guns and the Germans, who had the advantage in numbers, but for sheer bulldog courage our gunners take the cake. They simply would not give it best. They pounded away with a grim determination that had to succeed, which they eventually did by forcing the Germans to beat a very hasty retreat. I should like before I close to tell you how hard the drivers of the motor lorries worked; they seemed untiring, and there is no doubt about it they saved many a man that Wednesday who otherwise would never have got away.

SLAUGHTER ON A BRIDLE PATH.

A Lieutenant in the Scots Greys: We were holding a sort of sunk road, and we waited till the Germans were about 100 yards away before we let fly. They were coming up the road packed close in fours, and when they saw what they were in for they would have turned, but their officers drove them on with their revolvers. It was a murderous fire they were coming to, but they simply had to, and we continued to mow them down as fast as they closed up their ranks; unfortunately the rest of them somehow came through the woods on either side, and as we were in danger of being cut off we were told to retire.

18 September 1914

OUR COOL MEN.

BACON AND EGGS AND A GOOD VIEW OF THE BATTLE.

An officer writes:
I am sitting on the battlefield, with a good view of the battle, eating bacon and eggs! Nothing perturbs us. Even in the midst of our consolidating the enemy trenches the postman arrived with the day's letters!

Extract from a Scottish officer's letter:
For coolness in action our Scottish troops are unbeatable.

One great act of gallantry was recorded yesterday when our trench mortar battery was in action. The mortar shells, which are packed in cases, were being handed from man to man to the man working the gun, and as the shells were being passed one of the men heard the fuse burning inside a shell. Knowing that the shell would explode in a few seconds, he coolly walked with it in his hands to a trench, into which he threw it. The shell exploded immediately afterwards, and by this wonderful act of bravery he saved the lives of the whole of his section.

A private of the Scottish Borderers was wounded in the knee just after capturing two Germans. One of the Germans gave the Borderer a cigar, which the Scot began to smoke. Just afterwards he saw a stretcher lying on the ground near by; this he made the Germans bring along, and, seating himself on it, he directed them to our dressing station.

13 July 1916

Their officers drove them on with their revolvers. It was a murderous fire they were coming to.

He did **his** duty.
Will **YOU** do **YOURS**?

MILITARY MAP No. 2
LARGE SCALE
PRICE THREEPENCE

Daily Mail

FRIDAY, DECEMBER 11, 1914.

ALNELL/G CYDER

THE CARE OF THE WAR-HORSE AND THE STORY OF THE GUN

He has to be taught to lie still on the ground while he is being used as cover for his rider who snipes over his side

SAVE THE WAR HORSES!

MR. JOHN GALSWORTHY'S APPEAL.

"Honour to the Army Veterinary Corps! As far back as October 16 they had already 'dealt with some 27,000 horses . . . saving the lives of many.' They are a splendid corps doing splendid work. Please help them!" writes Mr. John Galsworthy, the author, in a stirring appeal for contributions to the Royal Society for the Prevention of Cruelty to Animals Fund for Sick and Wounded Horses at the Front, which has the approval of the Army Council.

"Twenty-five horse-drawn ambulances and twenty-five motor-lorries are specially required at once. Now that the situation is more in hand we can surely turn a little to the companions of man. They, poor things, have no option in this business; get no benefit out of it of any kind whatever; know none of the sustaining sentiments of heroism; feel no satisfaction in duty done."

Donations should be sent to Mr. E. G. Fairholme, hon. secretary of the fund, 105, Jermyn-street, S.W.

11 December 1914

Above: **Soldiers seemingly at a loss how to free a horse and its load, stuck fast in the glutinous earth.**

Below: **During the conflict it soon became obvious that the days of the cavalry charge were over and horses and mules were primarily used as a means of transport.**

ILL-TREATED HORSES.

To the Editor of *The Daily Mail.*

Sir,—There is one form of cruelty to horses to which I would like to draw the attention of people passing over the London bridges.

This is, the way many too heavily laden carts and vans are driven up the slopes of the bridges.

The way this is done is as follows: One of the men gets off the van, taking the whip with him; the other rushes the horse or horses at the slope, jerking and tugging at the reins; the first man runs alongside the horse hitting with all his might under the horse's flank and below the knees and hocks.

Instead of helping the horse it impedes him, as he is trying to get his legs out of reach of the whip instead of properly putting his feet to the ground and pulling the load; also, hitting under the flank with a whip ought to be forbidden, as it causes after-effects which may be fatal to a horse. WALTER WINANS,
Carlton Hotel, Pall Mall, S.W. 1.

1 August 1917

When war broke out, the British Army had 25,000 horses but needed four times as many, so animals were requisitioned from farms and businesses all over the country. Transporting them to France placed many stresses on the horses, but once trained and pressed into service they faced even more arduous and extreme conditions.

TRAINING A WAR HORSE.

You cannot just buy an animal and put him into a cavalry brigade. The real war horse has quite a long education before he is proficient, an education almost as severe and certainly as comprehensive as that of the recruit who ultimately rides him into battle.

It was in no small way due to the mettle of the horses they rode that Lord French was able to say of the British cavalry at the first battle of the Marne that they were able to do as they liked with the enemy. The well-bred cavalry horse possesses a highly strung nervous system, but when properly trained he will face barbed wire and even rush an entanglement when put to it, regardless of lacerated legs and flanks. But his education is begun carefully, or he may be ruined by a few careless lessons.

His education must not begin too soon after being brought to camp or his legs will not stand the strain, and the first step is the most important. If he is terror-stricken, or if his temper is aroused, he may never get over the incident. He is walked around free from the leading rein, and after he has been accustomed to have a man mount rapidly on his sensitive back he is taught to kneel with his rider.

This is an elaborate lesson. The first stage consists in getting him to bend his forelegs slightly before he gets to the stage of lying down on his side. He has to be taught to pull up in his own length from a gallop, to stand steady while his rider fires from his back and to lie still on the ground while he is being used as cover for his rider who snipes over his side.

*   *   *

One of the most difficult things required of a war horse is to get familiarised with the sword in fighting from his back. Here the greatest care is taken or he may be frightened at first and never recover his nerve. In real warfare it is a common trick for a cavalryman to aim his first blow at his opponent's horse. This is especially the case with lancers, for no horse will stand after being pricked on the nostril or lip. He will wheel round if he has room to turn, and the fight becomes a chase.

It is a peculiar fact, however, that when a horse knows his rider well he will face blows if properly handled such as would not usually be expected of him. A brigade have been known, for instance, to go through three lines of bayonets and then through a barbed-wire entanglement, trampling everything underfoot as if it were straw. Within the last year there was a case of a Canadian troop who charged two lines of German machine guns and rifles, wheeled and came back at them again, and rode through them for the second time, leaving a trail of dead and wounded Huns as a punishment. Seventy-five per cent. of the men who started on that charge were casualties—but practically all the Huns were dead or dying. And the horses stood it well, bless them.

When it is considered that the average weight, including equipment, carried by a cavalry horse is something like twenty stones it must be admitted that these fine, intelligent animals deserve every care. And they get it too. For when the big retreat begins it is they who will keep the Germans on the run. S. M.

1 July 1918

THE LAST MATCHES.
Corporal G. W. Cooper (16th Lancers).

I have now my fifth horse since we started. Two were shot under me.

I could do with some matches. We have about three matches left in our squadron, and when one is struck everybody crowds round. We have had a terrible shelling, but it has averaged a hundred German shells to kill three Englishmen.

19 September 1914

NEUVE CHAPELLE CHARGEFIERCE 90 SECONDS.

STIRRING ACCOUNT BY COMBATANTS.

At seven the bombardment began, 350 guns blazing at a short target. It was, I suppose, the most terrific bang a soldier has ever heard and the grandest sight one could imagine. It shook the trenches and the barricades. Shells burst everywhere with great flashes of flame.

We saw Germans breaking cover in all directions. It was a hard job to keep our men down; they were constantly jumping up to shoot. Our officers insisted on their crouching at the bottom of the trenches until they were wanted. Otherwise they would have been raked by our own shrapnel fire. They laughed and bobbed down. They sang and shouted, "That's one for Wipers!" (Ypres). "That's got them!" "Roll on, and let's get at 'em!" They were mad for a scrap with the cold steel.

The bombardment lasted three-quarters of an hour. Then a whistle blew, and our men came shinning out of the trenches, officers in front, carrying rifles and bayonets. They ran across the "No man's land" of 200 yards which divided the trenches, raked all the time by German machine guns from concealed positions.

A STEADY RUSH.

No firing from our chaps. Firing takes time. A swift, steady rush in open order. The first line of German trenches was reached. No Germans there saving the dead and wounded, as many as ten in a single traverse. On, on, over the bodies. The Germans were in a second trench line, a hundred yards or so behind the first. A yell and a dash and out jumped the Germans in swarms, as keen for a fight as our own men. They went for each other with rifles and bayonets—bang, stab, scuffle. One shot at close quarters, then the cold steel.

You can't miss. You may fall. You don't bother about that—there is no time. The thing is, bowl over as many of the enemy as you can and recover your bayonet quick. This scrap lasted, I should say, about a minute and a half. Many Germans threw down their rifles and held up their hands. My own battalion captured fifty prisoners in as many seconds.

1 April 1915

BROTHER HEROES.

CLARENCE LINNELL.   **PERCY LINNELL.**

These two brothers, sons of Mr. and Mrs. G. H. Linnell, 23, Mill-lane, Lincoln, were both killed by the same shell while they were talking together in a trench "somewhere in France." They were members of the 1/4th Battalion of Lincolnshire Territorials. A third brother, who is in the same company attended their funeral.

26 July 1917

"COME ON, THE KING'S!"

DYING OFFICER'S CRY.

IMMORTAL COURAGE AT NEUVE CHAPELLE.

(An Officer of the King's Liverpool Regiment writes.)

NORTH FRANCE, Saturday

I am writing to tell you what I can gather of the action of the 10th. The brigade was ordered to assault the German trenches, following a severe bombardment by the artillery. A and B companies of the regiment were detailed for the assault.

A company was commanded by Captain Feneran, who has spent all his life in the regiment and went out from Aldershot in August with us and was wounded on the first day of the battle of the Aisne. B company was commanded by Lieutenant Snatt, who was also one of the original band who sailed in August and was wounded during the battle of the Aisne.

The word being given, these two companies charged, but, unfortunately, the wire in front of the German trenches had not been cut by the artillery preparation, consequently the men got hung up on it and the Germans had time to bring their Maxims into action. The assault therefore failed and we lost heavily.

All eye-witnesses agree in saying the men behaved in a most magnificent way. I saw the artillery observing officer this morning. He said that they were absolutely splendid. Company-Sergeant-Major Jones actually stayed five minutes under the German wire trying to cut it. He got back without being hit. Lieutenant Millar also got up to the wire and, jumping into a side trench, cut off the enemy for a considerable time. He was wounded in the leg.

Colonel Carter himself is universally said to have behaved with wonderful gallantry, for, though wounded through the shoulder, he refused to come out of the fight and continued in command during the day. Poor Feneran was killed leading his men—a very sad loss, indeed, to us, but a gallant end. Snatt was shot through the leg, but managed to crawl back. But Madden, Webb, O'Donoghue, and Young were killed during the assault, the latter being hit actually on the enemy's wire entanglements.

Poor little Webb was heard shouting: "Come on, the King's" as he lay dying. He will not be forgotten by the old regiment. Hayes-Newington and seven men were killed by a shell. One of these was a son of a former officer of the King's.

We lost 219 all told, of whom 119 are wounded. The regiment was warmly praised by General Fanshawe, commanding the brigade, and he said that although the assault was brought to a standstill owing to the wire, still it pinned a great number of the enemy to their ground and made it easier for the rest of the first army to succeed on our left in carrying Neuve Chapelle.

19 March 1915

IN THE WOOD AT "WIPERS."

BREEZY TALES BY ONE OF THE CHESHIRES.

FROM OUR SPECIAL CORRESPONDENT.
BASIL CLARKE.

NORTH OF FRANCE, Saturday.

The sound of a good, honest Lancashire accent in a hospital on the French coast filled chiefly with French and Belgians was a welcome surprise and sufficient temptation to take one over to his bed for a chat. His name, James McManus, was tattooed on the forearm which lay on the bed coverlet. He belonged to the Cheshire Regiment, 3rd Battalion, but his home was at Ashton-under-Lyne, in Lancashire, and from that town and county came his welcome speech.

A hospital orderly passed at the moment and threw on to the bed a packet of cigarettes.

"Do you fine here," said the patient, with a smile, as he reached forward for them. He had been at La Bassée and later at Ypres.

"Pretty hot in both places," he said. "Lots of Germans there. Did their best to get through us, and we lost lots of men. But the Germans lost fair swarms.

"Near Ypres (not 'Eepre,' but 'Wipers' the soldiers call it) we were in a wood with rifles and machine guns. Some Germans came for us who were every man over six feet. I've heard since they were the Prussian Guard. Some of them seemed to think we couldn't shoot at all because they came up within easy range, took off their coats, and calmly started digging trenches. We popped off man after man of them before they decided that we were better shots than they had thought.

"There was some tough fighting in that

30 November 1914

WHAT THEY READ IN THE TRENCHES.

WHY WE MUST RECRUIT.

By W. BEACH THOMAS.

NORTHERN FRANCE.

People at home ought to know what a splendid confidence our soldiers show in the preparations being made in England. They express it in terms fit to shame every shirker who does not come to their help.

The Tommy loves to draw gorgeous pictures of the hundreds of thousands of men who will keep coming up from England to occupy and make sure the ground he has won. He tells you how this mass of men will shorten the war and save thousands of lives. He sits happy in his trench for twenty-four hours at a time and receives an attack of thousands quite cheerfully, joking even at the moment of a bayonet charge, because, as he has told me many times, these great reinforcements are on the way, and he has only to hold on to win the greatest war in the world. It is the recruiting news he looks at first when the papers reach the front.

THE BURDEN DOES NOT LESSEN.

Let there be no mistake—the burden he is bearing does not grow less. Though all is well, the German attack, especially against the British lines at Ypres, is still tremendous. It needs the utmost of pluck and endurance to resist it and conquer it. If the men were not splendid the Germans would still swarm through to the Channel ports and knock at the gate of England. The sleepiest village in England would know what war meant then, and the most selfish man understand that only the weight of the whole nation could save either his interests or his good name. I do not believe any man of military age could talk to one of our Tommies coming cheery and confident from the intolerable strain of the battle and not enlist at once. The mere knowledge of the number of men enlisting at home is worth a victory, because of the spirit it puts into the soldiers, British and French and Belgian.

12 November 1914

Above and opposite above: **Members of the Northumberland Fusiliers return from the front-line.**

Opposite below: **Soldiers receive intensive training sessions to prepare for the demands of trench warfare.**

Below: **The Royal Warwickshire Regiment enjoy a well-earned sleep in the open.**

BELGIAN STRUGGLES BY THE YSER.

(A wounded Belgian Soldier writes.)

I have been all through the war since Liège, but I assure you that never was there such fierce fighting as on the banks of the little River Yser.

I shall never forget a night which we passed, almost starving, in the trenches—a night which was followed by a very tragic morning. Indeed, very early (it was still dark) our sentries heard some noise in the water. The alarm was given and in a few seconds we, rushing forward, were much surprised to see a bridge which the Germans had made in haste—planks on little boats, the boats having wheels with pneumatic tyres—and almost without noise the work had been very cleverly done. Well, we were on the spot, our bayonets ready, and terrible hand-to-hand fighting began, while others of our men, by a well-directed fire, succeeded in destroying the newly made bridge.

Those Germans who had already crossed could not get back, but they defended themselves in a splendid way; only a few surrendered. The German bayonets are longer but our men were quicker and there were some very strong fellows among us.

The Yser will always be a glorious name for our Army, but will remind anyone who was in it for all his life of the horrors of war.

In many fights on the banks of the river, when preventing the Germans from crossing it, several men on both sides fell in the water. The badly wounded were not able to swim and were often drowned. In one of those fights I got a bullet in my leg, but could drag myself a hundred yards farther, when happily two comrades took me up and carried me to the ambulance.

23 December 1914

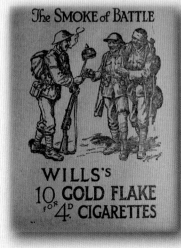

THE SPIRIT OF THE GURKHAS.

An Officer.— When the Gurkhas were told that they were wanted to fight in the great war they asked, "Shall we all be killed?" and the officer said, "Not all." They enquired, "Shall a great many be killed?" He replied, "Possibly." Then they asked, "Will a hundred come back?"

"Perhaps so." "That will be enough," they said, "our people will know that we have fought well."

Top: **Once the signal is given troops leave their trenches at Morval. A shell can be seen exploding in the distance.**

Above: **Gurkha Rifle battalions in the front line trenches in Palestine.**

THE FIGHT IN THE WOOD.
(From Lance-Corporal W.H. Seddon.)

There is no doubt whatever that our little Army saved Paris and France by our organised retreat from Mons and the terrible effect of our infantry's fire. No wonder that now the German infantry are half-hearted when they are told to attack British infantry.

Several Germans who were wounded and were lying with myself in an old barn at——, and who spoke good English, said that when our fellows fired it was like a row of machine guns but twice as deadly. I asked them why they fired from the hip in many cases when they advanced, but failed to get a satisfactory answer. (Poor devils!) I gave them some of my emergency rations as they had been feeding on nothing but swedes and raw potatoes for five days. One of them died in the night.

I myself was very lucky. My platoon was attacking the German trenches through the cover of a wood on the outskirts of the village of ——, and which at the time was being heavily shelled with shrapnel; and most of us knew it was a life-and-death struggle for each one of us, as the German guns had got the correct range and the leaves and branches were being torn from the trunks like chaff before the wind. Talk about Dante's Inferno! What with the whistling of the bullets and the shrieking of the shells, combined with the echo in the woods, made us all seek for the best available cover. Every now and then a cry would ring out which told us of somebody over. I myself dropped behind a thick tree to find head cover. Hardly had I got in a prostrate position when a shell burst with a terrific report on my right and over the tree tops. I must have been stunned, for on coming round I thought I was perched on a tree. Then I realised that half the tree with its branches and in full leaf had fallen over me. Happily the heaviest part fell over my ankle and I suffered nothing more than a dislocated ankle, several abrasions, cuts, etc. I was indeed lucky, as the effects of the same shell killed one and severely wounded several others sixty yards from myself. I was only sorry I could do nothing for them only to throw them any field service bandage, as the danger of exposing any of us would have been instant death, as for some hours after this machine guns and rifles kept up a heavy fire as well as the guns.

24 November 1914

GERMAN ALIENS.
FROM SIR ARTHUR CONAN DOYLE.

If these are to be treated exactly as the aliens are, then a British naturalisation paper has become as faithless a document as a German treaty.

GERMAN ALIENS.
FROM SIR A. CONAN DOYLE.

Sir,—Your correspondent "M.B.J.'s" remarks are beside the point. I have said nothing about German aliens. In fact, I reluctantly acquiesce in their internment, for though I believe them to be in the main inoffensive people, it is just that they should suffer for the methods of their country as exemplified by Stiefer, Graves, and others.

The cases I mentioned were those of Germans long naturalised with British wives. If these are to be treated exactly as the aliens are, then a British naturalisation paper has become as faithless a document as a German treaty.

A London newspaper quoted the other day with apparent approval the case of a citizen whose windows were broken because he harboured two distressed Germans. The same paper referred to the people who had subscribed to a fund for helping destitute German governesses, music masters, and others as "comforting the King's enemies." This is not patriotism. It is pure caddishness, and hurtful to our national reputation.

ARTHUR CONAN DOYLE.
Windlesham, Crowborough, Sussex.

SIR ARTHUR CONAN DOYLE.

Sir,—Sir A. Conan Doyle appears to have a very tender heart for "the enemy in our midst," and so one is not surprised to find that he is a contributor to the funds of "The Committee for the Assistance of Germans, Austrians and Hungarians in Distress."

Unfortunately he is not so considerate of the feelings of the British, otherwise he would not add to his income by writing tales for the consumption of the American and German public in which his own country, now in the supreme crisis of her history, is represented as utterly defeated. I have just received from a Canadian friend a magazine published at the end of last month in New York in which appears a story by Sir Arthur beginning with these words:

It is an amazing thing that the English, who have the reputation of being a practical nation, never saw the danger to which they were exposed. . . yet when the day of trial came all this imposing force was of no use whatever and might as well not have existed. Their ruin could not have been more complete or more rapid if they had not possessed an iron-clad or a regiment.

Published at this critical time doubtless this precious pen-picture of submarine warfare and the suggested downfall of the British Empire will be eagerly perused and gloated over by our enemies.

H.B.
28 October 1914

SIR ARTHUR CONAN DOYLE.

Sir, —Your anonymous correspondent "H. B." would have been wise to make sure of his facts. The story to which he alludes, "Danger," was written in the spring, published in July (Strand Magazine) and consisted of a warning of the growing power of the submarine with its special danger to Great Britain. Events have shown how far such a warning was justified.

ARTHUR CONAN DOYLE.
Windlesham, Crowborough.

To the Editor of the Daily Mail.

Sir, — "H.B.", who in his letter which you have published charges Sir Arthur Conan Doyle with having written an unpatriotic story, has got his facts all wrong. The story in question first appeared in the July number of the Strand Magazine a month before the outbreak of the war and was accompanied by a symposium of naval experts.

The object both of the story and of the symposium was to call public attention to the danger of submarines to British shipping and the best means by which it could be met, and was actually in type a little before Sir Percy Scott published his now well-known views, which are identically the same. To charge with want of patriotism one of the most eminent patriots we have among us is too ridiculous to require notice.

THE EDITOR OF THE "STRAND MAGAZINE."

Our correspondent "H.B." enclosed with his letter a copy of the World Magazine an American publication, dated September 27, 1914, containing the story "Danger," by Sir Arthur Conan Doyle.

29 October 1914

To charge with want of patriotism one of the most eminent patriots we have among us is too ridiculous to require notice.

Top: **The writer Sir Arthur Conan Doyle was too old to enlist when war broke out but frequently wrote to the press voicing his opinions. and thoughts. While the war was still raging he worked on his own history of the war entitled The British Campaign in France and Flanders, eventually published in six volumes.**

Above middle: **There were more than 50,000 migrants from Germany living in Britain before the start of the war. Half of these were in London.**

Above: **A young soldier equipped and ready to fight.**

Right: **A long, straggling line of captives leaves the battlefield.**

GERMANS SURE OF VICTORY.

Impressions of a Returned

GERMANS SURE OF VICTORY.

Impressions of a Returned Prisoner.

GERMANY'S IMPORTANT GAINS

A NEUTRAL VIEW.

[*The following appears in the "New York World."*]

Germany has not only kept most of the gains she made at the beginning of the war, but has succeeded in preventing her enemies from invading the Fatherland. With the exception of a small portion of Alsace at the extreme south of the western battle line there are no foreign foes on German soil.

While Austria is not yet entirely clear of Russians on her Galician border, and the Italians have made slight inroads on her southern frontier, the loss of territory sustained by the Dual Alliance is insignificant, and of no real economic moment.

The gains Germany has made, on the other hand, are of the utmost importance from an economic standpoint.

By conquering Belgium and the north-eastern portion of France, Germany has obtained possession of nearly two-thirds of the total ore deposits of Europe, and an even greater proportion of the steel mills and machine shops and factories that can be used for the manufacture of war supplies and equipment.

Likewise Germany is in possession of the great textile centres of France, and in Lille, Roubaix and Tourcoing has more than three-quarters of the textile factories of France within her grasp.

Besides, the great coalfields of Belgium and mines of Flanders and Artois further add to the economic advantages she has derived from the bold advance she made at the very beginning of the war.

28 July 1915

Above left and right: **Germany's hopes for a short, victorious war were dashed after the invasion of northern France failed to sustain the momentum vital to the success of the Schlieffen Plan.**

Below: **The first batch of British prisoners taken by the Germans at the beginning of the Somme Offensive.**

Opposite above: **A well-earned breakfast for members of the Black Watch.**

Opposite below: **A wounded soldier is helped to safety by a comrade.**

PRISONERS IN GERMANY.

THE QUESTION OF REPRISALS.

To the Editor of *The Daily Mail.*

Sir,—The answer to Mr. Fagan's contention that if reprisals become necessary the Huns will always outdo the British Government seems to be contained in this extract from a Russian official report:

On January 25 General Selivanoff informed the commander of the fortress that in view of the frequent cases of the use of explosive bullets by the troops of Przemysl, contrary to international agreements signed by the Austrian Government, the Grand Duke had ordered all Austrians found with these bullets to be shot.

General Kusmanek gave an evasive reply, and said that two Russian prisoners would be put to death for each Austrian shot. Nevertheless *after our firm declaration the firing of explosive bullets ceased.*

Has it occurred to Mr. Fagan that the son of the arch-pirate, Lieutenant Tirpitz, is in the custody of the British Government? Massacres of British prisoners by the enemy are unlikely in view of this fact. NAUTICUS.

To the Editor of *The Daily Mail.*

Sir,—With reference to the continual authentic reports of the atrocities—for there is no other name—to our wounded, our prisoners, and our countrymen interned in Germany, the time has now come for a public announcement from the Government that for each and every case a German official will be held fully responsible.

We are told that careful note is being taken of every act against the usage of warfare; it is to be hoped this is the case, although the texts may run into volumes.

But, knowing the jackal, cowardly nature of the German individually at heart, once let him know that the guilty culprits will be individually dealt with, once let these inflated, uncivilised bullies know that their necks are in danger, and the cruelties will diminish.

WHAT KULTUR.

27 April 1915

GERMANS SURE OF VICTORY.

Impressions of a Returned Prisoner.

" German confidence in absolute victory for German arms has not yet been shaken in the slightest degree."

This is the impression received by Lance-Corporal Edward Wells, who has returned after having been a prisoner of war in Germany since August 29.

" When we were travelling to the Dutch frontier from Erfurt," he says, " I saw that there was an abundance of men and war material, and we could see that the fields were all packed with growing corn. In fact scarcely an inch of soil was left uncultivated, grain and vegetables were growing everywhere.

" I am sure the people of this country do not yet half realise what they are up against.

" I had many opportunities to speak English to the guards at the camp. The Germans are satisfied that the Russians are practically finished with and that a month or so will see the end of their resistance.

" They recognise that England is now their strongest opponent and that the war with our country will continue well into next year, when a complete victory for German arms is in their opinion certain.

" 'We are so well organised, you know,' they would say; 'you are not like us. You do not know how to organise.'

" In fact, the one word they constantly harped on was organisation."

10 July 1915

BRAVERY OF TWO GERMANS
Officers Serve Machine Guns to the Last.

The Germans left alive in the trenches, half demented with fright, surrounded by a welter of dead and dying men, mostly surrendered. The Berkshires were opposed with the utmost gallantry by two German officers, who had remained alone in a trench serving a machine gun. But the lads from Berkshire made their way into that trench and bayoneted the Germans where they stood, fighting to the last. The Lincolns, against desperate resistance, eventually occupied their section of trench and then waited for the Irishmen and the Rifle Brigade to come and take the village ahead of them.

18 April 1915

OFFICER KILLED WHILE SAVING GERMAN OFFICER'S LIFE.

(An officer of the Yola Column of the Nigerian Field Force writes home from Soratsi of the fighting in the Cameroons.)

When I last wrote you we had just got news of the war and orders to proceed to Yola. We set off that afternoon, and reached Yola by forced marches on the 14th, six days' march. We averaged over 26 miles a day—good going for an infantry column with a scratch lot of carriers. We got a telegram from the commandant congratulating us on our performance.

The Benue is very low this year, and the other companies were a long time turning up. We were a week in Yola, and all feel better for a good rest. Our mounted infantry turned up on the 21st and at once crossed the river. We followed the next day—a very tedious, tiring day. We did two forced marches, and reached the border on Monday, leaving Tepe on our right front, with a German force in it. On Tuesday we crossed the Tiel, and were into German territory. We had not been over half an hour before heavy firing took place on our right front, so we halted in square till news came from the mounted infantry.

Alas! when it did come it was none of the best. Colonel Maclear had ordered them to clear the Germans out of Tepe. They started before us, and within half an hour of crossing the Tiel were heavily engaged at Tepe. The Germans let through the scouts, and the advance guard and the main body got somewhat bunched. The German soldiers evidently had orders to pick off the white men. Wickham and Sherlock were killed, and Lord M. Seymour who commanded, dangerously wounded, and McDonald severely wounded—four out of the six white officers. Only two rank and file were wounded, both badly.

It was very sad about poor Sherlock. The action was practically over and Sherlock had just come up in time to save a German officer's life. He turned away, and the officer's orderly let drive and got Sherlock through the throat. Needless to say, both officer and orderly didn't survive half a minute.

The Germans retreated into the native town, and McDonald, though wounded, got the Maxim turned on and gave them a bad sprinkling. In some way the town got on fire and the German wounded were burned to death, including at least two white officers.

I don't know how the mounted infantry took the place, as they hadn't more than sixty men, and the Germans had between fifty and a hundred, under five officers.

When the news reached us we set out for Tepe, and got there in two hours—a grilling march. Trumper and myself got Seymour and McDonald made as comfortable as possible. They left for Yola by canoe the next day, both wonderfully well. Neither wanted to be sent away, but of course, it was impossible to take them on.

We advanced to this place yesterday. The mounted infantry who were screening us had a brush with a patrol and killed a white officer and one native soldier. When we came in we were sniped, but no casualties on our side.

We are halting here today while the country is being reconnoitred. I think we are pretty certain to have a scrap tomorrow. We are only twenty miles from Sarus, and should get there in two days. It will be a hard nut to crack, and I am afraid we cannot expect to get off cheaply. Our real hope is in our guns. Given a good position they may make Sarus untenable; but there will be some sharp fighting to get a good position. Nobody is underestimating the job before us.

5 November 1914

FRENCH BOY HERO.

FATE OF A GERMAN OFFICER BULLY. PARIS, WEDNESDAY.

M. Pauliat, the senator, relates the following of a French lad at Lourches, near Douchy:

A German officer who had insulted a woman was shot by a wounded French soldier. The soldier was about to be shot when Emile Despres, aged fourteen, arrived and the condemned man asked for water. The lad brought a glass and was immediately brutally beaten. His eyes were bandaged and he was placed with his countryman for execution.

Then the German Officer suddenly changed his mind, and taking the handkerchief from the boy's eyes told him he would spare his life if he would shoot the soldier. The boy took the rifle given him, made as if to aim it at the soldier, and then, turning suddenly shot dead the officer. The boy was immediately transfixed with the bayonets and riddled with bullets, the soldier sharing his fate. — Central News

SHELL NEAR GEN. JOFFRE'S CAR. PARIS, SUNDAY.

From a Frenchman, who volunteered his motor-car and is now driving it for officers of the General Staff, I hear that General Joffre had a very narrow escape some days ago. He was being driven by Boillot, the French racing chauffeur, and the Germans seem to have laid an artillery ambush for him along a road by which they knew that he would have to travel.

As soon as the car reached the portion of road on which the German guns were trained a group of shells fell all around it. One fragment "as large as a teacup" struck the bonnet, but neither the general nor his chauffeur was injured.

Boillot dashed on at full speed and was out of the danger zone before the Germans could fire again.

16 November 1914

AUSTRALASIANS' GREAT DASH.

AUSTRALIANS, ARISE!

NEW-AUSTRALIA GERMANY

Save her from this Shame!

4 June 1917

IMMORTAL ANZACS.

AUSTRALIAN PREMIER'S PRAISE FOR GALLIPOLI HEROES.

Hundreds of war-seasoned Australians, heroes of Gallipoli, stood in the Australian headquarters in London yesterday and listened to a glowing eulogy of their deeds from Mr. Hughes, the Prime Minister of their homeland.

The little statesman has a trenchant and eloquent tongue. He spoke of the "many and grievous vicissitudes" through which the men had passed, and the "meagre stories" of their valour which had reached Australia. Mr. Hughes told the men that they had earned a name which in the history of the world would never die.

"In Australia," he said, "we have imagined in some fashion what dreadful things you went through. We have seen, we have heard, and we have gloried in your achievements. When you have been overwhelmed by the storms of circumstance we have wept with you, and when you have been victorious we have rejoiced with you, but always we have been prouder to call ourselves Australians since you won your name for us in Gallipoli."

There was about the Australian, he said, that dash and that readiness to endure and dare all things that had made him one of the best fighting men in the world. Australia had pursued resolutely the course she set out upon when war was declared. A little State had recruited at the rate of 13,000 or 14,000 in a fortnight, in spite of the terrible lists of casualties. The Australian Navy, too, had played its part in the war.

"It stands now a small but resolute partner of the British Navy, behind whose shield England, the Empire, and civilisation have been able to prepare themselves to meet our ferocious and cruel enemy."

15 March 1916

HEROIC AUSTRALIANS.

RUSH TO DEATH OF LIGHT HORSE BRIGADES.

Captain C. E. W. Bean, the official Press representative with the Australian Forces in the Dardanelles, in an article issued by the High Commissioner for Australia, says that "for sheer self-sacrificing heroism there was never a deed in history that surpassed the charge which two Australian Light Horse Brigades made in the first light of Saturday, August 7, in order to help their comrades in a critical moment of a great battle." The men had volunteered to fight on foot or in any other way provided they could get to Gallipoli to help the other Australians there.

Describing the action Captain Bean says that Colonel White stood by the parapet of their trenches watch in hand, and at the word "Go" the men were over the parapet like a flash. Then a tremendous fusillade broke out, and rose from a fierce crackle into a roar in which neither rifle nor machine gun could be distinguished, but just one continuous roaring tempest. No one could live in it.

"Exactly two minutes after the first line had cleared the parapet, the second line jumped out without the slightest hesitation and followed them. No one knows how it happened. And probably no one will ever know. But some either of that first line or of the second line managed to get into the extreme right-hand corner of the enemy's trench. They carried with them a small flag to put up in the enemy's trench if they captured it, and the appearance of this flag was to be the signal for a party of the Royal Welsh Fusiliers to attack up the gully to the right.

"In the extreme south-eastern corner of the Turkish trench there did appear just for two minutes the small flag which our men had taken. No one ever saw them get there. No one will ever know who they were or how they did it. Only for those two minutes the flag fluttered up behind the parapet, and then someone unseen tore it down. The fight in that corner of the trench, whatever it was, was over; and it can only have ended one way.

"It was all over within a quarter of an hour. Except for the wild fire which burst out again at intervals there was not a movement in front of the trenches—only the scrub and the tumbled khaki here and there."

2 October 1915

26 April 1916

THE DOG WAS THERE !—Australian soldiers brought the dog which went through the Gallipoli campaign with them.

Australia pledged its support for the Allies immediately the conflict began and by November sent over the first 20,000 men of the Australian Expeditionary Force. Along with their New Zealand counterparts they played a crucial role in the Gallipoli Campaign, where over 8,000 were killed and a further 18,000 injured. The AEF then joined the fighting on the Western Front in March 1916. By the end of the war over 420,000 Australians joined the military operations but over 60,000 lost their lives with another 137,000 wounded. This casualty rate was one of the highest of the countries from the British Empire.

Above left: **Sergeant MacMillan of the Australian Imperial Guards organises musical entertainment while keeping watch for the Turkish soldiers, who are barely 30 metres away.**

Left: **Crosses made by Australian troops at Gallipoli – for themselves. On the wood the men carved their names and the words "Killed in Action". They left the date to be filled in later. Wherever the soldiers went they took their crosses with them.**

CANADIANS ON THE SOMME—THE PUSH OF THE BIG GUN.

COLONEL FALLS AT THE HEAD OF HIS MEN.

CANADA'S EAGER BRITONS.

(A French Officer writes.)

Colonel D—— was killed in action on January 30, while leading his battalion in a terrible charge. He knew the action would be hard, and decided to give the example, and took the head of the battalion. He was killed, but his men carried the position.

I am leaving the trenches to-day for a few hours to go to his funeral. We succeeded with great difficulty in getting hold of the body of our beloved chief. It was only five yards from the German trenches, and we asked for volunteers to go and fetch it at night. Several of my men offered themselves, but their efforts were vain. One at last draped himself in a white sheet so as not to be seen on the snow by moonlight. The cold was dreadful.

He went very carefully on his knees in the snow until he reached the body, which was adhering strongly to the frozen snow owing to recent frosts. He passed a rope round the waist, but the frozen snow cracked and the noise attracted the attention of the Germans, who started firing at him. Owing to the white sheet with which he was covered they could not easily see him and missed him in spite of a lively fusillade. A few minutes later he was back in our trenches.

When the Germans stopped firing he returned, this time being himself tied with a rope so as to allow his friends to pull him back into the trenches in case he was wounded. This time he succeeded, and brought back the body of our beloved chief. He was promoted corporal on the spot.

16 February 1915

"BRAVE CANADIANS."

"New York Sun" on a Memory the World Will Treasure.

The Washington correspondent of the *Morning Post* says:—

The *New York Sun* pays a well-merited tribute to the superb gallantry of Princess Patricia's Canadian Light Infantry. Noting that in August of last year the regiment mustered 1,015 men, that on May 7 of this year, after five months in the trenches, 635 answered the roll-call, and that on the morning of May 8 the strength of the regiment was 150 surviving warriors the *Sun* adds: "This is but a dull statistical measure of a sacrifice which is typical of the spirit of the Briton on the stricken field. The report of the regiment's Record Officer, printed in the *Sun*, is a narrative of military courage and devotion than which nothing finer was ever penned. The world must long treasure the memory of those brave Canadians."

1 July 1915

CANADIAN VALOUR.

Early on Monday morning we moved into our places in the front lines. The night was bitterly cold and wet, and the mud was up to our knees, in some parts up to our middles. Then we just stood still and waited. At half-past five to the second our barrage began on the front line of the German trenches. There has never been such a roar before. Three minutes afterwards we jumped over the top and our barrage crept up to the second line.

FRONT LINE WIPED OUT.

We moved up silently. There was no cheering, no yelling. No one could have heard you had you yelled; the guns drowned every other sound. We reached where the first-line Hun trenches ought to have been. They had disappeared. Our shells had wiped them out. There were no signs of them save little ridges and heaps of dead. It was the same with the second line, except that to one side and the other I could see that some German machine guns had been left and were making a fight of it. The German gunfire at this point was amazingly feeble. Someone told me we had 280 Huns guns facing us. If so, most of them must have been wiped out in a few minutes by our fire.

Fritz made his stand on the third line. We were up against the Prussian Guard. They held their ground even under our barrage. They stood up atop of their trenches to fling bombs at us. They were fine, sturdy chaps, most of them very tall, young, and fit. They put up a good fight, but they couldn't keep back the Canadians. We have been up against the Prussian Guard before, and we went clean through them. We reached our objective to time, 900 yards in 32 minutes, and then another brigade swept over us and went still farther on.

Other Canadians around joined in. "The Huns never stood up once against our bayonets," said one. "They called 'Kamerad' and put up their hands as soon as we got near." "I only saw them coming and going," said another. "They were either running away or running to us to surrender." "I took eight of 'em back with me," said a man with a bandaged arm. "I thought they might get into trouble if they went alone, so I grabbed a rifle with my one good arm, hunched them ahead, and hurried them along. They went like little lambs."

14 April 1917

Although a British dominion, and therefore automatically part of the conflict, Canada's Governor General immediately declared war against Germany on 5 August 1914. The Canadian Expeditionary Force was raised and for the first time the country fought as a distinct unit. The CEF played a key role at the Somme, Vimy and Passchendaele but by the end of the conflict of the 620,000 mobilised, 67,000 were killed and 250,000 wounded.

Above: **General Sam Hughes greets and inspects Canadian troops. Britain's Empire contributed considerable numbers of soldiers to the Allies' fighting force.**

Left: **Canadians go over the top.**

TO RAISE THE MALE BIRTH-RATE.

By DR. ARABELLA KENEALY.

The increase of male births during war—now exciting widespread interest—is simply explained.

Because of men's greater risks to life, Nature provides that to every 1,000 girls born normally from 1,045 to 1,050 boys are born. Our deplorable preponderance of women is aggravated by frustrating this important dispensation.

The sex of offspring is determined by the relative parental power of the parents. When the father possesses greater constitutional or vital power, daughters predominate. When the mother possesses greater vital power, sons are born.

Men making greater efforts as bread-winners, women's power is more conserved. Hence the natural surplus of boys. The father being thus the parent of the female child, so to speak, and the mother the parent of the male, each sex becomes endowed with a degree of the characteristics of the other sex. Whereas, were inheritance from father to son, and from mother to daughter, male and female characteristics, instead of being blended in both sexes and valuably modifying and enriching one another, would have become so much exaggerated from generation to generation in the opposite sexes as to have produced two incomplete and lop-sided species.

Parental power is not power available for output, however. It is power conserved and *locked up* in constitution—invested vital capital, not vital income available for everyday expenditure. And this it is, as with financial resources, that serves as heritage for offspring. But just as to meet an increase of daily cash expenditure one must realise financial investments, so to meet increased activities of brain or body one must draw on constitutional capital—by converting vital investments into vital currency.

Now, the stress of war falls most heavily on men, and to meet increased demands they draw on their vital reserves. Hence the constitutional (and the parental) power of men is impoverished by war conditions.

Women's vital (and parental) power is diminished, too, by war activities. But in less degree. The parental power of women in general becoming thus relatively greater than men's, male births increase.

5 August 1918

Below: **Crowds in Whitehall in patriotic spirit the day after Prime Minister Herbert Asquith declared war on Germany.**

BOYS OUT OF CONTROL.
FROM JUDGE NEIL, OF CHICAGO.

To the Editor of The Daily Mail.

Sir,—In my published statement about the absence of fathers from home I was speaking about one class of fathers only. Mrs. Curnock, in her article in *The Daily Mail*, takes another class of fathers altogether, and assumes that it is the same class that I was talking about.

I said a mother will do far more for her own than she will for any other children. Curiously enough, experience teaches that a father's interest in his own children is far less in advance of his interest in children generally.

Destruction of life is abnormal now not only because men are dying in the trenches but also because they are dying more rapidly than usual elsewhere, partly due to the fact that work is carried on at a tremendous pressure and partly to the fact that the absence of the strongest in the trenches frequently throws overstrain upon the weak and aged. When the State takes up the matter of soldiers' widows' dependent children, is it not an absurdity for it to neglect the equally grave question of other widows' dependent children?

Why, in Heaven's name, should a child be penalised because his father was not a soldier? That was not the child's fault. It makes his life of no less value to the community in future. Any reasonable pension system should include all widows and orphans.

The importance of fatherhood is mistaken by many who do not differentiate between the father's value as a provider of funds and his value as an ethical guide. Some fathers drink. Mothers could do better with their families if such fathers never saw their children. A very large proportion of fathers coming tired to their homes at night fuss, fume, and complain. Mothers could do better with their children if they never saw such fathers.

HENRY NEIL.

St. Enoch Station Hotel, Glasgow.

17 September 1917

Were both needed to serve the Guns!

FILL UP THE RANKS! PILE UP THE MUNITIONS!

MORE BOY BABIES.

12 SONS TO 1 DAUGHTER IN BIRTHS COLUMN.

The popular theory that during wars the proportion of boy babies to girl babies is greatly increased above the normal average is supported to a surprising extent in the birth announcement column of *The Times* this month.

Out of 414 births announced since November 1 the boys exceed the girls by no fewer than 32. In the last Registrar-General's annual report, dealing with the period before the war, the proportion of male to female births was 1,038 to 1,000. If *The Times* announcement column figures could be taken as representative of the country, they would show a proportion of male to female births of about 1,075 to 1,000.

The highest proportion of male to female births since accurate statistics have been kept was 1,054 to 1,000 in 1844. On only six days this month has the number of births of daughters announced in *The Times* exceeded that of sons. The excess of boys over girls on several mornings was most striking, as, for example, 12 boy babies out of the 13 births announced on November 11.

25 November 1915

To the Editor of The Daily Mail.

Sir,—A letter in *The Daily Mail* raises the question, "What Can a Boy Do?"

At the moment, working on the land is the most important. Why should not each boy who wishes to do so take a spade or other tool along with his dinner and go and offer his services at the nearest allotment?

There he will find a healthy day's work and he may be sure he is doing his duty. Headmasters and others in charge of boys could very easily make suitable arrangements with local farmers, allotment holders, gardeners, and the like.

JOSEPH E. BECKETT.

1, Alexandra-road, South Hampstead, London, N.W. 8.

To the Editor of The Daily Mail.

Sir,—Referring to the letter under the heading of "What Can a Boy Do?" the reply is apparently, "Not much."

I am a schoolboy, and for various reasons my school was closed a month before it should have been, leaving me with two months with nothing to do, so I applied at a local munition factory. They offered me work for 12 hours a day—72 hours a week—from 7 a.m. to 8 p.m., with one hour for lunch, for the munificent sum of 7s. 6d. a week, which works out at approximately 1¼d. an hour, and this after two years' munitioning at school! Is this encouraging for a boy who wants to help his country?

A BLUECOAT BOY.

29 March 1917

THE TAX ON TOMMY'S LETTERS.

Sir,—On the question of postal taxation, is it not very hard to increase the cost of sending letters to France? There are many people to whom the extra halfpenny will make all the difference—for instance, a widow with five sons serving. Our fellows cannot do without letters, however short and trivial they may be. Men have been known to cry because the post brought them no letters.

Why not tax bicycles and increase the tax on dogs, both of which I have?

DOUGLAS E. S. JERVIS.

25 April 1918

16 July 1918

MR. HENDERSON'S WAR VIEWS.

To the Editor of *The Daily Mail.*

Sir,—I am a working man and have been a Socialist for more than a quarter of a century, and I would like to ask whom Mr. Arthur Henderson represents when he calls for a peace by negotiation with the beastly Hun.

I come into contact with a large number of working men, and in no instance have I found any other feeling than that Germany must be smashed before decent people may hope to live in safety. I am of the opinion that Mr. Henderson represents only himself and the few Bolsheviks who constitute the discredited I.L.P.

The men who before the war were real Socialists, such as Hyndman, Blatchford, and Tillett, are among the best patriots.

I was never more proud than I am to-day to realise the great privilege I enjoy of being even a humble unit of the great British Empire.

ROBERT CLARKE.
252, Bedford-road, Bootle, Liverpool.

Above: **The walking wounded assemble ready to board a Red Cross train.**

Bottom: **Marble Arch in 1904. Many of the men in this photograph would eventually be destined for the front line.**

Mr. Forty-one says goodbye. Chorus of young 'indispensables' (from the right side of the fence) - "Are we down-hearted?"

BICYCLE THEFT EPIDEMIC.

150 A DAY STOLEN IN LONDON.

Young thieves have been giving the London police much trouble lately and bicycles are their favourite prey. It is estimated that during the past month the average number stolen in London has been no fewer than 150 a day. Even the police have not escaped. A constable who rode up to a house and left his bicycle by the kerb while he delivered a message found a minute later that his machine had disappeared.

Thefts from vans have also been very frequent. A carman at Holloway who could not deliver a load of boxes of chocolates because of premises being closed during the dinner hour was accosted by two young men, who offered to get another van, take the load of chocolates over, and deliver them. The carman was delighted, a van was brought up, the chocolates placed in it, and then all trace of them was lost.

19 September 1917

BABY NAMED "SHRAPNEL."

Born amid the dangers of the bombardment of Whitby, the seventh son of Edward Griffin, shipyard worker, has been named George Shrapnel Griffin, the first name after the King. His Majesty's attention having been drawn to the event, a letter expressing his pleasure that mother and child were well has been received from Lord Stamfordham, also congratulating the father on his magnificent life-saving record. Mr. Griffin has saved thirty-six persons from drowning.

4 January 1915

WOUNDED SOLDIERS AND OMNIBUS "FIGHTS."

To the Editor of *The Daily Mail.*

Sir,—On Friday, at the top of Bond-street, I saw a wounded officer try in vain to get into three different omnibuses. The stronger members of the crowd kept him back.

As I gave him a lift down the street he said, in reply to my indignation, "They do not realise that we have saved them from invasion."

Surely it is time that London realised, and that wounded soldiers had the first place.

E. M. GREEN.
Lyceum Club, 128, Piccadilly, W.1.

28 July 1917

WHO ARE THE THIEVES?

Sir,—My husband fell in action on July 1, and three weeks later I received his kit.

This consisted of extremely mud-caked clothes, a variety of old brushes and empty tins. His wristwatch, field glasses, revolver, and a photograph in a suede case are missing.

CAPTAIN'S WIDOW.

Sir,—My son joined up in September and was killed in the trenches early in October 1914. He was killed in action at Ypres on April 26, 1915.

I have not yet received a single article. All my letters have been returned to me marked "no effects," although he was in possession of cash, watch, cigarette-case, and two of Princess Mary's tobacco boxes (one in trust for a wounded comrade).

H. J. HOBBS
337 Grove Green Road, Leytonstone.

Sir,—On July 14 last my only son was killed. He had the usual personal belongings of an officer drawn from the middle classes.

Immediately the overwhelming news was received I communicated with the Effects Department of the War Office giving the details of these personal belongings. None of these things has been received. I have since interviewed the private who buried the body of my son, who informs me that he made a thorough search and only found in the pockets of the tunic a khaki handkerchief and charged revolver cartridges. Not even his identification disc, which I placed around his neck myself on a silver chain, was found upon the body.

A SUFFERER.

Sir,—On July 25, before going into action, my son wrote home saying that he had that day sent off home a kit-bag, packed with things he no longer needed. Among these he mentioned a valuable pair of field glasses engraved with his name and address, a number of technical books, with his name written in, which he wished us to take care of for him. We have not received the bag and cannot learn anything about it.

On August 1 my son was killed, and on September 8 we received a bundle which consisted of a few old clothes, boots and the like. Ring, watch, and everything of value were missing.

SUBALTERN'S MOTHER.

7 October 1916

Sir,—I have had a son killed in France, on July 1, and his kit sent to me. It contained none of his personal belongings.

I have written over and over again, to France, to the War Office, and to Messrs. Cox, and received nothing, although my son was killed on July 1. His ring, watch, field glasses, and two Colt pistols I have not received, nor a bundle of letters, which I know he kept, congratulating him on his coming of age. I have offered to pay for a search, for I want these things so very, very much, but after months of inquiry I have nothing.

My son's effects were stolen in France—not in transit—as an officer of the A.S.C. sent me a list of all he was sending and they arrived. I could tell you the names of numbers of parents who, like "Junius" and I, have received nothing but parcels of worn-out clothes. You, Sir, have been so helpful in such numerous ways in this cruel war that I feel you will do what you can, for it is a scandal that the personal belongings of those who have made the supreme sacrifice should be stolen.

MATER

Sir,—My brother, after recovering from gastritis, went down to the store to obtain his private belongings. He found fourteen articles missing—fountain pen, ink pellets, shaving mirror, cigarettes, and the like.

M. C.

Sir,—On September 29 my son was killed on active service in France, and on Friday last his kit arrived after various forms had been duly completed.

The entire contents consisted of old boots, a few military books, diary, and his collar studs. His wrist-watch and other articles are missing. That a regular traffic is being carried on is very apparent.

B.

Sir,—My dear son was wounded on July 1 and reported missing. He left his few treasures five miles behind the line as ordered, which were to be sent home, all properly addressed. Nothing has come.

EDITH M. ROBINSON

Sir,—On August 23 a near relative of mine was killed in action in France. On about September 20 his kit arrived at his father's house, but not his watch, revolver, field-glasses, fountain pen, and money (the purse was empty).

He was beloved by everyone —"idolised" by his men, I am told—and an only son.

A. A. E.

25 October 1916

MORE DAYLIGHT.

To the Editor of *The Daily Mail.*

Sir,—What are the "many disadvantages" that the Home Office fears would result from the proposed extra hour's daylight during the mid-summer months?

I have received dozens of letters supporting the proposal, and, of those which do not, the only valid objections come from farmers and such factories as start very early. In both these cases it would surely be a simple matter to start an hour later by the clock.

The advantage of the extra hour to the great mass of townsfolk would be enormous. Hundreds of thousands of men and women would be freed for an extra hour of war work: the rearing of live-stock, allotments, Volunteer drilling, special constabulary work, and the host of part-time National Service duties that present conditions demand would all be possible with less serious loss to the business community, and if the present train restrictions are maintained town workers could get home in daylight.

Furthermore, the extra hour *must* automatically reduce the use of artificial light. "Dora" should be glad of the help of—shall we say?—a 30 per cent. increased output by her huge army of home workers, who are keen on doing all they can to help her to get on with the war.
SAMSON CLARK.
Moleside, East Molesey, Surrey.

REPRISALS PAY.

To the Editor of *The Daily Mail.*

Sir,—Please permit me to be one of the many —I trust and believe the million—who will write to thank you for your article in Friday's *Daily Mail* entitled "How to Handle the Hun."

In Heaven's name, Sir, back up the seafolk of Britain! They have saved us before and will save us again—by the will of the people and the patriotic Press. C. F. BRYCE.
15, Woodburn-terrace, Edinburgh.

WHY NATURALISE THEM?

To the Editor of *The Daily Mail.*

Sir,—I trust England will do away with all naturalisation and impose a tax on all foreigners who set foot in Great Britain and her Dominions over-seas, either on a visit or to settle.

I married an Englishman and am now English according to both French and English laws. I am very fond of England, but my sympathies are far stronger for France than for England in spite of mother English, husband English, and 33 years spent in England. FRANCO-ENGLISH.

TOO MUCH "SENTIMENT."

To the Editor of *The Daily Mail.*

Sir,—Many officers have noted with regret the letter entitled "Too Much 'Sentiment'" in Saturday's *Daily Mail*. While sympathising with Mrs. Hope of Luffness in her great loss, I do not think she is quite justified in calling von Richthofen "a low, murderous Boche."

The men who fought against him are better judges of his character, and in their opinion he was a sportsman and a clean fighter, hence he deserved to be treated as such.

In most cases men who die in the hands of the enemy are decently buried. If all Germans are not sportsmen—as we know they are not—nevertheless let us keep our name clean.
B. McK.

2 May 1918

HUN TORTURE OF OUR MEN.

To the Editor of *The Daily Mail.*

Sir,—I hope the generous offer of financial support from Mr. C. B. Cochran, made in a letter to *The Daily Mail*, will be accepted and a committee formed without delay, as he suggests, to inquire into the treatment of all Germans in English prisons or internment camps, and that the said committee will do all in its power to see that Germans in this country are treated with the "same measure" as our boys are being treated in Germany. (Rev.) F. C. BAKER.
69, Cunningham-park, Harrow.

WOMEN CLERGY.

To the Editor of *The Daily Mail.*

Sir,—Our Church congregations are composed chiefly of women, a condition likely to be accentuated in the near future. There are gifted women in our Churches who could cater for the needs of their own sex, and so set free a considerable number of ministers.

One of our religious bodies has an "order" of nearly 300 women, trained, qualified, and, in the main, prepared for such work. Other bodies have similar organisations. A few of these women are filling ministerial posts. The majority, however, are debarred from this opportunity of service on one pretext or another.
Chesterfield. ELEANOR ROBINSON.

ALIENS SHOULD FIGHT OR GO.

To the Editor of *The Daily Mail.*

Sir,—The alien who is fit should be conscripted into the Army or given the alternative of returning to his native country at his own expense. We are asked to eat less food while many thousands of foreigners in the British Isles are consuming our foodstuffs and enjoying the same freedom an immunity from invasion as ourselves without rendering service or sacrifice.

We were promised legislation on this subject in 1917 by Mr. Bonar Law, but nothing has yet been done. Every elector should drop a card to the M.P. for his constituency demanding his support for this principle. G. HEARON.
Didsbury.

AN HEROIC "M.O."

To the Editor of *The Daily Mail.*

Sir,—Will you permit me to convey my heartfelt thanks to an Army surgeon whose identity I have been unable to establish?

During the Amiens offensive one of my sons, a signaller attached to the King's Shropshire Light Infantry, was severely wounded on Good Friday just as his battalion had received orders to retire, and his fall being unnoticed he was consequently left behind.

My son writes: "Later on I was found by an M.O., who had hung back to search for missing wounded; he twice went off to look for a stretcher without success and finally improvised a splint for my fractured thigh, hoisted me on to his back, and so carried me until we got in touch with another unit." F. LLOYD BECKETT.
Crofton Lodge, Higher Runcorn, Cheshire.

15 April 1918

QUEER WAR WEATHER.

To the Editor of *The Daily Mail.*

Sir,—In view of the present abnormally severe weather, it is curious to note the fact that during this phenomenal war (whether as a coincidence or a part of the general scheme of things) the weather conditions have been more or less disturbed, several records having been made, remarkable for occurring so close together.

The following are the chief data:—

1914.
December: Wettest December on record.

1915.
January: Severe floods; Salisbury Cathedral flooded.
August: Extraordinarily frequent thunderstorms; nine within eleven days.
December: Very wet and stormy.

1916
January: Mildest January for half a century.
March: The severest March for 58 years. On March 28 greatest gale for a century.
August and September: Wettest since 1903.

1916-1917.
Coldest winter for 22 years.
JULIUS ROBINSON.
4, Margravine-gardens, Baron's Court, W. 6.

16 April 1917

---

25 July 1918

Left: A workman removes the brass plate from the German Embassy. Hostile crowds had begun to gather outside on the day war was declared and the German ambassador Karl Max, Prince Lichnowsky, immediately returned to Germany. He had made valiant attempts to maintain peace between the two countries.

Above: A female railway porter. By the end of the war the number of women taking on this type of unskilled employment had increased ten-fold.

OUR BIG JOB IN GALLIPOLI.

GOOD CHEER FOR GALLIPOLI.

GIFTS TO SEND.

LIST OF DELICACIES AND HOW TO PACK THEM.

From an officer out there.

This is an effort to tell in the most practical way how life can be made a little easier for troops in the Dardanelles during the winter.

I have been here with the British Mediterranean Expeditionary Force since the later spring and through the parched summer. Now we are at the edge of winter. Violent storms render transport very difficult by water and life rather comfortless on shore. We are very far away from home, and, without grumbling, we feel very far away, because our postal service is by no means ideal and letters and parcels are few and far between; it is no easy task to handle the correspondence of a force that stretches from Alexandria to the Greek Islands, from Lancashire Landing to Salonica, with units constantly shifting, and with the drift hither and thither of sick and wounded to the hospitals, rest camps, and convalescent camps as far away as Cairo or Cyprus.

Although our food is good and water more plentiful than it was, our diet is necessarily monotonous, and there are plenty of little things, cheap to buy and easy to send, which would make life a great deal more comfortable. Only it is but little good sending indiscriminately, and it is most important to send small packages, not bulky ones, and to see that they are properly packed.

It is disappointing to receive in one's twilight dug-out a tin of apricots which has leaked and smells like sin, a cake as hard as a rifle-barrel and smeared all over with a stale mess of crushed prunes that have oozed out of a brown paper bag and have incidentally ruined those longed-for new socks and handkerchiefs.

TREASURED LOCAL PAPERS.

Send letters first, of course, and always more letters. Then newspapers. If you pay a direct subscription to a newspaper office the papers come singly with printed labels and arrive with fair regularity. Also send the soldier his local paper too. I have never seen local papers so much treasured and so eagerly read as they are here. The village gossip, the small events of suburb or country town—these bring the thrill of home to the soldier in the Dardanelles, and he likes to think that the old life whose serenity and comfort he is fighting here to protect is going on unimpaired. But not more than two or three papers in one package and good strong brown paper and string. Sixpenny novels, please, as well.

Next, chocolate. No doubt about this. Speculators might make fortunes selling chocolate to the force. I have heard of some astonishing bargains on a small scale among the troops. Toffee, too, in cakes. Cigarettes, of course, and in the air-tight tins of fifty, which never go back on one.

Potted meat of all kinds, and, please, bloater paste. What a revolution bloater paste creates round a camp fire when bread has run out and there is only that horribly hard and dull biscuit! Home-made potted meat, if possible, we prefer, but it must be put up in very strong little tins. Not jam, I think, for the ration jam is good, but marmalade, for the ration marmalade is apt to be insipid, and really good marmalade puts heart into a damp and cramped man.

SWEET BISCUITS, PLEASE.

Biscuits—and sweet for purposes of contrast, for a pall of hard biscuit hangs daily over every soldier's life! Cake, if properly packed, but then only; small rock cakes always seem to travel well and are most welcome. Big sultana or Madeira cakes I hardly recommend unless bought from some firm accustomed to send things abroad.

Cocoa and soup tablets and lemon squash powders, those pleasant tins of excellent 'café au lait', and, if you insist on spoiling us, cream. A tin or so of ox tongue or lamb and peas that can be cooked in our 'dixies' some evening over an extempore fire in an oblong hole in the ground—these are luxuries, yet they would mean a good deal. Especially with Worcester sauce. Don't forget those; they make 'bully' palatable.

3 December 1915

The Allies decision to try and 'force the Dardanelles', the narrow strait along the Gallipoli peninsula in Turkey, aimed to force a route through to the Black Sea to assist Russia and neutralise the threat from the Ottomans by using the strength of the navy. Beginning in February 1915, the disastrous land-and-sea campaign lasted nearly a year, ending in an Allied withdrawal with over 157,000 men killed and a further 123,000 wounded.

Top: **Lord Kitchener visits the troops in Gallipoli.**

Above: **Australians on the beach at Gallipoli surrounded by their supplies.**

Right: **In the final withdrawal operation led by Sir John de Robeck, over 35,000 troops, nearly 4,700 horses, 127 guns, 328 vehicles and 1,600 tons of equipment were safely removed from the battlefield. The disastrous campaign finally over.**

THE PENINSULA ONE GREAT FORTRESS.

ALLIED TROOPS OUTNUMBERED BY TWO TO ONE.

MACHINE GUNS ALL-IMPORTANT.

> "The Army of Sir Ian Hamilton, the Fleet of Admiral de Robeck, are separated only by a few miles from a victory such as this war has not yet seen."—*Mr. Winston Churchill at Dundee, June 5.*

TWO important messages from the Dardanelles will help the country to correct its early misapprehensions on the campaign there.

Lack of information led everyone to believe that the Allied Fleets would quickly smash the forts and batteries of the Turks to powder and open the way to Constantinople.

To-day the nation understands that the Straits and Gallipoli can not be won from the water alone, and that the operation is a great war in itself—the most complex in history and one of terrible severity.

As Mr. Churchill has said, "only by a few miles" are we separated from victory, but every square yard of those miles is a natural defence, enormously strengthened by all the instruments of destruction.

Reuter's correspondent and Mr. Granville Fortescue of the "Daily Telegraph," de-scribing the obstacles, make us feel proud of the troops who face them with such splendid bravery, and Sir Ian Hamilton's latest report of an advance of a thousand yards on the left shows that their almost superhuman courage is not fruitless.

The messages of the two correspondents tell us that:—

The enemy has two soldiers to our one.

He has trenches loopholed at every yard, and

A great supply of machine guns, grenades and cricket ball bombs, and howitzers.

He enfilades us from the Asiatic shore.

Every ravine is a field of obstacles, every ridge a fort.

Mines abound in the water, guns are along the shore.

All Turkey is an armed camp, and the soldiers are training grimly and have the kind of fighting job that suits them.

Naval gunfire is accurate, but disappointing in its results.

Gallipoli is, in fact, "one great fortress."

1 July 1915

THE GALLIPOLI "GAMBLE."
To the Editor of *The Daily Mail.*

Sir,—If the men responsible for the Dardanelles tragedy are allowed to go free, can we ever again, in common fairness, punish the driver who in a moment of forgetfulness has wrecked his train and brought death and disaster to his passengers?   EMILY EDWARDES.
119, Manor-road, Wallasey, Cheshire.

14 March 1917

THE MEN OF GALLIPOLI.
To the Editor of *The Daily Mail.*

Sir,—When are the men of Gallipoli to be officially recognised—the men who performed the "impossible," and in the face of a withering fire and sunken barbed wire landed and clung to that small strip of Turkey for eight months against 400,000 of the most experienced fighters in the world? The Turks were not our only obstacles. There was the lack of drinking water and also disease, from which scarcely a man escaped.

The Anzacs, I understand, are to receive a decoration from their respective Governments, and even now they are permitted to wear the symbol A" on their sleeves.

Surely it is time somebody raised the question of recognition for Gallipoli men in this country?
ONE OF THE OLD 29TH DIVISION.

20 December 1917

"WHERE DID THAT ONE GO?"
With apologies to Captain Bruce Bairnsfather.
The Dardanelles Commission's Report has burst like a veritable "Jack Johnson" over the Old Gang's dug-out in Abingdon-street.

Above right: "Where did that one go?" (with apologies to Captain Bruce Bairnsfather). The Dardanelles Commission's Report has burst like a veritable 'Jack Johnson' over the Old Gang's dug-out in Abingdon-street.

Above: An injured Australian soldier is carried to safety.

Right: The Lancashire Fusilliers prepare to go ashore at Cape Helles.

NO SLACKERS AT THE FRONT.

NOTHING MATTERS BUT SUCCESS.

The following are the concluding paragraphs in "Eye-Witness's" contribution to-day:-

If there is one thing—and it has become even more noticeable during the last few weeks—which strikes those who go about among our men, whether in the trenches, in billets, or in the hospitals, it is that the thought uppermost in their minds is not of their own hardships and sufferings but of the progress of the war in general and of the operations on our front in particular. The first question that a wounded man usually asks is: "How far did we get? Did we take such and such a trench or position?" He may have been maimed for life; most of his comrades may have been killed; but these things concern him little in comparison with the point of whether his battalion or company accomplished the task assigned to them.

Nothing else matters. All these questions of hours of work and wages which are agitating his friends at home are utterly strange to him. He accepts everything, the heaviest losses to his unit as well as his own personal misfortunes, in complete cheerfulness so long as he knows that we are winning. Not that the feeling throughout the Army has ever been other than one of supreme confidence in the eventual result; but there is now something more than that. Every man feels that the long, dreary winter is past and that it is no longer a question merely of "sticking it" in wet trenches under a rain of high explosive from above and in the ever-present danger of a mine from underneath. He feels that the time for the realisation of his hopes is arriving and that he is, in his own words, "going to get a bit of his own back."

1 April 1915

MAYOR WHO WAS A SPY.

(From Mr. J. Elder, a Kingston-on-Thames postal clerk doing duty at the front.)

We have to be most careful in our conversation, for there are spies everywhere, and of a most dangerous and treacherous kind... In one instance the mayor of a place turned out to be an ally of the enemy, and he was the chap whose duty it was to receive the British troops and find billets for them. He, I am glad to say, paid the extreme penalty, but only after considerable loss had been sustained.

2 November 1914

CHEAP PLEASURES FOR HEROES.
To the Editor of *The Daily Mail.*

Sir,—In Blackpool all men wearing the King's uniform travel at half-rates in the tramway-cars, and at all places of entertainment they are admitted at a reduced rate—in many cases half the sum charged to civilians.

This practice has been in force for more than two years, and is greatly appreciated. Why cannot London follow this example?

Blackpool.   P. M. HUMPHREY.

---

5 September 1917

THE "NELSON TOUCH."
To the Editor of *The Daily Mail.*

Sir,—Among the muddle and babble of those who would have us fight for our life without disliking the enemy, it is refreshing to get back a glimpse of the winning temper of England a century since. In Nelson's diary there rings out, year after year, like a trumpet call, the phrase that was the secret of his victories, "Down, down, down with the enemy!"

We shall never win till the hearts of our people pulse in unison, "Down, down, down with Germany."   W. M. W. PITCHFORD.
Lamport Rectory, Northampton.

28 August 1917

DADDY'S OLD CORPS.

(Lance-Corporal G. Hawkins, of the 1st Lincolnshire Regiment, writing home to Lincoln, says.)

I was wounded in the trenches, where we had been for about fifteen days, and during that time we had nothing to read but "Fray Bento's Corned Beef," and that soon tired us, especially as the tins were empty and we could not get supplies up. However we gave the Germans a good supply of lead pills, so that consoled us a bit.

"Daddy's Old Corps," as we call the Lincolns, caught a lot of prisoners who seemed glad to get caught. One man was asked if he spoke English. He replied, "English none," and on being asked if he wanted some biscuits he said, "Ah, yes I'm hungry," so he was evidently a typical German—good at telling lies. He also knew how to demolish, for he got through six biscuits and a 12oz tin of bully in a twinkling of a gnat's eyebrow, and then said "More."

2 November 1914

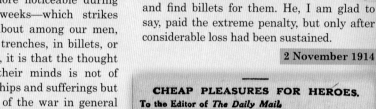

Above: **In July 1917 policemen began to patrol the streets carrying notices displaying the message "Police Notice-Take Cover"** if an air raid was expected. They blew whistles as they walked and afterwards Boy Scouts toured the area blasting on bugles to give the all clear.

Above: **A British intelligence sergeant examines a civilian's papers.**

Left: **Troops try to keep warm as they face the daily challenges of fighting on the Western Front.** There were clear plans in place for rotating the men; on average a soldier would spend about eight days on the front line.

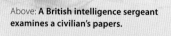

ZEPPELIN RAID ON ENGLAND LAST NIGHT

AIRSHIP ATTACK ON YARMOUTH, SHERINGHAM,

Above: Quartermaster Sergeant Rabjohn with his wife and daughter Mary after an air raid on Colchester in February 1915. Five hundred people had been killed in air raids by the end of the conflict.

Below: On 16 December 1914 the German High Fleet set out to bomb Scarborough, Whitby and Hartlepool. Scarborough, the first target, was subjected to ninety minutes of shelling, with the castle, the Grand Hotel and various properties and churches hit.

Below: Bomb damage left in Bury St Edmunds after the April 1915 Zeppelin attack. During the course of the conflict Germany conducted over fifty bombing raids on England. Beginning with attacks on King's Lynn and Great Yarmouth in January 1915, the terrifying airships appeared without warning, inflicting fear and panic in the civilian population.

SCARBOROUGH'S VICTIMS.

"MURDER" VERDICT URGED BY JURY.

"THE ENEMY WILL KNOW ALL ABOUT THIS."

The inquest on the seventeen Scarborough victims—eight women, four children, and five men—of the German raid on Wednesday, was held yesterday at Scarborough.

The coroner, Mr. George Taylor, said they were assembled to inquire into the circumstances of a tragedy such as had been unknown in that town for a thousand years. It had resulted from a bombardment of Scarborough by the ships of an enemy who were conducting war contrary to all the rules of civilised nations. It was an attack on an unfortified and defenceless town.

It might be that this method of conducting warfare was intended to terrorise the inhabitants of English towns, and at the same time to inspire confidence in the minds of the German people. A great deal was heard about German "Kultur," but he thought this nation was not disposed to imitate it. A similar visitation to our coast might be made again unless the British Fleet should be in a position to defend it, but our Fleet had a great deal to do, and a duty to discharge much more vital and important than that of meeting occasional attacks on defenceless populations.

FOUR ENEMY SHIPS.

Chief Petty Officer Arthur Dean, chief officer of the coastguard at Scarborough, said he was in his house at breakfast when the first gun from the German ships went off at 8.5 a.m. on Wednesday. "I walked out of my door and saw the walls of the castle tumbling down. I stayed outside about two minutes, and then saw two large cruisers come in sight from behind the castle towards South Bay. They opened fire with all their guns on the starboard side. They kept up an incessant fire. After-

16 December 1914

CLERGY AND AIR RAIDS.

To the Editor of *The Daily Mail.*

Sir,—Mrs. Ella F. Thompson asks, "Where are our clergy and Church workers when the tubes are crowded during an air raid?" And she goes on to say, "Surely this is the opportunity for our clergy at last to do something." I imagine that what is being done is not published, as we do not seek cheap advertisement.

But, at the same time, many of us who are not at the front are "doing our bit" among the people in our parishes who live in rottenly built little houses, walking through our streets regardless of personal danger and persuading people to go indoors and take cover. Mrs. Thompson should ask the police what we are doing. They know if we are funks or not.

In my own church crypt and in the cellars each evening this week we have taken in 600 to 700 men, women, and children, and by short services and other means have succeeded in allaying their anxieties until the "All clear" is given.

W. J. J. CORNELIUS, C.F., Vicar.
All Saints' Vicarage, Sumner-road, North Peckham, S.E.

30 September 1917

DISGUST IN U.S.

"IS IT THE MADNESS OF DESPAIR?"

FROM OUR OWN CORRESPONDENT.

NEW YORK, Wednesday.

Indignation and disgust are the keynote of American comment on yesterday's air raid.

The *New York Herald*, under the heading "More Slaughter of Innocents," asks:

"Is it the madness of despair or just plain, everyday madness that has prompted the Germans to select for attack the peaceful, undefended resorts of England's east coast? First a squadron of German cruisers swooped down upon Hartlepool, Whitby, and Scarborough to take their toll of death of non-combatants—'women and children first'—and now it is an aerial attack on Yarmouth, Sheringham, and King's Lynn. What can Germany hope to gain by these wanton attacks upon undefended places and this slaughter of innocents? Certainly not the good opinion of the peoples of neutral nations."

The *United Press* observes:

"Once more the futility of an offensive attack from the air has been demonstrated; once more women and children have been killed as the result of useless experiments with aerial weapons. The science of warfare has not mounted to the heavens. Valuable observations can be made from above, but death and destruction cannot be rained down except upon the innocent more than the guilty. Civilians are prohibited from making war upon the enemy, and the strict application of the German military code in Belgium has demonstrated what fearful penalties are imposed on the civil population that takes up arms against the soldiers in uniform. But attacks, it seems, can be delivered against women and children by aerial soldiers, not only without incurring penalties but also without loss of military honour.

"The civilian has no rights. He can be murdered with impunity if military reasons require; no warning of bombardment will be given him, and if he resists he makes himself an outlaw, to be summarily shot.

"Probably air raids on England will encourage daring and heroism by force of example among the German troops. German public opinion, too, which has pinned great faith to the effectiveness of aircraft, has influenced the present raid. Nevertheless, the killing of women and children is a hard price to exact, even though it stimulates battlefield courage and keeps public opinion contented."

22 January 1915

"OVER THE TOP."

BY AN OFFICER.

The Infantry will advance to the attack of the First Objective at 1.30 p.m.—Operation Orders.

8 a.m.—Since dawn two lion-hearted servants, who came up five miles under shell-fire during the night, have been busy with mysterious rites in the bottom of the trench.

It is quite a good trench, as trenches on the Somme go, about shoulder deep, with long holes scooped at intervals in the sandy parapet (rather like the tombs of Christian martyrs in the catacombs), where one may sleep, if one can. The trench is just the breadth of a man. To pass along it, crowded as it now is with men, requires the agility of the jungle ape blended with the patience of Job.

The previous occupants of the officers' corner of the trench, who displayed such indecent joy on being relieved last night, have scooped out a niche in the parapet to serve as a table. On this one of the servants deposits a teapot, a loaf, a plate of cold boiled bacon, a saucer of butter, and two tin cups, and announces breakfast.

We stop studying the view. The trench is not deep enough to prevent one's enjoying the landscape, a stretch of undulating pasture in front, then a reddish, greyish tangle of wire running in front of a yellow scar gashed in the grass. Beyond it is a village wreathed in dense clouds of smoke. The noise—not to forget a detail— is ear splitting. That is why we all eat breakfast standing up. If you sit down the thud of the shells bursting in the German lines rattles your eardrums till your head aches.

We are only four officers, with the two companies that are going to lead the attack for we are going in "under strength." While we breakfast, my company commander and I pore over our maps spread out on the parapet of the trench. For the hundredth time we discuss the plans we have made for keeping our direction as we advance to each successive objective. We disagree violently as to whether we turn half left, on leaving the trench, as he maintains, or a quarter left, which is my opinion.

8.30 a.m.—We still breakfast. The subaltern of the other company, pointing at the landscape with a piece of bread and jam, says: "Doesn't their wire look beastly?"

8.45 a.m.—The sun comes out and floods the scene with light, even tingeing the shell-bursts with gold. You catch yourself looking at your watch. "Only a quarter to nine!" is what you say. What you are thinking is that in five hours, anyhow, this rotten waiting about will be over, one way or another.

9.30 a.m.—The other company commander retires to his Christian martyr's tomb and reads the Field. His subaltern is still eating bread and jam. My company commander writes a note to the company sergeant-major. I watch two grey-coated Huns plodding stolidly along among the shell-bursts, carrying a plank. They disappear.

10 a.m.—Three aeroplanes come out from over our lines. Rather more noise in consequence, "Archies," machine-gun fire.

10.30 a.m.—German "H.E." shrapnel, very black, very smelly, very noisy, very erratic. The other company commander leaves his hole and demands to know why the blazes we are kept loafing about like this all the morning; people always attack at dawn; why make a blessed matinee of it?

11 a.m.—Frantic demands down the trench for Sergeant Bradawl: "Pass the word down for Sergeant Bradawl." One of the servants vouchsafes the information that the sergeant was killed last night. "On the water fatigue, sir," he says. "I saw him dead myself." More aeroplanes, more noise, more German shrapnel, most objectionable, but wide.

11.30 a.m.—Two hours more! My company commander and I agree we will stay where we are till one o'clock, then go along the trench to the right where the company is, see that the men can all get out of the trench easily, and pick a good jumping off place for ourselves.

Noon.—The servants produce a bottle of port. It betrays considerable signs of the agitation of the night. We partake of "port wine and a biscuit" in approved style. Wine does not taste well out of a chipped enamel mug, especially port after it has been under shell fire.

12.15 p.m.—We lunch off tongue, bread, and sand. The port is by this time so thick that it fortunately veils the interesting mineral deposits in the bottom of the mug. I retire to the Christian martyr's tomb and read several pages of the Field without understanding them.

12.30 p.m.—One hour more! Great map and compass work by everybody. Much discussion about the final objective, somewhere beyond the smoke wreaths round the village. My company commander produces a two-franc piece. "We'll toss who goes over with the leading platoon," he says. "Winner goes second." I win.

12.45 p.m.—My servant, wearing the chastened yet hopeful air of a second in the prize-ring, divests me of my raincoat and cap and hands me my helmet, then girds about my waist my belt with all the complicated paraphernalia of modern war—revolver, compass, field-glasses, gas helmet. The other officers are similarly occupied. Conversation languishes.

Right: **Allied troops leave the cover of the trenches to launch an attack at Gallipoli.**

---

9 SOLDIER BROTHERS.

EIGHT KILLED OR MISSING; ONE WOUNDED.

Nine brothers in the Army and eight killed or missing and one wounded is the war record of the Restorick family, of Birmingham.

The youngest brother, Private Thomas Restorick, of the Cameronians, fought at Mons and Neuve Chapelle, and was so badly wounded by shrapnel on July 15 that he has been invalided out of the Service.

All the Restoricks were in different regiments, and it is from other soldiers who have been in contact with his brothers that Private Thomas Restorick has learned of their fate. The father and mother of this family of soldier sons are dead, but there are four sisters living.

Private Restorick is at present in Berwick, staying with his father-in-law. He is thirty years of age, a fitter by trade, and his injuries have left him unfit for the performance of any but very light duties.

TWO BROTHERS KILLED.

News has reached Belfast that the brothers Joseph and James Murray, privates in the Inniskilling Fusiliers, have died.

They were in the same battalion, fought together in the Dardanelles, were sent together to another front, gassed at the same time, taken to the same hospital, and died on the same day.

---

9 September 1916

12.55 p.m.—Our orderlies appear, mysteriously, unbidden, at out sides, as is the way of orderlies. We four officers compare watches. My company commander and I set off along the trench.

1 p.m.—The British soldier is as full of angles as he is in a Nevinson war picture. He and his equipment stick out all over the trench. We are squeezed, battered, and bruised as we force our way along the trench foot by foot. The men are singularly quiet—the old ones phlegmatic, the young ones thoughtful.

1.10 p.m.—The din is awe-inspiring; the very air seems to tremble with noise. This must be the intensive bombardment. It makes the nerves tingle with excitement. The men are waking up. You look at your watch and wonder how much longer you can bear the strain of waiting not for what may happen but to fight—to get at them.

1.20 p.m.—We find a good spot to get out from, right in the centre of the company. The men of the platoon that is to lead are standing in the niches they have cut, ready to leave the trench at the sound of the whistle.

1.25 p.m.—Five minutes to go! We get our whistles out. My company commander gets up in our niche. The noise is deafening. You have to shout to make yourself heard.

1.27 p.m.—"Three minutes more I make it!" bawls my company commander in my ear. I nod, without lifting my eyes from my wrist.

1.28 p.m.—A man beside me points excitedly to the left. "They're off!" he yells. I see a stream of figures moving forward, ever so slowly, on the extreme left. It is a false start but they keep on.

1.29 p.m.—We are still waiting. My company commander has one foot on the parapet. He turns round and grins at me.

1.30 p.m.—A whistle just above me, whistles all along the line, men scrambling, stumbling on every side. The first platoons are off. Lord! What a row!

1.31 p.m.—How leisurely everybody seems to be moving forward! My platoon is tumbling out of the trench; I presume I blew my whistle. Smoke and noise and figures swarming through the haze. My company commander waits for me as I come up and roars in my ear: "Half left;

you see I was right!" A man beside you exclaims, "Oh!" in pained astonishment, as it seems, and you see him at your feet with the blood gushing out of his head.

Then you realise you are "over the top"—and you never knew it.

22 October 1916

A man beside you exclaims, "Oh!" in pained astonishment and you see him at your feet with the blood gushing out of his head.

18 July 1916

FOOTBALLERS' DUTY TO THE ARMY.

In 1914 there were over 5,000 professional footballers in Britain and 2,000 enlisted during the course of the war. Edinburgh City Pals Battalion was established in November 1914 as part of the Royal Scots, from players and supporters of Heart of Midlothian Football Club; the following month the Football Battalion was formed as part of the Middlesex Regiment.

The football league continued through the 1914-15 season with the FA Cup being played according to schedule. After this, association football was suspended until 1919, although regional competitions were allowed to take place.

Below left: **The professional footballer Walter Tull was the first mixed race officer in the British Army. He was killed in action on 25 March 1918. Tull was cited for his "gallantry and coolness" during action at the Piave river in Italy.**

Opposite: **Highland Territorials cross a German communication trench during the attack on Flesquières in 1917.**

Below right: **The 1915 FA Cup Final was a subdued affair, held at Old Trafford on a damp afternoon before a crowd of only 50,000; many were servicemen displaying signs of the injuries sustained in battle. Sheffield United won the match against Chelsea 3-0.**

FOOTBALLERS' DUTY TO THE ARMY.
To the Editor of *The Daily Mail.*

Sir,—I was surprised to find in *The Daily Mail* a statement from Colonel Grantham that only 122 professional footballers had joined the Footballers' Battalion.

Now in the country there are probably 4,000 or 5,000 professional footballers who, because of their calling, must be young men in the prime of life. The majority of them are single, and it is sad to think that only 122 have joined the battalion specially formed for them.

One who has officiated often in Southern League football and has frequently gone into the players' dressing-rooms, can easily imagine what a fine battalion 1,000 footballers would be—"hard as nails and fit as fiddles."

I see arrangements are already being tentatively made to continue football next year. There are two ways to stop it absolutely: (1) For the War Office to take over all professional grounds and utilise them as drill grounds; (2) for the present referees and linesmen to refuse to officiate in further matches after this season until the war is over. I intend to refuse. LINESMAN.

2 April 1915

FOOTBALL TO STOP.

NO MORE PROFESSIONALISM TILL WAR OVER.

The Football Association have decided that no Cup-tie or League football matches shall be played next season until the war is over. A statement to this effect was made by Mr. Charles Crump, the senior vice-president of the Football Association, in presenting the cup and medals to the winners of the Amateur Cup at New Cross.

A resolution to this effect will be adopted probably at the council meeting to be held on the eve of the Cup Final at Manchester on Friday. At the last council meeting on March 29 the Football Association passed a resolution giving itself power to suspend the game either sectionally or entirely if it thought desirable.

Mr. F. J. Wall, secretary of the Football Association, said that no agreements would be entered into for next season. A very large number of players are now engaged on Government contracts and munitions of war.

20 April 1915

FOOTBALLS FOR THE FRONT
Soldiers' Appeal to Home Clubs

From our own correspondent, Boulogne, Monday.

Men of the A. S. C. and the R. A. M. C. who are quartered here take every advantage when the tide is out of playing football on the fine stretch of sand.

Corporal H Whitcomb, a member of the R. A. M. C., who has been out here since the beginning of the war, told me how the football clubs in England could do the soldiers over here a really good turn.

"When we came out here," he said, "we brought with us a football, for we can't do without a game now and then. Since we've been here we bought one, but the price we had to pay was altogether too much. Now if the clubs at home will only send out to us all the old balls they can spare they would be doing us a real service. Now that the winter is coming on a game of football is as good as an overcoat. We can keep ourselves warm and at the same time exercise ourselves."

20 October 1914

FOOTBALL, NOT FLIGHT.

A Tyrone Officer.—Heard this morning that a German telephone which our intelligence intercepted said, "Men running about furiously in the square and in great commotion at British headquarters." Very amusing, all caused by our men kicking a football about the street.

An officer of Guards.—One of our men did a splendid thing three days ago. There was a thick fog and a group of three men was out in front as a patrol.

The fog lifted very suddenly and before they had time to get back into the trenches they were fired on. One was killed, one slightly wounded, and managed to crawl back, and the third badly wounded.

A man volunteered to go out and help him in. So he started off and crawled out with bullets striking close all round him (one took the heel off his boot), got to the wounded man, and crawled in again. Then he and another man crawled out again with a stretcher.

Having once got the man in the stretcher they stood up and walked in with him, as, of course, they would not then be fired at. The whole thing took an hour. The one man has been recommended for a "V.C" and the other for a "D.C.M."

14 October 1914

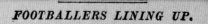

FOOTBALLERS LINING UP.

There was quite a rush at the recruiting office of the Footballers' Battalion in Kingsway yesterday, over 200 men being sworn in. The authorities, it is stated, are more than pleased with the physique of the men. Among the new recruits is Satterthwaite, the old Woolwich Arsenal player. Many of the officers are Blues and Double Blues. Internationals are to be found among officers and men.

13 January 1915

FOOTBALL RESULTS BY TELEPHONE.

(An Officer writes.)

The German trenches are about 100 to 150 yards away. We are on quite good terms with them, and exchange a shot occasionally, just to show we are still here. Neither of us shell the other, as our trenches are too near, and consequently the gunners might do damage to their own side; so we are quite "comfy." Our trenches are not dug down, but breastworks of sandbags and earth, etc. We have fires going day and night, and we are O.K.

Sometimes we shout across to the Germans. We can easily hear them singing at night, and our men sing ragtime and hymns all day long. We cannot, of course, move about much by day, so there is a telephone up to headquarters and to the trenches on either side of us. The telephone operators spend most of their time sending through the latest football results, and then shouting them down the trench. Having got these through yesterday, they condescended to send through the news that we had sunk a German cruiser, and all the other news, but it is always the football first. So we are quite happy. Please send me some catapult elastic, as we are going to play about with them, and hope to add to our menu thereby.

13 February 1915

(An officer writes.)

We got in at dark and ploughed our way through the same old mud. Now and again a little variety was caused by falling into "Johnson", holes full of water. This is very amusing when someone else falls in, but rather trying to the temper when you suddenly find yourself up to the chin in water. When one arrives in trenches one becomes at once a cross between a navvy and a farm labourer, and we dig till we are too tired to go on, and then we continue digging by way of a change, for we run no risks through having bad head cover which the wily sniper could get a bullet through. Work at night is in a way a blessing in disguise, for it helps the time to pass; it's the waiting, waiting, which wears your nerves, and I am always glad to trot about and see sentries and listening posts, for it's a break in the monotony. That night there was a keen frost—so keen that places where one went knee deep in mud at seven in the evening would bear your weight easily at six in the morning.

But it's rather unpleasant feeling your wet socks and boots freeze, though life is made up out of minor worries like this.

With daylight come the shells. It's marvellous how callous one becomes. I heard one—a new type, which goes "Whiz, Bang!" in one breath—which we have named "Whistling Rufus." I leaped lightly—i.e., crawled backwards out of my dug-out to see where it was, and found it a good fifty yards away, so returned and slept. Just behind me was a pond with a few defunct animals in it.

25 January 1915

A COLONEL IN COMMAND OF AN AMMUNITION COLUMN WRITES.

Orders to advance come in at any time, and within half an hour we are packed up and on the road. First come a few motorcyclists looking very smart and workman-like, with rifles slung across their backs. They whiz on ahead when required at fifty miles an hour, but usually keep within sight of the head of the column, which glides along at about twelve miles an hour, each section of twelve or thirteen lorries being led by an officer in a motor-car who is responsible for the pace and selection of proper roads.

These heavy motor vehicles bear the names of various English firms in London or the provinces. Thus one meets with "Harrods" or some well-known brewery at every turn. Not content with the name blazoned in gold letters on the side of the vehicle, Chauffeur Tommy christens his own van anew, and such names as "Slumbering Sam," "Furious Fanny," "Blundering Bill," "Lumbering Luke," and "Mustard Mike" are painted in neat white characters on the side of the bonnet.

The leading lorry contains an armed guard to protect the precious contents of Sam, Luke and Fanny from the possible assaults of lurking Uhlans who may have escaped the vigilance of the first-line troops. Softly the long train glides along when the roads are good, or lumber noisily over the rough pave. Sometimes Fanny skids into a soft place and has to be extricated by a first-aid lorry with jacks and towing ropes.

Barricades erected on the roads have to be carefully twisted through or even dug away to pass. And now the French interpreter spins ahead to the destination to interview M. le Maire to procure the best billets the village can afford, and soon the column comes up, each lorry halting on the right side of the road in its allotted place, and in a few minutes fires are going and tea (relished by Tommy at all hours) is made.

The guard is mounted, sentries put out, and soon the men are making friends with the villagers and buying any eatables and drinks available to supplement their already generous ration. As darkness draws on the sounds of merriment are heard, and "It's a long, long way to Tipperary," "Rule Britannia" the "Marseillaise," and finally "God Save the King" are rendered by the choir. Roll-call is at 8.30. and then, camping under the shelter of hospitable Sam or Luke, the men are soon asleep.

4 November 1914

THE KAISER BLAMES SIR E. GREY FOR THE WAR.

A REMARKABLE INTERVIEW.

"I never desired this war. Every act of mine in the 26 years of my government proves that I did not want to bring about this or any other war."

—The Kaiser's Statement to Herr Ballin.

HERR BALLIN.

BULLIES MUST BE THRASHED.

To the Editor of *The Daily Mail.*

Sir,—Surely no more brutal outrage has been committed, even by the German butchers, than that just reported by the Secretary of the Admiralty. Forty men of the crew of the Belgian Prince were done to death with no possible chance of escape, while their foul murderers were no doubt revelling in safety in their U-boat over their fiendish work, and looking forward to their due reward by the archfiend the "All-Highest."

Will our cooing doves at home never realise what we are "up against"? There has only been one way of dealing with a cowardly bully, and that is by thrashing him till he howls for mercy.

Stock Exchange. EDWARD F. DE ZOETE.

7 August 1917

CRIPPEN WAS A GERMAN.

FROM ALICE COUNTESS OF STRAFFORD.

To the Editor of *The Daily Mail.*

Sir,—Referring to your leading article in *The Daily Mail,* headed "Bombs on Hospitals," you truly add, "Dr. Crippen was a mild and humane man compared with Mr. Ramsay Macdonald's 'German friends.'" Perhaps you may not be aware that Crippen was a German. His real name was Cribben. I know this.

A. H. F. STRAFFORD.

13, Lower Berkeley-street, W. 1.

29 August 1917

BOMB THE RHINE TOWNS.

To the Editor of *The Daily Mail.*

Sir,—Cannot the Hun be paid back in his own coin for his latest "frightfulness" on the homes and harmless women and children of this nation?

We read of our airmen bombing the Hun aerodromes in Belgium, but why not bomb the Rhine towns as often as, if not more frequently than, the Hun bombs England?

Something more than the mere bombing of aerodromes must be done to satisfy the British public. J. H. B. R. (twice wounded).

7 September 1917

JUSTICE FOR THE KAISER.

To the Editor of *The Daily Mail.*

Sir,—It is a great satisfaction to learn from General Smuts, whose conscience can safely be trusted, that in our operations against Germany we will avoid German abominations.

But, on the conclusion of this war, are the Kaiser and the Crown Prince to be punished for their violation of all law, both human and Divine? That is the supreme question. In my humble judgment, we owe it to the world and to posterity to make a terrible and never-to-be-forgotten example of these miscreants. Unless we do, the lesson to bloodthirsty ambition will be thrown away.

More important than the evacuation of Belgium, the safeguarding of France, the destruction of Prussian militarism itself is the vindication of eternal justice. *Fiat justitia, ruat cœlum.* Let justice be done, though the heavens should fall.

A. KIPLING COMMON.

Cocoa Tree Club, St. James's-street, S.W. 1.

8 October 1917

Above and opposite below: More than two million German men would meet their deaths before the war was over.

Above right: A German officer walks towards Allied lines after being captured by Canadians during the Battle of Hill 70. It had been hoped that this localised conflict would draw German troops away from the main offensive, but the tactic was only partially successful.

The "Pus...

To the Editor of *The Daily Mail.*

Sir,—While we English-born women married to Germans and separated from them by a gulf wider and a thousand times safer than any law are patiently waiting until the new divorce laws are passed, which promise hopes of freedom, can nothing be done which will alter our present unbearable position as German aliens?

We are always under unnecessary observation and suspicion; our movements are curtailed; the police calling at our homes to inquire if we still live at them; and life made so miserable that even in dreams we are haunted by the situation into which we are helplessly thrust. Our hearts and minds are turned always and only in one direction, to our Mother-country, but our hands and lives are fettered and bound.

I have three brothers in the English Army, and when one of them came to bid me "good-bye" before being sent to the front I could not even go to see him off at the station without special permission, as it is slightly beyond the five-miles limit in which I am allowed to travel. M. G.

28 August 1917

HATE IN A GERMAN TRENCH.

OFFICER'S OUTBURST.

(A R.A.M.C. Sergeant writes.)

The Germans played the game decently and, needless to say, so did our fellows. They asked us to discontinue using dum-dum bullets. They are apparently under the impression that we use them, and we were almost certain they did, seeing the mess one or two of our fellows who were hit were in, but we have come to the conclusion that, owing to the (a) pointed bullet, (b) extremely high velocity, and (c) extraordinarily short range—viz., less than a hundred yards—bones being struck get splintered and smashed. I am forwarding a copy of a letter received on Christmas Day. The Germans asked for no firing, not us.

"Gentlemen, —You asked us yesterday temporarily to suspend hostilities and become friends during Christmas. Such a proposal in the past would have been accepted with pleasure, but at the present time, when we have clearly recognised England's true character, we refuse to make any such agreement. Although we do not doubt that you are men of honour, yet every feeling of ours revolts against any intercourse towards the subjects of a nation which for years has in an underhand way sought the friendship of all other nations so that, with their help, they might annihilate us; a nation also which, while professing Christianity, is not ashamed to use dum-dum bullets, and whose greatest desire would be to see the political disappearance and social eclipse of Germany.

"Gentlemen, you are not, it is true, the responsible leaders of English politics, and so are not directly responsible for their business, but all the same you are Englishmen whose annihilation we consider to be our sacred duty. We therefore request you to take such action as will prevent your 'mercenaries,' whom you call soldiers, from approaching our trenches in future.

"LIEUTENANT OF LANDWEHR."

21 January 1915

HERE IS MY FRIEND MAX.

When 1914 was young and before the Kaiser had removed the "Lid," I found sustenance in Cocoa—diluted as a beverage and concentrated in the Press. Over many brews of the brown liquid I fraternised with a Hun whom my Press exhorted me to love brotherly. Max was a charming young fellow engaged in the study of the British insurance system – a worker in the cause of "peaceful penetration." He belonged, of course, to a German club, the members of which spent their Sundays in the pleasant and harmless amusement of exploring and photographing the environs of London. Every Sabbath, wet or fine, winter or summer, the club visited different outlying suburbs—as Max jokingly suggested—"to select and photograph gun positions for the 'day' when a German Army Corps invested London, as your Daily Mail would say." How I laughed as I looked up momentarily from the comfort of Cocoa! But Max laughed louder and longer than I. Together we visited Paris for the Easter holidays.

Max knew his Paris as thoroughly as London. I was very English and obtuse, and there were moments when he no longer troubled to conceal his superior German intelligence.

We visited the Invalides, and Max sorrowfully regarded the captured Prussian standards. "War!" he exclaimed. "To steal your neighbour's property and then exhibit it!"

But the sight of the Arc de Triomphe restored his good humour.

"How our glorious lads must have thrilled when they marched with conquering stride past here in '71!" he cried enthusiastically.

When we were on top of the Eiffel Tower he surprised me. The wireless was crackling busily, and Max lapsed into a brown study.

"Do you know," he murmured dreamily, "that when war comes this is the first place we will shoot down?"

I was perplexed, but I returned to England—and Cocoa—and forgot.

Max "providentially" returned to Germany just before the fourth of August. I saw him on the eve of his departure, and I wondered at his emotion.

"Ach, you English!" he exclaimed at my question. "You do not know what war is. That strip of blue water that separates you from the Continent is wider than you think…"

In the following November I received a letter bearing an English postmark and enclosing Max's photograph as a Bavarian soldier.

He was on the "eve of going to the front in Northern France" to fight against Englishmen, yet he was "concerned about the fate of his luggage in London." He wished me to care for it while he proceeded with his job of killing Englishmen! Possibly he thought I still imbibed Cocoa.

Sometimes, in the trenches, I wondered if Max was on the other side of the parapet. But Max, going to the front opposite Ypres in '14 to fight the old "Contemptibles," would hardly be termed, in insurance phraseology, a "first-class life." Yet he may survive.

If he does, his hope that the "war will not interfere with our friendship" is futile.

Yes, Max, I can say with "Sir John Rhead," in Milestones, "We live and learn."

SIDNEY HOWARD.

21 June 1918

WE DO NOT HATE ENOUGH.

To the Editor of The Daily Mail.

Sir,—Mrs. "Maude Annesley," in her downright article "Do We Hate Enough?" in Thursday's Daily Mail, has voiced the views of millions.

We do not hate enough, because it is impossible. No hatred can possibly be great enough for the Huns and their accursed deeds. And no contempt is too great for those who have the glory of being British-born subjects and who yet palter with "spiritual-brotherhood slush," to quote Mrs. Annesley's vigorous expression. They are self-confessed Bolos or Ignorants, or they lack all imagination to appreciate what others have lived through during a three-years-and-three-months' storm of unbridled murder, lust, and devilry.

I have seen in France what the Huns have wrought on human bodies, in human souls, on land and property; others have seen that, and more, in Belgium, Serbia, and Rumania—all done, not in any righteous cause, but with the sole idea of fulfilling their own insensate ambition of subordinating the whole world to their bestial notions of life.

What I have seen with my own eyes and heard with my own ears has made me take a solemn vow, a vow which, in my opinion, every subject of the Allied nations should take and keep while life lasts:

> Never, knowingly, to speak to a German, or to touch a German's hand in friendship.
>
> Never, knowingly, to buy German goods, or to enter a place where a German is employed.

Hatred of incarnate brutality, wickedness, lust, and murder is not a vice. It is a righteous and a virile sentiment. E. ALMAZ STOUT.

LORD NORTHCLIFFE'S WARNING.
FROM LADY PRIMROSE.

To the Editor of The Daily Mail.

Sir,—Every mother in the Empire must thank Lord Northcliffe for his outspoken words in his letter to the Prime Minister.

All down the centuries British mothers have known that their sons' first duty was defence of their native land. The doctrine of pacifism—a sort of twin brother to "Wait-and-See"-ism—can only be the result of degenerate nerves.

Boloism thrives in this atmosphere.

Those who are not prepared to defend their birthright can have no stake in the interests of their country, and therefore should have no vote as to its government.

The unfettered action of the pacifists is not only prolonging the war by hampering our Navy and Army, thus causing unnecessary loss of life, but it is also endangering a successful issue to this titanic struggle.

One of two things: we must change our ways, or America will take control.

HELEN PRIMROSE.

44, Ennismore-gardens, S.W. 7.

17 November 1917

WEEK. | VICAR'S BUTTER | BRITISH REPRISAL ... TO BR ... A. ARM ... TONS DIV ...

OLD POTATOES FOR THE WOUNDED
To the Editor of *The Daily Mail.*

Sir,—Is it fair that soldiers in hospital should be expected to eat the oldest potatoes in the world when the whole of England is revelling in cheap new potatoes?

This is the case in a large South London military hospital, where the potatoes are practically impossible when boiled and just edible when fried. OBSERVER.

5 August 1917

Above: A large banner encouraging citizens not to waste food flies above a recruiting campaign held in Trentin, New Jersey.

Left: Christmas dinner for these men is bread, jam and tea in a shell hole at Beaumont Hamel, next to the graveside of one of their comrades.

Bottom:Food queues form outside a shop on Stamford Street at Blackfriars.

Opposite above: Soldiers home on Christmas leave buy their turkeys at a stall near Victoria Station.

Opposite below: British and French troops combine forces to cook a meal.

HORSEFLESH FOR FOOD.
To the Editor of *The Daily Mail.*

Sir,—There is a Hunnish coarseness about the term horseflesh. In this country we do not speak of oxflesh, sheepflesh, or pigflesh. There is no ignorance of the origin of beef, mutton, and pork, but our nomenclature, very rightly I think, does not "rub it in." If it be desired to popularise horseflesh as a food it should be given a popular name. I suggest *carquin* (or the simpler *carkin*), derived from the Latin *Caro equina*. F. SOUTHERDEN.
Exeter.

"WHAT HORSES THINK"
To the Editor of *The Daily Mail.*

Sir,—My letter headed "What Horses Think" in last Wednesday's *Daily Mail* has brought me a shoal of letters from horse-lovers from Land's End to John o' Groat's, which I find too numerous to answer individually.

May I therefore trespass upon the hospitality of your columns to thank the writers collectively and to say how deeply interesting I consider their correspondence and how much pleasure I shall miss owing to the utter impossibility of answering them personally? AUSTIN LATHAM.
113, Empress-avenue, Ilford, E.

OVERFED DOGS AND STARVED HENS.
To the Editor of *The Daily Mail.*

Sir,—The case of Miss Evodia Hughes, who in ten days obtained at Carmarthen 100lb. of meat for her dog, shows to what lengths some people will go in feeding their dogs. Yet there is no restriction on the number of dogs we may keep, and no additional tax has been imposed on them.

On the other hand, poultry, which produce a quantity of valuable food, are to be restricted severely, and we are told that three-quarters of the present stock may have to be killed off. While these anomalies exist, can it be said that our Government is taking the present food shortage seriously? F. L. S.
Farnham, Surrey.

6 August 1917

THE POOR MAN'S POTATO.
To the Editor of *The Daily Mail.*

Sir,—All persons who are in receipt of an income of more than £2 10s. a week should at once refrain from eating any potatoes whatever.

This would surely be the means of at once putting our poorer brothers and sisters in a very much safer position as to the food they require, and would mean cutting out the potato until better times came from every hotel and restaurant and well-to-do household; in fact, any man who ordered a potato in a public place or before his servants in his own home would then be entirely eligible for the highest distinctive order for bravery at the table. SEYMOUR HICKS.
The Princes Theatre, London, W.C.

FOOD CONTROL OR PROFITEERING.
To the Editor of *The Daily Mail.*

Sir,—Already the Food Controller has seen fit to control the prices of potatoes, tea, and parsnips, and those of milk, sugar, and coal have also been fixed. The shortage of potatoes has led to a "run" on every other kind of vegetable, and rice, peas, beans, lentils, and the like are greatly in demand. But the "food profiteers" are wide awake, and already extortionate and unwarrantable prices are being charged for those commodities.

Is it too much to hope that the Food Controller will instantly, and not three months hence, put a stop to the nefarious exploitation of the public which is now in progress? A. L. REED.
Temple, E.C.

21 March 1917

LONDON SQUARES AS HEN RUNS.
To the Editor of *The Daily Mail.*

Sir,—In view of the general shortage of food, could not the London square gardens be used as chicken runs?

Hens could easily be kept there, as all the gardens are enclosed by high railings, and in most of them are some small building, shed, or summerhouse that could be easily converted into a henhouse.

The gravel walks are particularly suited to hens, and either the owners of the houses or their servants could look after them. Eggs are important items of food at present when we are asked to be so sparing with meat and bread. No damage would be done to the gardens save that no bedding-out flowers would be practical; but surely no patriotic citizen could allow this to weigh in the balance, and it would not prevent the old or the young or the sick using the gardens.

In view of the serious scarcity of eggs and the gravity of the situation before us, it seems to me an absolute duty that these valuable open spaces should be put to a use of this sort.
15, Gloucester-square, W. NINA COHEN.

15 February 1917

TOO MUCH TEA FOR SOLDIERS?

Sir,—I wonder how many people realise the amount of tea that is drunk by "Tommy" in the British Army?

The average soldier drinks perhaps three or four times as much tea in the Army as he did in civil life. He has tea for breakfast, if possible tea in the middle of the morning, again tea after dinner, and tea at his tea-time, and very often a cup of tea with biscuits at night before turning in to bed. Altogether, perhaps, 5 pints of tea a day!

Is this good? The business man, clerk or working man in peace time would probably have tea once a day—at tea-time, for the average man has coffee for his breakfast. Why doesn't the Army provide coffee at the morning meal for Tommy? I believe from a medical point of view there is much more heat-giving property in a cup of coffee than in a pint of tea.

The French poilu, besides having his coffee ration, has in addition his allowance of red wine—there is nothing provided for Tommy's midday meal.

Is this tea-drinking the cause of all the gastritis in the Army? For any medical officer will agree that the number of gastric stomach cases is abnormal, and this trouble is very difficult to cure, especially on Army food.

I suppose some day when this war is over and the ex-director of Army food supplies is sitting in front of his hearth his wife will say, "My dear, why didn't you supply the troops with a ration of coffee?"

"My love," he will reply. "it never entered my head."

A GASTRIC CORPORAL.

2 October 1918

GOLF COURSES AND AGRICULTURE.
To the Editor of The Daily Mail

Sir,—Your mention of the Sandy Lodge Golf Course makes me ask whether you cannot fix public attention upon these wasted lands. There must be hundreds of miles of them in England. We have two in Cambridge, one of which is near my house; it contains over 200 acres taken from farm land, and it is still kept carefully, the grass cut short regularly, although it is hardly used at all. But just think—200 acres of farm land wasted throughout this war in one place! Golf is all very well on sand dunes and waste land, but it is a crime to use wheat land for this old women's game.   W. H. D. ROUSE.
Perse School House, Glebe-road, Cambridge.
    ** Agricultural land does not make a good golf course; and vice versa.

2 January 1917

DEARER TEA.
To the Editor of The Daily Mail.

Sir,—We hope that the Tea Controller will take measures to stop profiteering in tea. The Government controls a proportion of the tea output under grades A, B, and C to be sold at 2s. 4d., 2s. 8d., and 3s. per lb.

It is very difficult to procure these " control " qualities as the wholesalers apparently prefer to sell their own blends bearing a larger profit. We have just been informed by a traveller that by the end of November tea will cost 8s. per lb. Cannot the Controller step in and control all supplies?   JONES, SONS, AND CO.,
                    Pharmaceutical Chemists.
Warrenpoint, Co. Down.

23 August 1917

WHAT THE SOLDIER EATS.
"RATIONS."

By A SUBALTERN.

Rations at the front consist of five chief items—biscuits, cheese, jam, tinned meat, and tea. It might be thought that this fare day after day for week after week would become monotonous. But appetites remain keen, the items themselves are slightly varied, and the general verdict of the soldier in the trenches is that he is well fed.

Army biscuits are of three kinds—ordinary, brown and crackly, and buttons. The ordinary are the least appetising; they are of a whitish brown hue, with no particular taste. They are, however, very much better than nothing, and with jam or a slice of bully beef quite good. The brown and crackly have a taste of porridge and brown sugar; they are very nice indeed, and pleasant to eat by themselves. The buttons have not much flavour but are fascinating little biscuits, small and fat, about the size round of a two-shilling piece. They are not often issued, but when they are the custom is to stuff one's pockets with them and dip into them throughout the day.

Cheese does not vary much. The richer kinds, such as Gorgonzola, are for obvious reasons not issued. At the front it would be impossible to extend the disciplinary measures which govern the issue of rations to the control of Gorgonzola cheese. The cheese issued is of the good plain dark yellow variety, and each man gets a handsome wedge a day.

Jam is issued in 1lb. tins—a tin roughly to every seven men. The idea is that one man should carry the tin and the others share it with him at a chosen time. In practice men outside the " firm " join in the banquet and the tin is finished and thrown away or kept for bomb manufacture. At a later hour in the day the ones who joined in produce a tin of their own, which the first firm share and help to empty. By this means the difficulty of carrying an open and half-empty tin of jam in the haversack is overcome. It has happened that in the excitement of an attack an opened tin of jam instead of a bomb has been thrown by mistake. Jam at the front is of many kinds—strawberry, raspberry, apricot, greengage, marmalade. The best-known variety is " plum and apple."

Tinned meat also varies. There is Fray Bentos—generally known as " bully." This is pink, stringy, and of a salt flavour. When nothing else can be procured—as often happens—the men eat it gladly enough. Cut in slices on a biscuit it is quite palatable. But it is not a thing which anyone would eat out of sheer gluttony. Stewed with potatoes it is quite good, and this is the way the men generally have it when they are in billets or anywhere where they can cook. The French peasants near the firing line quite like Fray Bentos and get a good many tins given them.

22 October 1915

As soon as the conflict began the British government put in place measures to protect the food supply. The country was still able to import food but on 1 February 1917 Germany began its campaign of unrestricted submarine warfare with merchant ships regulary hit, thus severely limiting food supplies. The public responded by converting gardens into allotments and keeping small livestock such as chickens. Three million acres of farming land was created with the Women's Land Army and conscientious objectors pressed into farming duties.

Despite this, food shortages became a serious issue with malnutrition becoming more common so in 1918 rationing was introduced.

Below: **The 11th Battalion of the East Lancashire Regiment, known as the Accrington Pals, was one of the worst hit on the first day of the Somme. Out of a force of around 700 men, 585 were reported dead or injured in one day.**

Opposite above: **British soldiers marching through France buy oranges from a local girl.**

Opposite below: **This official photograph of a warm, dry, well-fed, smiling "Tommy Atkins"— the generic name for a British soldier — created an impression far removed from reality.**

THE PRECIOUS SARDINE.

(From an officer to his mother.)

Of course I can't say anything about the war, for we only know what immediately concerns us.

The Germans' guns do shoot well. (So do ours.) I watched a battery being shelled by the Germans; two shots just short, two over, and then twenty all within 50 yards of the guns; about the fifteenth shot hit a gun and lifted it clean off the ground. Another time one of our heavy batteries was firing with an aeroplane directing their fire by wireless. Within fifteen minutes they had put the opposing battery out of action and disabled three of their guns, dropping two shells actually into the gun pits.

But of course guns are much easier to hit than men in trenches, as the shell has to drop slick into the trench to do any harm, and a trench is only 2ft. to 3ft wide. Yesterday they shelled our trenches near a village from about 6.30 a.m. till dusk. They must have fired some 1,000 or more shells. My trench was filled with mud, bits of beetroot, and one crow!

I found a tin of sardines the other day and was eating them when one fell into the mud, but he was too precious to waste. So he was picked up, wiped down with a very dirty handkerchief, and eaten, and tasted none the worse.

The other night we suddenly made an advance and that was beastly in the dark and rain and mud. Well, we advanced and then lay flat in the mud. Then advanced again, and after sometime got the order to entrench, which we did and just got finished at dawn in time to stop an advance by Germans. We were a mass of mud and slime, and still are, as we have no water to wash in. I've only had my clothes off once in three weeks and that was when I had my one and only bath.

11 November 1914

MEAT SUBSTITUTES.

Sir,—Would it not be better to encourage the consumption of poultry, rabbits, and pigeons which are produced in England by offering some inducement to consume them in the place of meat, which is more required by the Army and manual workers?

I would suggest that 3lb. of poultry, game, rabbits, or pigeons should be considered the equivalent of 2lb. of meat in computing weekly household consumption allowances. This might tend to reduce the consumption of meat still further.

FROM SIR HENRY HOARE.

9 February 1917

I found a tin of sardines the other day and was eating them when one fell into the mud, but he was too precious to waste.

"SHOOT THE BIRDS!"
To the Editor of *The Daily Mail.*

Sir,—I am glad to see from "G. S.'s" le [...] *The Daily Mail* that some one has the courage as well as the good sense to advocate the destruction of bird pests, or at any rate of a modicum of them.

I have here at Putney, within three minutes of Putney Bridge, what I believe to be the finest cherry tree in Surrey; this, with one or two other trees here and hereabouts, being the remnant of the great orchard that once stretched from Chiswick and farther to Wandsworth.

For some years past I have got practically no fruit on account of visitants in the shape of blackbirds, thrushes, and especially starlings, which have lately increased in such numbers. The tree, a full-grown one, is too large to net except at great expense, although I have managed to net isolated branches. The birds will peck at a cherry, and in nine cases out of ten it falls to the ground. Every morning during fruit time at least a bushel of such half-eaten fruit is found strewn upon the ground, good human food wasted.

Let us, as a set-off to the Wild Birds' Protection Act, have a Tame Human's Preservation Act. Save nourishing food and help the war at the same time. **G. WOOLLISCROFT RHEAD.**
Doune Lodge, Oxford-road, Putney, S.W.

10 January 1917

RESTAURANT PRICES.
To the Editor of *The Daily Mail.*

Sir,—The unfortunate business man, compelled to lunch away from home, wonders what ultimate extortions the *à la carte* restaurants will practise in their profiteering.

On Monday I lunched at a well-known but by no means luxurious restaurant near the Haymarket. The charge for six oysters, a small chop with *half* a grilled kidney, potatoes, bread, butter, and a small bottle of Guinness's stout, was 6s. 4d. The charge for two potatoes was 9d.

Yesterday, in a restaurant near Temple Bar, I was charged 2s. 10d. for a small fried flounder (alias "lemon sole"), potatoes, bread, butter, cheese, and a pint of ale.

These charges bear no relation to the actual rise of food prices. The only way for the business man is to bring his luncheon from home in a bag. His father was not too proud to do this in days when either of the meals instanced could have been obtained, in similar restaurants, for less than half these charges. **T. B.**

DRINK RATIONS.
To the Editor of *The Daily Mail.*

Sir,—Prohibiting off-sales will drive the workman to the public-house, in many cases for an article far more injurious than he would get in bottled form. And what of those people who are prohibited by their medical advisers from taking any stimulant but a little weak whisky and water? Is every invalid to be deprived of a stimulant in case of emergency?

The word "rations" is in the air; why not rations of whisky? Everybody is registered. Why not let those who must have spirits apply at the post office, produce their registration card, get it stamped, and receive a permit to buy one bottle per week or fortnight, the permit to be ruled in squares like a National Insurance card, and be crossed when delivery was made by the publican or off-licence holder, and in the important areas stop sales on draught if necessary?
CHAS. A. PALMER.
Palmeira House, 16, Mitcham-lane,
Streatham, S.W.

3 January 1917

PERCH IS GOOD TO EAT.
To the Editor of *The Daily Mail.*

Sir,—It may be of interest to some of your readers to know that perch are delicious if they are skinned before being fried.

A knife or scissors should be run down the centre of the back from head to tail, when the skin will come away with very little trouble. Many of our friends find perch treated in this way as good as freshly caught and fried trout.
A FLY FISHERMAN'S WIFE.

GIVE UP AFTERNOON TEA.
To the Editor of *The Daily Mail.*

Sir,—Let all who eat breakfast, lunch, and dinner or supper give up afternoon tea, and a huge saving in flour will result.

Busy people will not miss afternoon tea, and if idle people miss it it does not matter.

In French hospitals two good meals a day is all the patients are given. They increase in weight on this régime, which proves it is sufficient. Many English people eat four times daily and never give their digestion a moment's rest.

Will not other women join me in omitting afternoon tea during the war? It will not be found difficult if once tried. **E. LE BLOND.**
The Empress Club, 35, Dover-street,
Piccadilly, W. 1.

29 March 1917

MEAT WASTE IN CAMPS.
To the Editor of *The Daily Mail.*

Sir,—For the last week I have kept my household strictly on the prescribed limit of flour, meat, and sugar. It has been a little difficult, naturally, but all the inmates have done their best to assist. There has been no grumbling upstairs or downstairs.

I have a hospital, which, of course, I do not attempt to keep on the rations, as our wounded soldiers must be well fed, but there is a point to which I wish to draw attention.

Most of my patients tell me that there is terrible waste of meat both at home and at the front at some of the military camps owing to the vileness of the cooking, whole joints being thrown away because, by the ignorance or inefficiency of the cooks, they are rendered uneatable. Stews are served with fat, and so greasy that the soldiers throw the food away in disgust in preference to eating it.

Could not some good women cooks be supplied and so save this great waste? **ECONOMIST.**

DISTRIBUTING THE FOOD.
To the Editor of *The Daily Mail.*

Sir,—The most practical means of getting more food from the cottage garden to centres where wanted would be for the authorities to send a motor-van from one principal centre, calling at each village one day every week, the villagers being paid a fair price for their produce.

It would encourage the people who have the knowledge and land to grow more, and also supply the missing link between country and town. Tons of good food would in this way be collected which is now wasted through lack of a market. **S. HODGES.**
Bradpole, Bridport.

15 February 1917

WHAT YOUR FOOD COUPONS WILL BUY.

28 February 1918

IS IT JUSTICE?
To the Editor of *The Daily Mail.*

Sir,—My son, aged 24, was killed fighting the Huns. I am now asked to live on 4lb. of bread and 2½lb. of meat per week while we supply the Hun with 10½lb. of bread and 3½lb. of meat per week. I only ask one question, "Is this what my son died for?" **E. TURNER.**
23, Chandos-road, Cricklewood, N.W.

** Mr. Hope stated in the House of Commons that the whole scale of rations for German prisoners was being revised.

FOOD TREACHERY.
To the Editor of *The Daily Mail.*

Sir,—If, as Lord Lytton stated in the House of Lords, the standard of food consumption as laid down by the Controller "is very far from being complied with by the whole country," would it not be advisable for Lord Devonport to issue a plain warning that those who fail to comply are actually assisting the enemy? Such a statement might be effective, in the case of those with whom obligations of honour have apparently no weight at all.
Royal Automobile Club. **E. LOWNDES.**

15 February 1917

It is very difficult to do a man's work and remain a clinging woman.

Below: A woman confidently controls the trains in Birmingham. The first railway jobs offered to women were level crossing gatekeepers.

"MAGNIFICENT WOMEN."

To the Editor of *The Daily Mail.*

Sir,—With "Raw Colonial," whose ideas are recorded in an article in *The Daily Mail* headed "Magnificent Women," I am in constant wonder at the attitude towards women in this country.

They seem to be looked on as a nuisance. There is the greatest indignation if they are put into a job—"robbing the men" it is called.

Men must have all the work, women must be kept out. Even when men go wrong, it is the fault of the women. It is never the men who lead girls astray; it is the girls who tempt the poor, innocent men, who blush and keep their eyes down.

It is curious this pretended hatred of women; it is only pretended, and hypocrisy.

A Frenchman frankly avows he is fond of women. If one talks of women here the man gets up and says, "I am a single man; this is no place for me," as if he were a young girl.

In France the man's wife and daughters help in the book-keeping and running of his shop; in England they are not allowed to come near it, and a lout of a boy loafs round the shop yawning and thinking of his football or betting.

Why not save his wages and give the wife and daughters an interest in the business?

A BUSINESS MAN.

12 August 1917

HOW OUR GIRLS CAN GET HUSBANDS.

NATIONAL MATCH-MAKING.

I once won a competition on "Why I Have Never Married." In fun I said, "Because I had not a match-making mother."

The truth of it has only just come home to me with regard to other girls. A match-making mother is more or less a necessity when a girl is young. There are some things a girl cannot do for herself. Encouraging the man she likes is one of them.

In the working classes there are more opportunities for girls to meet with men; in the middle classes it is solely "by invitation." If a mother is not a match-maker she asks the wrong people. The girl is too shy to tell her so. If a girl never meets any men how can she get married? She needs a constant succession of men passing before her in order to form her judgment.

The nation is at the moment exactly like a short-sighted mother. It has the opportunity for match-making and it is not using it. It has crowds of attractive young girls and an army of fine, healthy over-seas men, and it does not bring them together. It leaves the men to get bored and lonely; it leaves the girls with the chances of marriage receding day by day.

What happens to the men? Girls who would not stoop to introduce themselves pass them by. The men are left to find what company they can—or to let it find them. They also have no chance of selection, for they do not know a sufficient number of girls to draw a comparison. Everyone knows the tragedy of the wrong girl and the hasty marriage repented at leisure. Oh, for a matchmaker!

13 September 1917

WAR CHANGES WOMEN.

THEY WILL NEVER BE THE SAME.

There are some people who think that women will be "as they were" after the war. Some of them may want to be so, but it is not in their power.

The other day a girl sat looking at herself in the glass as a hairdresser waved her hair. She noted the lines on her own face—lines of determination, lines of endurance. "I can never look young again," she said to herself. "You never see marks like those on young faces."

A man said to a capable woman war-worker: "I was glad when you wrote and said that you cried over Marjorie. I was afraid that you never cried nowadays."

The woman looked at him in astonishment. "Surely you don't think it is good to cry?"

"It seems that you are changing completely if you do not," he said. "It means that you are developing the masculine qualities at the expense of the feminine."

"That is good," she said quickly, "if it means fewer tears. They only demonstrate self-pity."

*   *   *   *   *

Women do not themselves know how their engagement in men's occupations is changing them—changing their looks, their manner, and their character.

At a recent women's farm competition young girls killed the chickens. They seemed not to mind the job, but whether they did mind or not the work was having its effect upon them. Either their natural sensitiveness had become dulled or they were holding it strongly in check.

Women's very walk is becoming different to-day. You cannot often be in a hurry without unconsciously increasing the length of your stride. Their manner is taking on a certain determination. Even pushing for a place in an omnibus does away with indecision of movement. The girl who has to look after herself develops a natural resourcefulness—she has difficulty in preventing it from becoming pushfulness. It is very difficult to do a man's work and remain a clinging woman.

The question is: Do women want to remain so? Are they willing to have the lines on the face which denote a certain strength of character? Are they willing to give up the weapon of tears, if instead they have gained self-control?

Some women are too willing to do so. Their obvious aim is to be as like men as possible. They cut their hair short; they stride, they call each other by their surnames, they smoke, and—they swear. Women have always stood for the ideal to men. These women are doing their best to drag it in the dust. If only they would be content to remain women! They cannot help acquiring masculine qualities when they face the same conditions as men; but they can still preserve the best of the feminine. Tears do not make a woman; gentleness and refinement do.

The new woman takes some "getting used to." No one expects her to have the qualities she has acquired. She is still judged by a pre-war standard. A girl who lost a very dear brother in action resolutely put her own feelings to one side and continued her war work. A man actually asked her what her attitude meant. "It is not callousness," he said, but there was a doubt in his voice. That is where the breaking point comes in woman's new-found endurance.

It is not certain that men want this self-possessed counterpart. They rather want to keep certain qualities to themselves, but the war has taken the matter out of their hands. Women will never be the same again.

PEGGY SCOTT.

6 September 1917

At the beginning of the conflict the initial role for women was to support the war effort through voluntary activities. However as casualties increased and conscription was introduced, the Board of Trade called for women to register for paid employment. They were called into industries previously the preserve of men such as transport, agriculture and engineering. Auxiliary arms of all three services were also formed. By doing this women were able to support their menfolk fighting abroad and by the end of the conflict began to change women's expectations and demands for more equality.

TOO MANY IDLE GIRLS.

There are two very common fallacies about many of the girls of the well-to-do classes of this fourth year of the war. One is that the leisured class is "a very small one"; the other, that girls who have grown up since the war must be having a very dull time in comparison with the pre-war gaiety enjoyed by their elder sisters.

Do not believe either.

"Betty has been to 17 dances this month," said Betty's mother, the wife of a very successful professional man, the other day. "You see, there are not only our own boys to be entertained, but also cousins from overseas and their friends, as well as a great many Allies. We mothers are not worried that our girls won't marry, I assure you."

I know another mother, a bright, energetic woman, who works long hours at the War Office while her 19-year-old daughter just "gads about" with her boy and girl friends.

I do not suggest that all the girls as they grow up are merely having "a good time," only that the percentage who are doing so is far too large. The majority of the girls of the upper and middle classes are working just as hard as their working-class sisters, and in many cases are working side by side with them. But too many of them are not working at all.

* * * * *

Many of the girls who are not working have been kept out of the labour market not so much by indulgent parents as by the very ill-advised appeals of some war-workers' committees. "Educated women and girls wanted to harvest potatoes" were asked for by one of these the other day—surely the most ridiculous of many silly calls. The "educated," well-off girl is wanted merely because she can afford to take low wages, which she ought never to be asked to take, since her "education" should have fitted her for more highly skilled work. By taking them she not only throws away what she has, but also keeps down the level of the genuine "uneducated" women's wages.

Betty and her friends may not be expert typists and stenographers—indeed, I am certain they are not. But their education has taught them enough for them to be just simply clerks—to write legibly, to add up simple accounts, to sort papers, and keep an office tidy. They can offer themselves as unskilled clerks in the Women's Army where they will not be taking anybody else's work, and at the end of a year—perhaps less—they can go back to their pleasures—if they want to do so. Nearly a month ago the Army asked for 10,000 women by October 1. Eighteen hundred "possible" applicants have been selected, and all these have come from other wage-earning occupations!

There are roughly three million women working for wages in England. There are eight million families. Surely these can spare a few more healthy daughters.　　　　G. C.

29 September 1917

GIRL ENGINEERS.

"We work automatic machines, but we are not thought worthy of being trained to do highly skilled work or to design," complained a girl "engineer" the other day. It was the truth. The engineering workshops have been flooded with women who do simple operations under the supervision of skilled men. Many of them are intellectually superior to their supervisors.

In the early days of the war, when quick adaptation was a first consideration, this was understandable, but conditions have altered. The war machine is now running smoothly, and we ought to consider if we cannot utilise the labour of women to greater advantage. If a little foresight had been exercised three years ago, and girls of fifteen or sixteen had been apprenticed to the highly skilled sections of the engineering industry, a great and increasing number of men would have been liberated for the Army. Instead, however, we have thousands of young men in their teens and early twenties in munition works who cannot be spared.

The Government advertise for women who are willing to be trained at certain centres as fitters, electricians, and draughtswomen, but everyone knows that these recruits will be "one-job" artisans. They will be specialists in the narrowest sense. Specialisation is necessary nowadays, but the successful specialist is he, or she, whose specialised and expert skill has sprung out of a wide knowledge of a craft.

It would be a national calamity if women were to be driven out of engineering after the war. There is a general recognition among thinking people that they have come to stay. They have proved a great asset, and in the days of stress to come the nation that will soonest recover from the effects of the war will be that one which to the fullest extent utilises its resources.

12 October 1917

CONSCRIPT THE WOMEN.
FROM MRS. FLORA ANNIE STEEL.
To the Editor of The Daily Mail.

Sir,—You have urged many measures which after intolerable delay have at length become law. Will you add to the number of your victories and urge the conscription of women?

We are at last, thank Heaven, to be counted as citizens and so must bear the full burden of responsibility for the protection of the State. The great mass of us are ready to do so, but there still remain hundreds, nay! hundreds of thousands, of young women who seem to think that perfunctory trapesing about after sick soldiers is an honest day's work.

The domestic servant class is undoubtedly being drained of its younger members. Apart from patriotism the freer life of munitions and the land has its share in this movement. We find this if we look to the shopgirls. Here freedom has already been gained, so the recruiting is slow. But these girls, spending their lives in tempting other women to be extravagant, are the very ones we require to grip if the England of the future is to be worth more than the England of the past.

And without conscription we shall never get them, never rouse them to a sense of their duty to themselves and to their fellows.

So let us have it—and as soon as possible.
　　　　　　　　FLORA ANNIE STEEL.
Court of Hill, Tenbury.

8 May 1918

Top: **The "Tar Women" spraying the roads in Westminster.**

Above right: **Coal was frequently delivered by women.**

Left and above middle: **During the conflict the number of women employed in munitions factories, familiarly known as the "Munitionettes", increased from just over 200,000 to nearly one million.**

SUFFERING FROM SHOCK.

Mr Lees Smith in the House later drew attention to a letter written by 2nd Lieutenant Sassoon, of the Royal Welsh Fusiliers, which, he said, raised the question of what policy the Government were going to adopt towards men who broke through the King's regulations.

This officer, he said, had one of the finest records of service in the Army and was granted the Military Cross for conspicuous gallantry. He wrote to his commanding officer, in wilful defiance of military authority, as he said, to declare his view that the war was being deliberately prolonged by those who had the power to end it. The war into which he believed he entered as a war of defence and liberty had now become a war of aggression and conquest; its original end could to-day be obtained by negotiations.

The lieutenant said he could no longer be a party to prolonging such sufferings as he had seen for an object which he considered to be unjust. He was, he pointed out, not protesting against the conduct of the war but against the political errors for which men were being sacrificed. He hoped that his action might do something to destroy the callousness with which people regarded agonies they did not share and had not enough imagination to realise.

This gallant officer, said Mr Lees Smith, was at once sent to hospital for shell shock. He asserted he had seen him and there was nothing wrong with his nerves. He was a man of unusual mental power and exceptional determination of character. How, he asked finally, were the Government going to deal with soldiers in uniform who broke up meetings contrary to the King's regulations?

Mr Macpherson replied that his attention had been called to the case of this gallant officer. The telegram he received from the War Office in answer to his inquiry was that no disciplinary action had been taken as the medical board reported that Lieutenant S. L. Sassoon was not responsible for his actions. He was suffering from nervous breakdown, and had proceeded to Craiglockhart Hospital, Midlothian. Mr. Macpherson said he had greater respect for military boards than to believe they would report in this way of a man because he wrote such a letter. It was not in the interests of the cause which Mr. Lees Smith had at heart that such use should be made of a letter written by a gallant young officer in such circumstances. (Cheers.)

31 July 1917

MEDICAL OFFICER'S SHOCKING EXPERIENCES.

(A Royal Army Medical Corps officer writes to a friend on October 5.)

We had more than we liked yesterday. The brute's aeroplane followed our empty motor-ambulances which were coming up as usual to take our sick and wounded down the line. Three minutes after they arrived the infernal blackguards sent shell after shell into the middle of the barns which we have fitted up as a hospital for the wounded. They smashed the glass of all the windows, showered shrapnel on the roof and through windows, and sent several shells clean through our roof.

All the people we could we put in the cellars—wine cellars (every French house has them, and these here are very spacious). A lull came and we loaded up very quickly and sent the convoy off. Just then the shelling began again vigorously, direct at our hospital—there is no question about it; gunners and all who were watching us and the shells said there is no doubt whatever they shelled us deliberately.

I went round to our guard and found some of our men very excited, They said unanimously they saw a red flag run up and down several times on a large barge in the canal. Spy signalling; no question. I jumped into a motor-ambulance and told the driver to go for all he was worth to the canal. I brought one of my own men with me.

We were just in time to catch two villainous-looking men who were legging it away. We brought them back and handed them over to an armed guard for which I sent to the provost marshal. Scarcely had I finished and was entering the ambulance when a gunner came galloping up and told me that a lot of the King's Royal Rifles had been killed or wounded by a shell a little distance away.

We went off at great speed and found two dead in the house, one dying (the officer), three seriously wounded, and two lightly wounded. We dressed and took them off in a very short time and now they are well on their way to England.

I was not back long when I got an urgent message for a motor to go to a station five miles away, where I have three officers and a bearer section. The road to the place is under both rifle and shellfire and no one can go along it in the day time. So at dusk we started off. It soon began to rain and got pitch dark, and the road became terrible greasy; in addition, we were told we would have to put our lights out after the first two miles. The motor skidded, went sideways and every other way, and the wheels revolved without gripping. We could only get along four miles an hour. The road was full of shell holes, which nearly brought us to grief. There was nothing for it but to light the lamps again.

This we did, and in a few minutes both rifles and guns were popping away at us for all they were worth. The rain made us a bad mark and we got safely to the temporary hospital in a large château. The top of the house was literally blown away by shells and pitch darkness prevailed. At length a flicker of light appeared from the ground and my officers conducted us to the large cellars below, where they could only live.

There was an officer with a bad abdominal shrapnel wound; and a fine young French girl about 19 years whose arm my officer had amputated only a few hours previously (the poor girl did not know it had been done), as a shell had shattered it to ribbons from the elbow down.

We loaded with difficulty in the dark, lit our lights and made off down the incline, "homewards." We were potted at constantly, but our backs were now to the woods, the rain increased, and we got back well pleased with our day at 3 a.m., very, very tired. The mother and father of the girl we brought away with her—and oh! how thankful they all were for our looking after them—with two more officers and men.

After some hot coffee and cocoa (made with new milk from my own herd of cows I told you of) I bade farewell to the convoy as it started off down the lines of communication to the large stationary hospitals.

This is a sample of our work.. We look after, in addition to our own people, wounded French soldiers, Zouaves, Turcos, etc., and villagers of all ages and both sexes. We now have treated 4,000 wounded officers and men of our own since we came here.

30 October 1914

SHELL SHOCK.

By the end of the conflict army doctors dealt with what came to be known as 'shell-shock', causing a myriad of symptoms from panic-attacks, inability to sleep or even walk or talk. The term was first discussed by physician and pyschologist Charles Myers in 1915, but little was understood about the condition and why it occurred and consequently reactions from officers and medical staff varied. Some men were sent back to the front-line while others were evacuated from the area and given time to rest and recuperate. Ten years after the war ended 65,000 British veterans were still receiving medical treatment for the condition.

Right: **British gunners watch German prisoners being escorted away.**

Below right: **Australia's ambulance men carry wounded soldiers to safety.**

Opposite: **Horse-drawn ambulances arrive at an advanced dressing station near Vimy.**

SHELL SHOCK.

CASES THAT THE DOCTORS CANNOT EXPLAIN.

By A PHYSICIAN.

Soldiers always believed that a cannon ball passing close to the person might cause internal injury without leaving any mark on the skin.

This was called "winding," an occurrence about which surgeons have been very sceptical. They explained the injury on the theory that a heavy mass of iron striking the body might produce no external mark and yet work serious mischief inside the body. Whatever may be the truth about "winding," there is no room for question now that the great pressure of air resulting from the explosion of a large shell may completely incapacitate a man, perhaps for many months, without producing the slightest trace of a bruise or scratch or causing any discoverable injury to internal organs.

There have been thousands of such cases in this war of high-explosive shells, and they constitute a puzzling problem for the medical man to explain or to cure.

Sometimes men are killed as suddenly as if they were struck by fragments of the shell, and, according to the *Lancet*, such deaths have occurred in groups, the men still in lifelike attitudes, in the acts of eating or drinking or smoking. So like living men do they appear that enemy soldiers hesitate to approach them.

More commonly the explosion of the shell throws the men down unconscious, either from the direct concussion or from the impact of a mass of earth. These may never recover consciousness, but die soon after from collapse; or in a few minutes they may get up feeling dazed but able to continue their duties. But if later on these men get a slight wound they collapse utterly and have to be taken to hospital. Then a great variety of nervous symptoms develop.

The patients may become deaf, dumb, or blind. In nearly all cases the nerves of vision are affected in a peculiar way. The field of vision is contracted and the victim can see only straight in front of him. Sleeplessness, nightmare, and vomiting are often very troublesome, and worst of all is the despondency from which most of the men suffer. Probably the most frequent effect is loss of control of the muscles, so that some men tremble in every limb and others can scarcely walk, but shuffle sideways like a crab.

26 August 1915

SHELL-CONTEMPT.
A FRONT LINE "AILMENT."

Everyone has heard of "shell-shock." It is one of the minor accompaniments of modern warfare meaning "Blighty" and a long spell at home to the unfortunate victim.

In actuality it is a nervous breakdown, distressing and sometimes terrible in its symptoms, a kind of derangement, in which the sufferer feels that he has won the war or has lost the war according to the mood. The disease is one of the inevitable consequences of a war in which half-tons of destruction are thrown about like confetti at a wedding. Nature, it is said, has her counterpoise in most things. In this war she has balanced shell-shock by a condition which I can only describe as "shell-contempt."

It is not a disease; it is hardly a philosophy; it is a peculiar condition of mind for which Boche heavies have no terror and which enables many soldiers to keep calm and collected throughout the most strenuous bombardment.

7 September 1917

EFFECT OF SHELL-FIRE.

An interesting analysis of the physical results of shock from shell-fire appears in this week's Lancet by Captain C. H. Myers, of the Royal Army Medical Corps. In the three cases analysed in detail, those of three separate soldiers near whom a large shell had burst, the sense of hearing was practically unaffected. On the other hand, the senses of sight, smell, and taste were temporarily absent or greatly reduced. Badly blurred vision and an inability to taste salty and acid substances, and, in two out of the three, loss of memory, were characteristic symptoms.

Under treatment by rest and hypnotic suggestion a gradual improvement took place in all the cases.

7 November 1917

The medical board reported that Lieutenant S. L. Sassoon was not responsible for his actions. He was suffering from a nervous breakdown.

THE MENTAL EFFECTS OF SHELL-FIRE.

There has recently been much public interest in the question of sending wounded men back to the front. The matter has been discussed chiefly from the standpoint of military necessity or its utilitarian aspect in connection with the supply of man-power to the fighting Army; but the case of the wounded man himself and his further value as a fighting unit also deserves consideration.

It is enlightening to make a comparison between the mental attitude, towards the ordeal of the trenches, of a man who has served in them for twelve months and that of a recruit on his first visit to the front. However keen the latter may be to take his place in the fight and however high-spirited and confident he appears as he sallies forth to his "baptism of fire," he has at the back of his mind certain fears of definite things anticipated in detail as a result of his previous attempts to form an idea of the material side of modern warfare.

It is a characteristic and peculiar fact that in nine cases out of ten these particular fears are of being bayoneted, blown up by a mine, or sniped through the head. These are things which, by virtue of their inherent simplicity, are readily assimilated by the mind and assigned to a foremost place. But the actual psychological effect of the ordeal of warfare is of a totally different and more complex kind. The matter may be summed up in the statement that the fundamental difference between the outlook of the layman and the veteran is that the former is unaware and unsuspecting of, and the latter is familiar with, the effects of the outstanding terror of modern warfare and the terror which completely swamps all others—namely, shell-fire.

The wounded man fears to return to the front; but he never has in mind the horror of being sniped through the head or blown up by a mine or bayoneted. The sole thing he dreads, the thing which has exclusively made its impression upon his mind during his time at the front, is shell-fire.

by George F. Sleggs.

7 September 1917

WOUNDED.

Shortly before zero (the time chosen for the operation) the men of the first wave stand, rifles in hand, fingers fumbling nervously with cartridge slings, belt, helmet—anything. They do not talk much; they are not afraid, but they are tense with excitement and expectation.

Suddenly the storm breaks. The deafening crash of gun after gun mingles with the swift rush of shells and the whistle of machine-gun bullets. The darkness becomes an ever-changing scene of fitful lights and flashes; the noise re-doubles as enemy guns answer our barrage.

The subaltern looks hastily at his watch, a message passes quickly down the trench, and following closely on his heels the line of khaki climbs slowly over the parapet and commences a steady jog-trot across No Man's Land.

It is no easy matter to keep in touch with sixty or seventy men extended in line several yards apart; when the only light is the flash of the Vérey lights. The subaltern runs along the line hoarsely shouting commands which are never heard.

Men drop—wounded or killed—no one must stop to help them. Forward they go. What are these men doing in that shell-hole? "Get out! Get on!" Forward again!

Suddenly a blow like that of a sledge hammer catches his arm. He swerves, then stops; there is no pain, just a numb sensation, and looking down at his side it is almost laughable to see the way in which his arm is swinging backwards and forwards without any effort or sense of feeling.

The wave has passed him now. He sits down on a low mound and looks at his arm in a dazed, detached sort of way. Suddenly he looks up, hearing the shells still shrieking overhead, and dives for the nearest shell-hole. There he feverishly scrambles out of his equipment, makes a temporary sling for his arm out of a leather brace-strap, and then sits quietly watching the dark blood ooze out of the tiny hole in his arm.

Soon dawn comes, and looking behind he can see the grey line of the British trench. Here and there are men lying still—very still; others, wounded, are beginning to make their way back; stretcher-bearers are hurrying to and fro with their burdens. The noise of the battle seems to be dying away in the distance, so restful is the comparative calm after the hell of the first few minutes.

A smile slowly flickers over the subaltern's face. "A Blighty for a quid!" he murmurs, and joining the motley stream of wounded, trudges wearily back to the dressing-station—the first stage on the journey home.

R. G. T.

13 September 1918

No one must stop to help them. Forward they go.
What are these men doing in that shell-hole?
"Get out! Get on!" Forward again!

AT A CASUALTY CLEARING STATION.

SOMEWHERE IN FRANCE.

The first impression I get is of the silent intentness of the walking wounded. They are quiet because they are dead-tired, and also because they are taut with military discipline.

That boy is 19 and looks like one of my choirboys. I sit on a form, which collapses. At home he would snigger at my downfall; he now watches me dispassionately, even sympathetically.

But they are intent because dominated by one absorbing hope—that their wound is a "Blighty one." The padre has no doubt whatever, embroidering cheerfully his very slight medical knowledge, and sends them away happy to the base, where they learn their ultimate fate.

The reception room is very soon ankle deep in bandages. The field ambulance dressing are removed, wounds probed, cleansed, and redressed. Teeth are set, and the pain-sweat breaks out, but a groan is rare, and a cry provokes interest as an unusual phenomenon.

Three hours' hard work finishes the walking wounded, and then come all the stretchers. We are advancing all along the line, and there are many prisoners. The first stretcher case tonight provides, unexpectedly, entertainment. The bandages are removed and reveal a gaping back. Tenderly the orderly puts his hands under the shoulder to get the best position for examination. The patient writhes and twists, and—there is no other word for it—squeals. "Bite on it, sonny," says the orderly; the padre puts a sympathetic hand on his head. And it turns out that the squeal is laughter, and the twists and writhes because the sufferer is ticklish and can't bear being touched near the armpits!

There is no cessation of work day and night in a casualty clearing station during a battle. Two side by side, working independently, alternately receive. Between them they have taken in during 12 days of this battle nearly 7,000 wounded, by far the majority surprisingly light cases.

The lightning diagnosis of the M.O.s in the reception room is marvellous to behold. They are untiring and never rest for a moment when on duty, rapidly examining the wounded and marking them for immediate evacuation, or X-rays, or operation.

The Boche prisoners are also dealt with. Their number is the surest sign that we are doing well up the line.

E. G. E.

1 September 1918

THAT WINTER COLD.

NOW IS THE TIME TO AVOID IT.

By A DOCTOR.

It seems early in the year to think of winter colds, but a long experience has taught me that the only way to avoid them is by taking timely precautions.

To begin with, anyone who is not in the habit of taking a cold bath in the morning should begin now. The weather will be warm enough for some weeks for the beginner, and his reaction will be developed before the chilly days arrive. Some cannot take a bath dead cold, but there is nothing to prevent any but the very delicate from having first a tepid bath and then making it colder each day until a very little added hot water suffices. The bath should only last a few seconds; when the weather becomes really cold it should be a case of jump in, plunge under the water, jump out, and dress as quickly as possible. Thorough drying is less necessary than quick dressing.

For everyone who can take it, and there are few who cannot, cod-liver oil is a sovereign preventive of colds. Just one teaspoonful morning and night immediately after—or, better still, half an hour after—meals is quite enough. This small dose aids the digestion, whereas the customary tablespoon dose disturbs it.

But there are many other little things to be attended to. Resistance to disease of every kind is largely a matter of nervous energy. Consequently whatever can be done to brace the nervous system should be done. Nothing is so requisite for this purpose as a sound night's sleep every night in the year. For an adult nine hours in bed, with eight hours' sleep, are not too much. Quietness, darkness, and good ventilation of the bedroom are essential.

In connection with nerve energy, it is necessary to control the smoking habit. There is a popular belief that smoking is a good preventive of colds and other infectious diseases. It is no such thing. It keeps the mucous lining of the nose, mouth, and throat in a state of depressed vitality, the very condition most favourable to the development of microbes. Often I have cut short a cold by giving up my pipe for a few days. Therefore the person who wants to avoid winter colds should begin now to limit the number of his daily cigarettes, cigars, or pipefuls of tobacco. For the average man I would put the limit at 1oz. to 1½oz. of tobacco, or 12 to 14 cigars or 40 cigarettes a week.

A person taking these precautions in time will be saved from probably two-thirds of his usual share of winter colds.

13 September 1917

The Royal Army Medical Corps had been established in 1898 and at the height of the conflict numbered around 140,000 personnel. A triage system was established to assess a man's wound and move him to the appropriate base or hospital for treatment as quickly as possible.

Opposite above: **Refreshments are provided for the walking wounded.**

Opposite below: **Red Cross ambulances on hand to support the medical services.**

Below left: **American troops advance through a gap in the enemy's barbed wire.**

Right: **A wounded man is lifted from an ambulance wagon at a farmhouse hospital station.**

COMPULSION AT LAST!

SINGLE MEN FIRST.	SINGLE MEN FIRST.	VOSGES GAIN.	SERBIANS' NEED.	"DAILY MAIL"	BIG GUNS FOR
	"THE DAILY MAIL" CAMPAIGN.	GERMAN TRENCHES CARRIED.	A CALL TO BRITAIN.	FREE INSURANCE FOR 1916.	SALONICA.

The government appealed for volunteers and by the end of January 1915, over a million men had enlisted. This rose by another 1.5 million by the end of September but many volunteers were unfit to serve and others were reluctant to enlist so by the end of the year the number of men coming forward had dwindled significantly. Many more were needed, as the casualty rates grew so advertising was used to either encourage or shame men into signing up. The 'Derby' scheme gave men the opportunity to agree to serve at a later date if needed, and once attested were given an armlet to wear. Eventually the Military Service Act of January 1917 began the process of conscription, initially requiring single men between the ages of 18 and 41 to enlist which extended to married men in May. As the war continued many height and age restrictions were relaxed to harness as much manpower as possible.

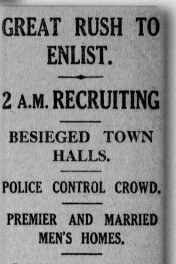

THE KING'S CALL.

MORE MEN AND YET MORE.

MAKE GOOD THE SACRIFICES.

"THE END IS NOT IN SIGHT."

BUCKINGHAM PALACE.

TO MY PEOPLE.

At this grave moment in the struggle between my people and a highly organised enemy who has transgressed the Laws of Nations and changed the ordinance that binds civilised Europe together, I appeal to you.

I rejoice in my Empire's effort, and I feel pride in the voluntary response from my Subjects all over the world who have sacrificed home, fortune, and life itself, in order that another may not inherit the free Empire which their ancestors and mine have built.

I ask you to make good these sacrifices.

The end is not in sight. More men and yet more are wanted to keep my Armies in the Field, and through them to secure Victory and enduring Peace.

In ancient days the darkest moment has ever produced in men of our race the sternest resolve.

I ask you, men of all classes, to come forward voluntarily and take your share in the fight.

In freely responding to my appeal, you will be giving your support to our brothers, who, for long months, have nobly upheld Britain's past traditions, and the glory of her Arms.

George R.I.

6 May 1915

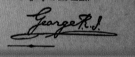

M.P.s WHO SHOULD GO.

To the Editor of *The Daily Mail.*

Sir,—*Quis custodiet ipsos custodes?*

Mr. Lloyd George's Committee has recommended that everyone of enemy origin shall be discharged from Government employment. Presumably members of Parliament fall to be dealt with in this category. Even if they do not, I think we might stretch a point and include them. If Germany admitted a full-blooded Englishman *as of right* to every secret session of the Reichstag, we should say she was mad. And yet. . . . It is like playing poker with your cards on the table. And we have done this for four years and have not been cleaned out yet, though we have lost pretty heavily. It is enough to make Simon de Montfort and John of Gaunt rise from the dead.

Members of Parliament of enemy origin may be out for the Allies to win; but they may not, and that is a risk we cannot afford to take.

I have always understood that if a man found that the people he represented were not quite sure of him he withdrew of his own accord. I suppose I was wrong. All the same, the man who in such circumstances does not withdraw I do not trust out of my sight.

ONLY A SOLDIER.

12 July 1918

"ENLIST OR GO"

Employers' Offer to Single Men

TORRENT OF RECRUITS

The War Office has issued a statement suggesting that employers should copy the patriotic example of certain firms who have posted notices to single employees with no dependents, urging them to join Lord Kitchener's Army and 'promising to find them work at the end of the war'.

The Associated Portland Cement Manufacturers, Limited, of Portland House, Lloyd's-avenue, E. C., who are instanced by the War Office, to add 5s. a week to their employees' Army pay, and they also give notice that the services of unmarried men with no dependents will be dispensed with after September 12.

Harrod's have issued a notice to their staff strongly supporting Lord Kitchener's appeal and offering a bonus of £2 to young single men who enlist. Recruits from the staff are to be taken on again after the war, and the directors are prepared to consider granting half salary during absence to those with widowed mothers partly dependent on them.

The Great Central Railway treat all single men joining the colours as on 'leave with pay'.

14 September 1914

GREAT RUSH TO ENLIST.

2 A.M. RECRUITING

BESIEGED TOWN HALLS.

POLICE CONTROL CROWD.

PREMIER AND MARRIED MEN'S HOMES.

Recruiting took a real spring forward yesterday, and especially last night. Men released from business thronged to recruiting stations that were already overflowing.

Doctors and officials toiled in many instances until long past midnight. Everywhere men who could not possibly be attested promised cheerfully to return this morning. All realise that the recruiting officials have been ready for weeks, and that now the great rush has come every nerve must and will be strained to cope with it.

6 September 1917

MEN OF 45.

THEIR REAL HARDSHIP.

The extension of the Military Service age has led to absurdly conflicting estimates of the physical capacities of men of 45.

The man of 45 who *cannot* walk fifteen miles is the man who is most likely to die suddenly. A run of a quarter of a mile, at a jog-trot pace, only takes 2½ minutes. Thousands of stout City fathers often run for more than 2½ minutes for their morning trains. Sexagenarians often play two rounds of golf and think nothing of it. An octogenarian, writing to *The Daily Mail*, tells of his walk of 40 miles. I knew a septuagenarian cyclist, of apparently frail physique, who constantly rode 80 miles during a day. My father, when 81, covered daily his 20 miles, shooting in winter, walking in summer.

There is certainly something grievously wrong with any man of 45 who cannot, when out of training, leave his desk any day and walk fifteen miles. It is not a walk, it is an amble. I have a physical trouble that disqualifies me from military service, but in the first week of my convalescence, after twelve weeks in bed, I walked twelve miles in a day.

*   *   *   *   *

The real hardship of calling up men in their forties is not physical, but financial. Their real trouble is not the march of fifteen miles or its equivalent in physical effort that they will have to do in a day's Army training, but the march of *hundreds of miles* that most of them will have to do to find positions in civilian life again. A young man, if he emerges from the war unmaimed, has lost nothing. He was at the start of his career; he has merely postponed the start a few years. The man of 45 is in the noon of his career; he cannot recapture the morning. He cannot start again; he cannot rebuild. If he was a master he has lost his business; if a professional man, he has lost his clientèle; if an artist, he has lost his touch; if an employee, people will say, "We want younger men."

Not hammer-toe, but hammered homes; not arthritis in the joints, but arthritis of the income-tax return are what tribunals ought to consider most tenderly in the men of 45.

       T. B.

30 June 1918

HOW TO GET THE MEN.

Sir,—There is but one primary question for us all. It is the provision of the largest number of fighting men in the shortest possible space of time. All other questions are subsidiary to this one of men. The Board of Agriculture and the Board of Trade are hobbling the War Office in its business. You can shorten the war by a year or more if you will press for some such scheme as this:

1. Every exempted man to be examined by a medical board at barracks or locally by January 1.

2. The War Office to have unfettered control for the Army or other Government work of all single men of military age and all married men under the age of twenty-eight who pass A or B.

3. All soldiers and all single civilians of military age who pass C and who are not required by the War Office for other work to be at the disposal of recruiting officers for substitution of labour purposes.

4. All other persons of military age to be under the rules of tribunals as at present.

5. Practising professional men not to sit on tribunals or to act as military representatives.

6. War Office inspection of tribunal clerks and recruiting offices to be constant.

I venture to ask to be allowed to express an opinion as I have been hard at work khaki-hunting since the war began, and I do feel it is not just that I, for instance, should contribute four officer sons at various fronts—one no more, alas!—while certain Government Departments are keeping back so many of their fit young men at civil work that their elders can do.

     J.H. FARMER,
Military Representative to Three Tribunals.
Fairfield, Mundesley, Norfolk.

24 October 1916

ENLISTED AT 50.

MAGISTRATE ON NOBLE EXAMPLE TO YOUNG MEN.

A private in the 12th Battalion Middlesex Regiment, named John Williams, stationed at Colchester, was charged at the North London Police Court yesterday as an absentee. He had overstayed his leave.

Mr Hedderwick: I see you are fifty years of age. How was it you were accepted?

Williams: I enlisted as thirty-four, sir. You were anxious to defend your country?

—Yes, sir.

That is very noble of you. Do you want to get back?

—Yes, sir; very much.

Mr Hedderwick: I think it is a very fine thing for you to offer yourself at the age of fifty, but they must have been passing men in a great hurry to accept you for thirty-four.

In ordering the man to be detained for an escort Mr. Hedderwick said: I hope you will be able to give the commanding officer a good excuse. Although you are before me as an absentee you are a very great example to many men much younger than yourself who are shirking their duty to their country. I hope you will do well and come back safe and sound.

15 December 1915

Opposite above: **Men who had attested under the Derby Scheme hand in their armlets at White City.**

Below: British troops trudge along a wet road on the Western Front.

Below left: By the end of 1915 the number of men coming forward to enlist had dwindled significantly. Caption to the cartoon published 25 May 1915:
First strenuous youth:
"It's difficult to wealise the fightin' is less than sixty miles away.
Second: Ditto, Ditto: "Difficult? It's absolutely impossible."
(They turn over and go to sleep)

A Holiday Idyll.

FIRST STRENUOUS YOUTH:
"It's difficult to wealise the fightin' is less than sixty miles away."
SECOND DITTO, DITTO: "Difficult? It's absolutely impossible."

(They turn over and go to sleep.)

BOYS IN THE ARMY.

THE AGE FRAUD.

WAR OFFICE REPUDIATES BIRTH CERTIFICATES.

Under the voluntary system boys are being bullied or cajoled into joining the Army. They are enlisted by their own fraud, countenanced by the recruiting officer, and they are kept in the ranks against the wish of parents by official threats of fine and imprisonment for that fraud.

The lawful age for enlistment is nineteen. If a boy wants to join but says he is under age he is told to "go and think again," or "turn round three times and guess again." No attempt is made to ascertain his true age either by a demand for his insurance card or his birth certificate or by reference to his parents.

In the House of Commons it has been repeatedly asserted that any parent of a boy so enlisted can claim his discharge. In numberless cases parents have attempted this, only to be told by the War Office that their son is now officially "nineteen."

Proof of these assertions is contained in letters received by the organisers of National Service, 63, Temple-chambers, London, E.C. The facts are also known independently to many members of Parliament. One case was referred direct to Lord Derby last week and is now under his "careful consideration." Additional cases will be submitted to him to-day by the National Service movement.

FOUR EXAMPLES.

Here are a few typical cases:

1. The only son of Mr. J. Hamilton, of Longton, Staffordshire, Private A. Hamilton, enlisted in the Duke of Cornwall's Light Infantry on April 26, 1915, being then sixteen. On August 6 he was sent to the front, being then one month under seventeen. Appeal was made before this to his commanding officer, who advised an application to the War Office. The boy's birth certificate was sent there, and returned with the statement that "the soldier had declared himself nineteen." Five weeks ago a local minister wrote to the boy's company-sergeant-major in France, sending another birth certificate; no reply. These efforts were prompted by the poor health of the mother and her distress. The boy spent his seventeenth birthday in France on September 10.

2. The youngest son of Mrs. Eveny, of Green-lanes, Ilford, enlisted in the 4th Essex two weeks before war was declared, being then sixteen. His two elder brothers are now serving. He was put to work too great for his strength, and went into hospital, where he was operated on, remaining there three months. He has been under medical care ever since and has been declared unfit by a Medical Board. Several applications have been made for his discharge. The War Office has refused, and has informed his parents that he has incurred a debt of £4 in the regimental books. He was seventeen last April.

3. Private C. S——, son of Mrs. S——, of S——, was seventeen on February 12 last. The medical history of his family indicates that he ought not to be subjected to any physical or mental strain. He cannot write. The facts in his case have been laid before the War Office by his mother, a very poor woman, who had to borrow money twice to secure birth certificates to back her application. The War Office asserts that the boy is over eighteen, and refuses to release him.

4. Private S——, whose mother lives near York, enlisted last November when seventeen years old. His mother, a very poor woman, paid 1s. 1d. for a birth certificate, and asked that he might be kept on home defence work until he was nineteen. The War Office sent him to the Dardanelles, where he spent his eighteenth birthday. This woman, "a soldier's daughter, wife, and mother," remarks that her son is "a very fine young man for his age, and the Army will want such as him in a few years."

Under National Service these cases could not occur.

18 October 1915

SOLDIERS' PAY.

THE INFANTRYMAN'S 1/-.

'FIGHTING MEN WORST OFF.'

Members of both Houses of Parliament and representatives of the General Federation of Trade Unions met in conference at the House of Commons yesterday to consider the pay of soldiers and sailors. The federation ask that the rate should be raised to 3s. a day.

Mr. J. O'Grady, who presided, said the present rate of pay was wretchedly low. An infantryman was lucky, after paying certain deductions out of a shilling a day, if he received 4d. net a day. He estimated that the cost of increasing the pay to 3s a day would be about £125,000,000. When the pay of the over-seas and American troops was considered, 3s. a day was only a fair amount to ask.

Mr. Ben Tillett referred to the profits of ship owners and the engineering industries and urged that while advances of wages had been secured by industrial workers at home the case of the soldier who is offering his life demanded consideration.

Colonel Wilson, M.P., spoke in favour of equalising the pay of soldiers in all branches. It was a scandal that the men nearest the trenches got the worst pay of all. The infantryman was paid the worst.

2 August 1917

BACK TO "CIVVIES."

We deal with damaged soldiers at our camp. Some of them we mend and send back to the war, some of them are so badly damaged that it is not possible to mend them, and so they are sent out of the Army. Those of us who have been watching them go are feeling ashamed.

We have read of the treatment of the discharged soldier. Certainly he should be given a suit which does not suggest the more horrible recesses of a pawnshop, but that is not all. So much could be done to make his honourable exit from the Army a dignified and happy ending to his service. Of course those suits are detestable. They are ugly; they are nearly always creased and wrinkled, and they hardly ever fit. The failure to provide a collar and tie is the crowning insult.

You can see these men as I see them, day after day. They go before the special boards which deal with men who are to be invalided out of the Army. At that time they are soldiers, more or less smart according to their nature, but at the very least dressed neatly enough to absolve them from the fear of the criticism of sergeants and other bitter-tongued superiors. A couple of days later you see them wandering down to the station in twos and threes, looking like loafers.

6 October 1917

Above: "Father, I've heard you say you are opposed to compulsion in any form. I don't want to do any lessons today. I can please myself, can't I?"

To the Editor of *The Daily Mail*.

Sir,—I have been struck with the large number of youths from 19 to 23 still in civilian clothing.

With thirty-one months' active service to my credit I fully realise the importance of munition workers, but surely these young men have not reached the stage of efficiency which makes them indispensable as engineers?

Life in muddy Flanders demands young men, and however physically fit a man over 35 may be, if he has led a "soft" life he will not last long there. Our hospitals are always full of men whose only complaint is that the life is too much for them.

The tribunals should pay more attention to the young man of 20 and insist upon him donning khaki, filling his place with the older married man who is so often only a big expense to his country.

"Out there," I always found, I could drive youths of 19 to 25, lead men of 25 to 35, but I had generally to nurse men of over 35, and that, I believe, is the general rule. SAPPER.

6 September 1917

KHAKI ARMLET.

THE MARK OF THE WILLING MAN.

THREE CLASSES TO WEAR IT.

HOW IT AFFECTS YOU.

WAR OFFICE, Saturday.

The Secretary for War has decided to issue khaki armlets, bearing the Royal Crown, to the following classes of men :—

1. *Men who enlist and are placed in groups awaiting a call to join the colours.*
2. *Men who offer themselves for enlistment and are found to be medically unfit.*
3. *Men who have been invalided out of the Service with good character, or have been discharged "not likely to become efficient" on medical grounds.*

There will be a distinctive mark for each of the three classes. The armlets are in process of manufacture. Notice will be given when they can be issued, together with instructions as to issue.

WHAT IT MEANS.

THE WILLING AND THE UNWILLING.

The official announcement given above fulfils the suggestion made first in *The Daily Mail* on July 30. It means that the nation is divided practically into the willing and the unwilling.

If you have enlisted and are awaiting your call you will wear your armlet and everybody will know that you are as much a recruit as if you were in khaki.

If you have offered and been found medically unfit your armlet will prove your willingness and protect you from badgering.

If you have left the Army for good reason you will be equally unassailable.

The great advantage of the armlet is that

1 November 1915

Above: **Volunteers queue to enlist at their local recruiting office.**

Opposite: **A platoon of the Worcestershire Regiment marches to the front line in good spirits.**

1 November 1915

MORE MEN,
THE ARMY'S ANSWER TO THE KING.

The King, who has just spent three days at the front, has sent the following message to Sir Douglas Haig:-

My dear Field-Marshal,—My short visit to the battle front gave me an exceptional opportunity of seeing you and some of your generals engaged in the fierce battle still raging, and I thus obtained personal testimony to the indomitable courage and unflinching tenacity with which my splendid troops have withstood the supreme effort of the greater part of the enemy's fighting power.

I was also fortunate enough to see some units recently withdrawn from the front line, and listened with wonder as officers and men narrated the thrilling incidents of a week's stubborn fighting. I was present at the entraining of fresh troops eager to reinforce their comrades. In a large casualty clearing-station I realised what can be accomplished by good organisation in dealing promptly with every variety of casualty of greater or less severity and passing on by trains to the base hospitals those fit to travel. The patient cheerfulness of the wounded was only equalled by the care and gentleness of those ministering to their wants.

With these experiences, short but vivid, I feel that the whole Empire will join with me in expressing the gratitude due to you and your Army for the skilful, unswerving manner in which this formidable attack has been, and continues to be, dealt with.

Though for the moment our troops have been obliged by sheer weight of numbers to give some ground, the impression left on my mind is that no Army could be in better heart, braver, or more confident than that which you have the honour to command. Anyone privileged to share these experiences would feel with me proud of the British race and of that unconquerable spirit which will, please God, bring us through our present trials.

We at home must ensure that the manpower is adequately maintained and that our workers—men and women—will continue nobly to meet the demands for all the necessities of war. Thus may you be relieved from any anxiety as to the means by which, with the support of our faithful and brave allies, your heroic Army shall justify that inspiring determination which I found permeated all ranks.

GEORGE R. I.

1 April 1918

FOUR DAYS' IMMORTAL STRUGGLE.

THE GLORY OF THE CANADIANS THEIR EYE-WITNESS'S STORY.

The following is an account by the Canadian Eye-Witness of the glorious feats of the Canadian Division who "saved the situation" in the new German attempt to break through the Ypres line to Calais from April 22 to the 26th:-

The battle in the neighbourhood of Ypres was bloody, even as men appraise battles in this callous and life-engulfing war. But as long as brave deeds retain the power to fire the blood of Anglo-Saxons, the stand made by the Canadians in those desperate days will be told by fathers to their sons.

The Canadian Division consisted in the main of men who were admirable raw material, but who at the outbreak of war were neither disciplined nor trained, as men count discipline and training in these days of scientific warfare.

On April 22 the Canadian Division held a line of, roughly, 5,000 yards, extending in a north-westerly direction from the Ypres-Roulers Railway to the Ypres-Poel-capelle road, and connecting at its terminus with the French troops. The division consisted of three infantry brigades, in addition to the artillery brigades. The day was a peaceful one, warm and sunny. At five o'clock in the afternoon a plan, carefully prepared, was put into execution against our French Allies on the left. Asphyxiating gas of great intensity was projected into their trenches. The result was that the French were compelled to give ground for a considerable distance. The immediate consequences of this enforced withdrawal were extremely grave. The 3rd Brigade of the Canadian Division was without any left. Rough diagrams may make the position clear.

Below: **Soldiers watch for signs of any further enemy activity.**

Opposite: **A procession of limbers carry provisions and weapons to the front-line.**

As shown above, it became necessary for Brigadier-General Turner, commanding the 3rd Brigade, to throw back his left flank southward to protect his rear.

The attack developed with particular intensity upon the apex of the newly formed line, running in the direction of St Julien. It has already been stated that four British guns were taken in a wood comparatively early in the evening of the 22nd. In the course of that night and under the heaviest machine fire, this wood was assaulted by the Canadian Scottish 16th Battalion of the 3rd Brigade, and the 10th Battalion of the 2nd Brigade. The battalions were respectively commanded by Lieutenant-Colonel Leckie and Lieutenant-Colonel Boyle, and after a most fierce struggle in the light of a misty moon they took the position at the point of the bayonet. An officer who took part in the attack describes how the men about him fell under the fire of the machine guns, which, in his phrase, played upon them "like a watering pot." He added quite simply, "I wrote my own life off." But the line never wavered. The German garrison was completely demoralised, and the impetuous advance of the Canadians did not cease until they reached the far side of the wood and entrenched themselves there in the position so dearly gained.

TERRIBLE CASUALTIES.

The fighting continued without intermission all through the night. At 6 a.m. on Friday it became apparent that the left was becoming more and more involved. It was decided, formidable as the attempt undoubtedly was, to try to give relief by a counter-attack upon the first line of German trenches, now far, far advanced from those originally occupied by the French. This was carried out by the Ontario 1st and 4th Battalions of the 1st Brigade, under Brigadier General Mercer, acting in combination with a British brigade. It did not seem that any human being could live in the shower of shot and shell which began to play upon the advancing troops.

They suffered terrible casualties. For a short time every other man seemed to fall. The 4th Canadian battalion at one moment came under a particularly withering fire. For a moment—not more—it wavered. Its most gallant commanding officer, Lieutenant Colonel Burchill, carrying, after an old fashion, a light cane, coolly and cheerfully rallied his men, and at the very moment when his example had infected them fell dead at the head of his battalion. With a hoarse cry of anger they sprang forward (for, indeed, they loved him) as if to avenge his death. The astonishing attack which followed, pushed home in the face of direct frontal fire made in broad daylight, by battalions whose names should live forever in the memories of soldiers, was carried to the first line of German trenches. After a hand-to-hand struggle the last German who resisted was bayoneted, and the trench was won.

This charge, made by men who looked death indifferently in the face, saved, and that was much, the Canadian left. But it did more. Up to the point where the assailants conquered or died, it secured and maintained during the most critical moment of all the integrity of the Allied line. For the trench was not only taken but held until the night of Sunday, the 25th, when it was relieved.

OFFICERS' VALOUR.

At 4 a.m. on Friday, the 23rd; a fresh emission of gas was made upon the 2nd and 3rd Brigades. Two privates of the 18th Highlanders who found their way into the trenches commanded by Colonel Lipsett, 90th Winnipeg Rifles, 8th

Battalion perished in the fumes and it was noticed that their faces became blue immediately after dissolution. The Royal Highlanders of Montreal, 13th Battalion, and the 48th Highlanders, 15th Battalion, were more especially affected by the discharge. The Royal Highlanders, though considerably shaken, remained immovable upon their ground.

German troops in considerable though not in overwhelming, numbers swung past the unsupported left of the 3rd Brigade and slipped in between the wood and St. Julien. In the exertions made by the 3rd Brigade the fate of some of the officers of Royal Highlanders of Montreal attracted special attention. Major Norsworth, already almost disabled by a bullet wound, was bayoneted and killed while he was rallying his men with easy cheerfulness.

NOT A GUN LOST.

The case of Captain McCuaig, of the same battalion, was not less glorious, although his death can claim no witness. This most gallant officer was seriously wounded, in a hurriedly constructed trench. Peremptory orders were received for an immediate withdrawal. Unwilling to inflict upon the men the disabilities of a maimed man, he very resolutely refused to be moved, and asked one thing only, that there should be given to him as he lay alone in the trench two loaded Colt revolvers to add to his own, which lay in his right hand as he made his last request. And so, with three revolvers ready to his hand for use, a very brave officer waited to sell his life, wounded and racked with pain, in an abandoned trench. On Friday afternoon the 3rd Brigade was ordered to retreat farther south, selling every yard of ground dearly.

The enforced retirement of the 3rd Brigade reproduced for the 2nd Brigade, commanded by Brigadier-General Curry, in a singularly exact fashion the position of the 3rd Brigade itself at the moment of the withdrawal of the French (its left was in the air). It now devolved upon General Curry to reproduce the tactical manoeuvres with which, earlier in the fight, the 3rd Brigade had adapted

itself to the flank movement of overwhelming numerical superiority. He held his line of trenches from Thursday at five o'clock till Sunday afternoon. And on Sunday afternoon he had not abandoned his trenches. There were none left. They had been obliterated by artillery. He withdrew his undefeated troops from the fragments of his field fortifications and the hearts of his men were as completely unbroken as the parapets of his trenches were completely broken. Lieutenant-Colonel Lipsett, commanding the 90th Winnipeg Rifles, 8th Battalion of the 2nd Brigade, held the extreme left of the brigade position at the most critical moment. The battalion was expelled from the trenches early on Friday morning by poisonous gas, but, recovering in three-quarters of an hour, it counter-attacked, retook the trenches it had abandoned, and bayoneted the enemy. And after the 3rd Brigade had been forced to retire, Lieutenant-Colonel Lipsett held his position, though his left was in the air, until two British regiments filled up the gap on Saturday night.

The artillery never flagged in the sleepless struggle. Not a Canadian gun was lost in the long battle of retreat.

1 May 1915

The impetuous advance of the Canadians did not cease until they reached the far side of the wood and entrenched themselves there in the position so dearly gained.

TO HIS MOTHER.

This is a portion of a letter to the mother of a gallant young officer who died for our country in France, written by one of his comrades who was blinded in the battle. It speaks for itself. Every word in it goes to the heart as it comes from the heart. Its rare beauty will place it among the classics of war.

You know how we all loved the "Babe." He was the youngest and the livest thing I ever came across, and if one had happened to hold the dreadful old ideas about death, the passing of these wonderful boys would be enough to show how grotesque they were.

I can't feel somehow in writing to the "Babe's" mother that I am writing to a comparative stranger, so you must forgive me if I seem to trespass on too sacred ground. I have never yet lost any of those nearest to me and I know that one can never conceive what a loss like this must mean to you all. I think that somehow all of us who have been out there must always have a different perspective, in looking at death, from that of people at home—especially just before July 1, when we knew what was before us (right up to the day and hour) and we knew that very few of us would come through, one faced the issue squarely; and I know what we thought of death and how contentedly we faced the likelihood of meeting it.

My own particular experience seemed to take me even further and let me see what the actual moment is like. There was the one all-embracing flash and roar as the shell burst beside me, then—for a moment—nothing, and then life went on again, but, for me, in the dark. Well, I don't think that the men who were killed beside me by the same explosion experienced much else except the latter part. One moment they were going on with their work; then the whole world seemed to explode, then nothing, and then they went on again, but freed from the strain and the weariness and all the hampering circumstances of humanity. Nothing terrible about this.

I'm sure they're not less alive, but much more alive, going on with finer and more fascinating work, with greater scope for development, clearer understanding, and less to bewilder and hamper them. Things must be better in the next stage, and—freed from all the clumsiness of matter—we must have finer powers to work with, and keener enjoyment. If the "Babe" found something to enjoy in every minute here, we needn't doubt that he is doing so there.

Matthew Arnold, long ago, in "Rugby Chapel" said some fine things about the next stage, and Rupert Brooke, who was my first school friend, has some wonderful lines in one of his sonnets, where he says that there we shall

> Learn all we lacked before, hear, know, and say,
> What this tumultuous body now denies,
> And feel, who have laid our groping hands away,
> And see, no longer blinded by our eyes.

The grief and the loss are only for those left behind, and it is good to remember that the long lapse of time before we are together again is also on this side only. For time only belonged to this stage, and even here its existence is rather unsubstantial, for an hour under some circumstances passed as quickly for us as five minutes under others. So that the intervening years before he meets you again may not exist at all for him, but that day may follow straight on.

27 November 1917

One moment they were going on with their work; then the whole world seemed to explode, then nothing.

Above: **A sentry from the Worcestershire Regiment keeps watch. The sandbags filled with earth offered protection against enemy rifle fire, while the loophole provided a good vantage point.**

Opposite: **Soldiers pick their way through obstructions on the battlefield.**

SOME OF THE FALLEN.

MEN WE LOVED.

GAPS IN A CIRCLE OF FRIENDS.

By HAL MORTON.

On this anniversary let me look back and pay tribute to those men who went out, brave-hearted and great of soul, never to return. Before me are the names of eight brave men and good friends. They are names known outside the intimate circles of family and friendship, and, with one or two exceptions, their owners had lain down the pen, put aside the brush, and left the playing field at the call of the drum.

Rupert Brooke.

First, for several reasons, among those whose spirits are not dead must we place the young Adonais, Rupert Brooke, sub-lieutenant of the Royal Naval Division, who died from sunstroke at Lemnos. He was a young poet of genius, and therefore he had more to give than most men. He has gone down into silence taking his songs with him—the young poet is the only one of us who may carry riches

beyond the grave. As soon as war broke out there came into the verse of Rupert Brooke a fiery idealism, in which, it may be said, he forged his own sword. No man went into battle with a higher mind. Patriotism, not the flag-waving vagaries of the popular bard, but the deep love of English earth and the memory of all things English and good, came to him:—

God! I will pack and take a train
And get me to England once again!
For England's the one place I know
Where men with splendid hearts may go.

Dear, splendid heart, what is it possible to say? Those who knew you in the old days can imagine your scorn at the thought of anyone mourning the songs that might have been yours. You lived for your ideals and you died for them: it has made you a greater poet.
R. W. Poulton Palmer.

3 August 1915

AN ENGLISH TOMMY'S WORD.

(A PRIVATE OF THE GRENADIER GUARDS WRITES.)

A touching incident occurred in front of our trench. A German officer had been wounded in a charge and left in front of our trench. He was crawling, or trying to crawl, to our trench, but could not manage it. One of our stretcher bearers got up out of our trench and asked the Germans if they would shoot him if he went and pulled a German in, but they made no answer.

So our chaps shouted across and told them to fetch him and they would not shoot, so two Germans came over the trench and brought him in. The Germans said, "Thank you, English," and our fellows gave the Germans a cheer, which was taken up by the Germans.

The incident shows how a British "Tommy" will not take the word of a German but that a German knows that if an Englishman gives his word he will stick to it.

We have church service once a week. Every man attends, as his first thoughts are of home and God when he goes in the trenches.

22 February 1915

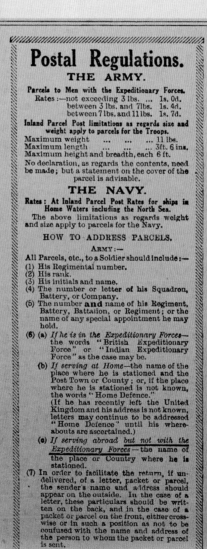

Postal Regulations.

THE ARMY.

Parcels to Men with the Expeditionary Forces.
Rates :—not exceeding 3 lbs. ... 1s. 0d.
between 3 lbs. and 7lbs. 1s. 4d.
between 7 lbs. and 11 lbs. 1s. 7d.

Inland Parcel Post limitations as regards size and weight apply to parcels for the Troops.
Maximum weight ... ... 11 lbs.
Maximum length ... ... 3ft. 6 ins.
Maximum height and breadth, each 6 ft.
No declaration, as regards the contents, need be made; but a statement on the cover of the parcel is advisable.

THE NAVY.

Rates : At Inland Parcel Post Rates for ships in Home Waters including the North Sea.
The above limitations as regards weight and size apply to parcels for the Navy.

HOW TO ADDRESS PARCELS.

ARMY :—
All Parcels, etc., to a Soldier should include :—
(1) His Regimental number.
(2) His rank.
(3) His initials and name.
(4) The number or letter of his Squadron, Battery, or Company.
(5) The number and name of his Regiment, Battery, Battalion, or Regiment; or the name of any special appointment he may hold.
(6) (a) If he is in the Expeditionary Forces—the words "British Expeditionary Force" or "Indian Expeditionary Force" as the case may be.
(b) If serving at Home—the name of the place where he is stationed and the Post Town or County; or, if the place where he is stationed is not known, the words "Home Defence."
(If he has recently left the United Kingdom and his address is not known, letters may continue to be addressed "Home Defence" until his whereabouts are ascertained.)
(c) If serving abroad but not with the Expeditionary Forces—the name of the place or Country where he is stationed.
(7) In order to facilitate the return, if undelivered, of a letter, packet or parcel, the sender's name and address should appear on the outside. In the case of a letter, these particulars should be written on the back, and in the case of a packet or parcel on the front, either crosswise or in such a position as not to be confused with the name and address of the person to whom the packet or parcel is sent.

NAVY :—
Name of man, H.M.S. (name ship), c/o General Post Office, Inland Section, E.C. This applies only to ships in home waters; for men in [...]

send out a little more OXO it would be greatly appreciated."
Letter received by the proprietors of OXO.

From a Captain in the 2nd East Lancashire Regiment.

By the way, you might tell some of those societies that send out tobacco and things to the troops to send cigarette papers as well. They get plenty of tobacco, but no paper to roll it in.—The Daily Mail, December 19, 1914.

Even those at home can form some sort of idea of the terrible strain which must be endured by the men who are keeping ceaseless watch and ward afloat and ashore. They say very little about their sufferings—but a chance word shows what they are enduring. The two following extracts are typical, and they will suggest to the senders of presents that a compact tonic should be included in the next parcel.

Letter from an Officer in the R.A.M.C.

It's something to be an Englishman after all. Of course, it's cold, wet, and miserable; a good many of us have coughs, colds, and neuralgia, but it is very good to be with gallant gentlemen.—The Evening News, January 25, 1915.

From Private Sainsbury, 4th Seaforth Highlanders. Dated January 9.

I am now in splendid health. The battalion has been sadly depleted through various causes, and sore throats and colds are very numerous.
The Evening News, January 21, 1915.

Matches are things which are in constant demand—for all the tobacco in the world would be useless unless its possessor had the means of lighting it. In fact, to have tobacco and a pipe, or cigarettes, would be only tantalising to the man who had no matches. It should be borne in mind that when matches are sent in a parcel they must be clearly declared in the statement of contents, and this applies even when they are enclosed in special packing according to the Post Office regulations.

From Pte. C. Butters, 82nd Co., Motor Transport, A.S.C., Indian Cavalry Supply Base, to relatives at Mansfield, Notts.

I received a letter from my landlady at Little Heath, and she thoughtfully sent me some soap and a dozen boxes of [...]

THE CHRISTMAS SPIRIT IN WAR-TIME.

CHRISTMAS TREES IN GERMAN TRENCHES.

TROOPS FEAST WHILE BELGIANS FAST.

FROM OUR SPECIAL CORRESPONDENT, JAMES DUNN.

ROTTERDAM, Friday.

Sentiment and shrapnel mingled in the German trenches this Christmastide. From correspondents at Sluis, Maastricht, Bergen-op-Zoom, and Sas van Gent I have received reports stating that great Christmas celebrations have taken place in the trenches, at the depots, and along the frontier. The enemy made merry in obedience to the military order, for notices were issued several days ago that the troops must do their best to enjoy Yuletide.

Hundreds of thousands of parcels arrived from Germany containing knitted articles, sweets, cakes, and tobacco. In addition the poor Belgian peasantry were bled to assist the German Christmas. Huge levies of wine and cigars were made in Ghent and Bruges, and the Belgian people were even asked to make Christmas cakes for the German soldiers. The Belgians in reply asked where the flour was to come from as they had eaten nothing but black bread for a long time, and even that was scarce.

While the German soldiers were feasting, drinking, and roaring wine songs the unfortunate Belgians were glad to have a Christmas dinner of half a loaf. Meat or vegetables are unknown, while butter and cheese are rare luxuries.

26 December 1914

CHRISTMAS IN THE TRENCHES.

GREAT PREPARATIONS IN FRANCE.

AN INFORMAL TRUCE EXPECTED.

FROM OUR SPECIAL CORRESPONDENT. GEORGE C. CURNOCK.

PARIS, Wednesday.

More than 3,000,000 French soldiers will spend their Christmas Day in the trenches, camps, and barracks of France, far from their children and homes. The roads to the trenches are filled to-day with wagons taking great stores of good and comforting gifts to these brave fellows.

One at least will receive with his Christmas parcel a little letter which I read yesterday. When he gets it I hope he will pass it down the trench. I am sure it will bring a smile, and perhaps a tear, to the face of these impressionable men in the blue coats and red trousers who are holding the line to-morrow.

Here is this charming little letter written by René Pierre Fredet: " I hope that the soldiers will put their shoes in the trenches, and that le Petit Jésus will fill them, for we are quite ready to give our share of good things in order that they may be well filled."

It was no copy-book sentiment which made little René Pierre write his letter, but the genuine expression of a thought which is filling the hearts of millions of children in France to-day. There is not a child in France who would not give up his Christmas gifts to make the soldiers in the trenches happier.

24 December 1914

CHRISTMAS IN THE GERMAN LINES.

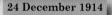

They shook hands with us and gave us cigars and wished us a happy Christmas. I got one of them to write his name and address on a postcard as a souvenir.

Below: **On Christmas Eve, British soldiers noticed Christmas lights appearing in the German trenches and the following morning they heard cries of "Happy Christmas".** The British responded with similar good wishes in German, giving rise to an informal armistice. Slowly both sides emerged from the trenches and met in no-man's-land to exchange pleasantries and gifts.

The ceasefire also gave both sides a chance to collect and bury their fallen comrades.

Above: **An opportunity for a member of the machine gun corps to kiss a French farm girl under the mistletoe.**

CHRISTMAS LETTERS FROM THE FRONT.

CONTENTED CANADIANS.

(A Sergeant in Princess Patricia's Canadian Regiment writes.)

At last we are where we wanted to be, and are contented with our little lot. We had a fairly good Christmas. Dinner consisted of bully beef and biscuits and whatever we could forage. My friend Sergeant —— and myself did not do so bad, as we had 1 carrot, ½ turnip, 2 leeks, 1 onion, 2 Oxo cubes, and 12 oz. of bully beef, with 3 hard biscuits, all mixed up and boiled in a bully beef tin. It sure made a tasty dinner. Today we had our Christmas pudding, ½lb. a man, 1lb. tin of jam between four men, and a small bottle of wine also between four men. We are all in good spirits, and also within sound of the big guns.

7 July 1915

Above: **Royal Scots Fusiliers dug in at La Bouteillerie during the winter of 1914.**

Below: **Scottish troops at the entrance to their hut enjoy the New Year festivities.**

"Business as Usual on Christmas Day.

[*From Cpl. J. Alldritt to his wife at 33, Highgate-road, Kentish Town, Dated December 15.*]

We shall be having our Christmas dinner in France, but I have the pleasure of knowing that we shall have as good a time as our friend the enemy in the opposite trenches.

I have been asking Dad to send me some cocoa and sugar instead of cigarettes; it is such a handy thing to have, and one cup of cocoa is worth two of tea.

I wonder if you imagine the troops as being tired and worn out. If you do so, you would receive a distinct shock at my measurements. European wars seem to be very beneficial to me. Truth to tell, I am afraid of getting too fat!

Don't forget to enjoy yourself as well as you possibly can this Christmas, and be sure I will be just as happy trying to cause as much discomfort as we can to our friends in the other camp.

CHRISTMAS AT THE FRONT.

December 1915

(Rifleman C. H. Brazier, Queen's Westminsters, writes.)

You will no doubt be surprised to hear that we spent our Christmas in the trenches after all, and that Christmas Day was a very happy one.

On Christmas Eve the Germans entrenched opposite us began calling out to us, "cigarettes," "Pudding," "A Happy Christmas," and "Englishmens good" so two of our fellows climbed over the parapet of the trench and went towards the German trenches. Half-way they were met by four Germans, who said they would not shoot on Christmas Day if we did not.

They gave our fellows cigars and a bottle of wine and were given cake and cigarettes. When they came back I went out with some more of our fellows and were met by about thirty Germans, who seemed to be very nice fellows. They shook hands with us and gave us cigars and wished us a happy Christmas. I got one of them to write his name and address on a postcard as a souvenir. All through the night we sang carols to them and they sang to us, and one played "God Save the King" on a mouth organ.

On Christmas Day we all got out of the trenches and walked about with the Germans, who, when asked if they were fed up with the war, said "yes, rather." They all believe that London has been captured and that German sentries are outside Buckingham Palace. They are evidently told a lot of rot. We gave them some of our newspapers to convince them. Some of them could speak English fairly well. Between the trenches there were a lot of dead Germans, whom we helped to bury.

In one place where the trenches are only 25 yards apart we could see dead Germans half-buried, their legs and gloved hands sticking out of the ground. The trenches in this position are so close that it is called "The Death Trap," as hundreds have been killed there.

A hundred yards or so in the rear of our trenches there were houses that had been shelled. These we explored with some of the Regulars, and we found old bicycles, top hats, straw hats, umbrellas, etc. We dressed ourselves up in these and went over to the Germans. It seemed so comical to see fellows walking about in top hats and with umbrellas up. Some rode the bicycles backwards. We had some fine sport and made the Germans laugh.

7 July 1915

6d. per packet of 8 Cards.

THE KING'S MESSAGE.

TO SAILORS AND SOLDIERS.

I send you, my Sailors and Soldiers, hearty good wishes for Christmas and the New Year.

My grateful thoughts are ever with you for victories gained, for hardships endured, and for your unfailing cheeriness.

Another Christmas has come round and we are still at war. But the Empire, confident in you, remains determined to win.

May God bless and protect you.

GEORGE R. I.

TO THE SICK AND WOUNDED.

At this Christmastide the Queen and I are thinking more than ever of the sick and wounded among my Sailors and Soldiers.

From our hearts we wish them strength to bear their sufferings, speedy restoration to health, a peaceful Christmas, and many happier years to come.

GEORGE R. I.

26 December 1916

THE KING'S THANKS.

SIR DOUGLAS HAIG'S GREAT VICTORY.

The King's message of congratulation to Sir Douglas Haig and his heroic armies sets the seal upon the victory on the Ancre. He has inflicted a terrific blow on the Germans just as they were telling one another that the British offensive had closed for the winter. He has been able to go forward through the mud and to penetrate deep into the enemy's line. The unwelcome discovery that he can thus attack and can continue attacking compels the Germans to keep vast armies in constant readiness to ward off a blow on the western front.

Among Sir Douglas Haig's captures of the past week has been the fortified village of Beaumont-Hamel, with its vast system of trenches and outworks and with its immense caverns which, in Mr Beach Thomas's picturesque phrase, are as "big as Buckingham Palace." The enemy believed and boasted that this place was impregnable. So long as it was in the hands of the Germans it was impossible for us to reach the high ground north of the Ancre, which is of immense importance as an observation post. The fortified village of Beaucourt, which has also been stormed was little inferior in strength to Beaumont-Hamel. Both threw into the shade the old-world fortresses of Sebastopol or Plevna.

The Germans have industriously spread reports of "enormous," "sanguinary" British losses—indeed the phrase recurs with the monotony of a refrain in their headquarter bulletins. They may have persuaded themselves that as the result of these absurdly exaggerated casualties the British infantry had lost its fire and vigour of attack. If so, they now know that the fighting quality of our troops is as high as it ever was, while the skill with which Sir Douglas Haig is using them is an entirely new feature in the war in the west. The nation will echo the words of its Sovereign. It owes to its soldiers a debt beyond human words.

17 November 1916

THE KING ON THE SOMME BATTLEFIELD

The King returned yesterday from another visit to the front. The following is the General Order to the Army in France which his Majesty sent to General Sir Douglas Haig:- Officers, N.C.O.s, and men.

It has been a great pleasure and satisfaction to me to be with my Armies during the past week. I have been able to judge for myself of their splendid condition for war and of the spirit of cheerful confidence which animates all ranks, united in loyal co-operation to their Chiefs and to one another.

Since my last visit to the front there has been almost uninterrupted fighting on parts of our line. The offensive recently begun has since been resolutely maintained by day and by night. I have had opportunities of visiting some of the scenes of the later desperate struggles, and of appreciating to a slight extent the demands made upon your courage and physical endurance in order to assail and capture positions prepared during the past two years and stoutly defended to the last.

I have realized not only the splendid work which has been done in immediate touch with the enemy – in the air, under ground, as well as on the ground – but also the vast organizations behind the fighting line, honourable alike to the genius of the initiators and to the heart and hand of the workers. Everywhere there is proof that all, men and women, are playing their part, and I rejoice to think their noble efforts are being heartily seconded by all classes at home.

The happy relations maintained by my Armies and those of our French Allies were equally noticeable between my troops and the inhabitants of the districts in which they are quartered, and from whom they have received a cordial welcome ever since their first arrival in France.

Do not think that I and your fellow countrymen forget the heavy sacrifices which the Armies have made and the bravery and endurance they have displayed during the past two years of bitter conflict. These sacrifices have not been in vain; the arms of the Allies will never be laid down until our cause has triumphed.

I return home more than ever proud of you.

May God guide you to Victory.

GEORGE R.I.

16 August 1916

Both pages: **King George V visited the Western Front several times, and on one occasion broke his pelvis when a horse rolled on top of him. He had previously served in the Royal Navy but was forced to end his service when he became second-in-line to the throne, following the death of his older brother Albert in 1892.**

"TRENCH-FOOT"

TO THE EDITOR **SIR,** —

The Regius Professor of Medicine in the University of Oxford, Sir William Osler, in his most excellent letter to the Lancet has laid stress on the fact that inertia of the various muscles of the lower extremities plays an important part in the very serious drawback known as "trench-foot" with which our brave fellows in their underground shelters are so much afflicted during the cold season.

The experience of those who have already spent a whole winter at the front will not permit of their agreeing with the dictum of the learned professor on the subject of "puttees," which are undoubtedly a contributory cause, producing a steady compression and constriction on the capillary circulation, a gradual stasis, leading to loss of caloric, cramp of the muscles entering into the formation of the calf (the gatrocnemii especially), and loss of sensation in the toes.

An unusual experience some years ago taught the writer of this letter the value of wearing "cork socks," covered on the surface next the foot with stout felt, and dusted with ordinary red pepper (Cayenne, not Nepal) once in twenty-four hours, this producing decidedly good results in keeping "alive" a better state of circulation. Changing the wool socks worn on the feet should be done as frequently as convenient, and painting the soles of the feet with the "B.P." tincture of iodine two or three times a week is always helpful.

E.M. BUTCHER
3, Oakhurst terrace, Benton,
Northumberland.

28 December 1915

TRENCH RATS.

Thanks to modern medical science, there has been little or no disease spread among our troops by the tens of thousands of rats that have dug themselves in among the billets and trenches in France and Flanders.

Rats thrive well and multiply rapidly in the trenches. Alas, they never go scarce of food! One thinks with a shudder of their loathsome feasts and impish gambols among the unburied dead of "No Man's Land." A constant torment to the soldier, they steal his rations, disturb his rest, ruin his harness, and spitefully bite him when he offers resistance. Unless properly attended to, a rat bite often results in a nasty septic wound. Their favourite tit-bit is the lobe of the ear.

In billets also they are ever present, though it is some satisfaction to know that they are on a different diet. If you waken in the night on your bed of damp straw in some old barn or ruin, their beady eyes peer out of the darkness as though in gleeful anticipation of a feast. They may have nibbled holes in your socks by morning, or lined their nests with leaves from your pay-book, or carried off your false teeth if you were foolish enough to take them out before falling asleep. They are bold and audacious. They have even been known to knock down a lighted candle and carry it off, leaving the surprised "poker" party in indignant amazement.

An active warfare is continually being waged against these pests. Ferrets, terriers, poison, and traps, all take their daily toll; but there is nothing so effective as a gas attack. After the trenches have been drenched with gas they are generally clear of rats for some time to come.

Sometimes the soldier gets an opportunity for a very satisfying revenge. He leans with his back against the parapet and steadfastly watches a rat hole in front of him. In course of time a sniffing be-whiskered nose appears. He lunges forward, catches it on the point of the bayonet, and, thinking of all the torments rats have caused him, gives a vindictive pull of the trigger.

E. J. S.

1 July 1918

Once the attrition of trench warfare was established, soldiers had no alternative but to endure the daily grind of life in their primitive surroundings. At times they feared for their lives as the bullets began to fly, but this was frequently replaced by monotony and boredom. Added to this were the health hazards created by poor sanitation and the presence of flies, rats and lice. The constant exposure to cold and wet conditions often led to trench foot, damaging some men's feet beyond repair.

HEALTH IN THE TRENCHES.

200 NEW FRENCH TRAVELLING LABORATORIES.

FROM OUR OWN CORRESPONDENT.

PARIS, Monday.

Two hundred travelling toxicological laboratories have been formed by the French Army authorities and will shortly leave for the front.

Their main utility will be to insure the health of the soldiers fighting in the trenches or resting in the cantonments. The chemists attached to each laboratory will analyse the water the soldiers drink and the foodstuffs brought to them, so as to ensure their perfect purity. They will also control the disinfection of the front-line trenches whenever that is possible.

A secondary phase of their activities from which, however, much is expected will be the analysis of new German methods of attacking by gas bombs, liquid fire, or gas clouds.

Each laboratory has attached to it either a skilled doctor or an expert analytical chemist with trained laboratory assistants.

10 August 1916

TRENCH FOOT.

HOW TO PREVENT IT.

The ideal protection for the feet of soldiers in the trenches was outlined by Dr. L. Hill last night in a lecture on the science of clothing and the prevention of "trench foot" at the Royal Institution.

"Trench foot" is caused by two things, he said. If water soaked into the tissues it damaged their vitality or killed the tissues. There was natural grease in the skin, but if the foot was in a boot full of water the grease was used up, bacteria grew, and it decomposed. A supply of grease was needed to keep that from taking place. The other thing was to keep the limb from getting too cold. It was a question of air and plenty of it. Soldiers must not have tight boots.

Producing an Army boot, Dr. Hill said it was rigid, full of metal, increasing its conductivity of heat. The boot unless too large would press upon the tissues of the foot, and there should be no pressure. Something beautifully supple and easily moved was needed so that the blood could get to all parts. It had to be dry and warm.

The Italian device for stopping water from soaking into the tissues was a piece of linen soaked in a preparation of tallow, lard with salicylic acid, oil of spikenard (aspic), and oil of lemon. The soldier stood on the linen and then wrapped it around the foot. This could be worn with a wader, and for protection against the cold plenty of dry air space, obtainable by wearing a fluffy woolly substance with a wader, was necessary. The grease cloth kept the feet sweet and clean, which was highly important. Dry air was the only remedy against excessive cold.

28 January 1916

BOBBIE.
THE TRENCH CANARY.

The general public knows little about that most useful and life-saving animal—the trench canary.

He or she, whatever may happen to be its sex, is quite unknown to the infantry. The gunners would scorn so insignificant a mascot. But ask the tunnellers of the Royal Engineers—those human moles whose greatest joy in life is "blowing the Boche"—and they will tell you that the canary has been an invaluable ally in underground warfare.

The trench canary does not flutter in a gilded cage or sing in the scanty sunshine of La Belle France. You will have to climb down a mine shaft or two and scramble through tiny, dark galleries to make his acquaintance.

He is usually to be found in a small wooden cage ensconced with several others of his tribe in a cosy dug-out far beyond the reach of the heaviest howitzers.

One does not hear much singing in the trench canaries' dug-out. They are most of them too busy recovering from gas attacks.

"Cruelty to animals!" a reader mutters over his meatless breakfast.

No, not cruelty. The canary is just "doing his bit," the same as everyone else.

Bobbie is the veteran of the canaries in one part of the line. If he were a man he would have many medal ribbons "up." He is "some" bird, is Bobbie! He has been gassed seven times.

"Surely the gas doesn't come as far underground as this?" you question.

"We don't mean the chlorine which they squirt out of cylinders on the surface," says an Engineer officer who is willing to explain to you. "That's a picnic in these days of gas masks! Besides, you can see it coming rolling along before the wind, and it gives you lots of time. Our gas, known technically as carbon monoxide, is invisible and has no smell. If you happen to get into it—for a few seconds only— it's all up."

"But if you can't smell it and can't see it, how do you know it's there?"

"That's where the canary comes in," says the officer. "When a mine is exploded, whether by Fritz or ourselves, gas is given off. It may find its way into our galleries or it may not.. You have your anti-gas apparatus all ready, and grab Bobbie's cage or that of any other canary in whom you have confidence. You keep the cage well in front of you and high up, and push on, watching Bobbie as you would for a rival for a lady's affections. Bobbie knows what to do—you can trust him. He sniffs like a dog on a strange scent. If there's gas, down goes the canary flat on his back, toes up in the air."

"I suppose you miners get plenty of honour and glory?" you ask.

"M.C.s galore and a few D.S.O.s but I don't know of a tunneller having got the V.C. yet," replies the veteran with the two stars and the ribbon of the Military Cross on his muddy tunic. "But there's someone I know who has certainly earned the V.C., and that's Bobby, and all he gets is an extra ration of his favourite seed."

E. C. S.

28 April 1917

Right and opposite: The trenches were frequently flooded, adding to the risk of trench foot. At times men would take off their boots in an attempt to warm them up, only to find their feet had swollen so much they couldn't put them back on again. This began to improve in 1915 when soldiers were ordered to change their socks twice a day and were supplied with whale oil to repel the moisture.

THINGS THAT HAPPEN IN THE TRENCHES.

BY ONE WHO HAS BEEN THERE.

People at home do not know much about what life in the trenches is really like. Most of them imagine it a "lark" or a picnic, but I can tell them it is anything but that. I will try to describe how my comrades and I lived it for ten days and nights on the bank of Aisne.

After having marched the whole day and most of the previous night we finally make a halt in the dark, eagerly longing for our well-deserved supper and still more well-deserved rest and sleep. But immediately after halting a shout goes up: "No grub! The supplies have been captured by the Germans!"

"D—— the Germans!" we say, and with empty stomachs we prepare for rest. But no sooner have we rolled ourselves in our overcoats than the order comes: "Trenches to be dug immediately and to be finished before dawn." Now the digging of such trenches is no small work. Each trench is about two yards broad and five feet six inches deep and from half a mile to a mile in length. One side is perpendicular and the other slants upwards to give easy access to the rear, or sometimes to the front, as the case may be. When the trench slants frontwards it is to enable the boys the more easily to get at the enemy with the bayonet, a thing that the Tommy loves but the German fears. He shudders before the steel, as a Tommy said, and he had occasion to know.

There is neither time to cover the bottom or the sides of the trench nor any material at hand to do it with. You just jump down into the raw earth and there you stand up and fire if you get the chance, and there you sleep and there you eat. But very soon the trench gets wet from moisture in the soil and the rain, and then the water soaks the bottom of the trench and you sometimes stand ankle deep in it.

In these comfortable apartments you stay day and night and night and day. Your "grub" is from your emergency rations—tinned beef and biscuits—and the water that you are able to get hold of. The beef is all right when it is tinned. But very often the tin is pricked when you come to use it by accidentally having been hit against something hard, such as the metal fittings of a wagon or a spur or a bayonet, or by having been actually struck by a piece of an exploded shell, and then the formerly red and nourishing beef is green and filthy and perhaps able to "walk by itself." But it goes down just the same, for your hunger has to be stilled in some way or other.

THE OFFICER AND THE BEEF.

There are several stories connected with "grubbing" which shows what a fine fellow our Tommy is. An officer's tin had been pricked, but of course he said nothing above some mild oaths all by himself and sat down on his coat to munch the green stuff which once had been beef. But suddenly a private stood in front of him with his red and fresh tin in his hand and held it out and said: "Let me have yours, sir, and you take mine; it makes little difference to me, I am used to it."

Of course the officer refused and sent the man back to his place, but he forgot neither the man nor his offer.

The trench being entirely uncovered is open to sun and rain and storm and shells. A covering of boards and earth and grass would be very nice against rainstorms, but nothing can protect you from the shells except perhaps a concrete roof a couple of yards thick at least. For when a shell bursts on the ground it digs a hole in the earth three yards deep. We in the trenches consider the "life danger radius" of the shell to be about fifteen yards, but there is nothing to prevent you from being killed by a shell bursting more than a hundred yards away from you. Once a shell exploded just on the surface of the Aisne and it threw up a spout big enough to drench every man in our trench, which lay about two hundred yards away from the bank. One can imagine the size of the spout. It was a magnificent sight and we wished the Germans would give us some more "water-pantomimes."

28 October 1914

The formerly red and nourishing beef is green and filthy and perhaps able to "walk by itself." But it goes down just the same.

4 December 1914

In summer you may be able to divest yourself of your trousers. On the other hand, you may not, and most likely won't.

WHAT 15 MONTHS MEANS TO A TRENCH.

TRENCH ONLY A CHAIN OF HOLES.

The trench so called may be no more than a yoked line of shell holes converted with daily toil and loss to a more perpendicular angle. And the tangled pattern of craters is itself pocked with the smaller dents of bombs. Indeed, you have three grades of holes: great mine craters that look like an earth convulsion themselves, pitted with shell holes, which in turn are dimpled by bombs. Imagine a place like this, a graveyard maze under the visitation of 8,000 shells falling from three widely separated angles: and when you have imagined it give all the admiration that is in you and all the help within your resources to men who have held it for fifteen months.

It is a change of air, as grateful as the move to a hill station in India, to pass from such a low-lying and stormy salient as Ypres, where a canal bank is a mountain, to many parts of the front south of Arras and towards the Somme. The stratum is often chalk; and if they so desire it a battalion headquarters can be most comfortably built in the security of its white walls. Trenches of any depth with the firmest walls provide pleasant security on the way to the front line. You may comfortably survey the German lines from wooded hills; and though some of those wooded hills make much too perfect targets, it is a very different thing being shelled where dug-outs are deep and dry and well roofed than in an earthwork on a plain a yard or two above sea level.

BY W. BEACH THOMAS.

25 February 1916

HOW SOLDIERS GO TO BED.

BY JAMES HODSON.

"Going to bed" is, of course, a highly imaginative description of what happens. The nearest I ever approached to the real thing was a mattress on the floor with rather doubtful blankets and sheets—for three nights only. But the human frame is an accommodating structure, and a knobbly floor or a plain boarded one is soft enough when one is tired enough.

I can say with all gravity that my life's best sleeps have been enjoyed on boarded floors in France. We have all heard, I suppose, of the soldier on leave who can't go to sleep in his bed (broad smiles from the lads), but it is certain that there is nothing to compare with the first night or two in billets among the straw when you can wake up—and go to sleep again; when night is one long blessedness, and when, even asleep, one seems to savour the joy and luxury of it.

In summer you may be able to divest yourself of your trousers. On the other hand, you may not, and most likely won't. Down goes the groundsheet; pack, covered with a woollen scarf, is comfortably arranged for a pillow, boots and puttees are off, tunic off, a blanket over you, and great coat too if necessary, and—'tis done. You sleep. You probably wear your cap comforter for protection from draughts, and you may possible keep your bayonet handy in case rats are frolicsome.

In winter it is a more serious business. Boots off, puttees wound round feet, feet and legs thrust into the arms of your greatcoat, skirt of greatcoat drawn up to the waist and fastened with a belt, tunic maybe on, and two blankets over you, scarf round neck and ears (like a man with toothache).

But you are not always in billets. In trenches you have no blankets, so you do your best with greatcoat and groundsheet. If you occupy a dug-out in reserve you may please yourself whether you wear your greatcoat or spread it over you. Fashions change. Some dug-outs require groundsheet under you; others are dry enough to allow of it over you. Sandbags are godsends. A few underneath and one on each leg work wonders.

In the front line your bed is likely to be the firestep. You just curl up or stretch out, dependent on space and the weather. You sleep sitting, crouching or lying. I have occupied shelters where in one case I reposed on a rum jar: in another a petrol tin; and in yet another I slept sitting bolt upright on the firestep. I once lay head and shoulders in a "cubby-hole," my feet trailing across the bottom of the trench. Each passer-by trod on me—but I slept in the intervals.

20 September 1918

Opposite above: **Welsh Guards resting in the trenches at Guillemont.**

Opposite below: **Stretcher-bearers transport a Canadian infantryman to safety.**

Above: **The Allies were able to use creeping barrages to great effect, sending the gunners ahead of the troops to lay a network of high explosives and shrapnel shells.**

Left: **Whenever possible, field telephones were used during the conflict to provide instant communication between battalions and the troops.**

THE STRUGGLE AT THE CORNER

Lance-Corporal J. H. L. Smith (Royal Irish Lancers). —I was in as tight a fix as ever I want to be one day at ——. There, were just about eighteen of my troop out by ourselves. Up came a galloper to our officer with orders to cross the bridge at ——by a certain time, so we tracked off. Of course we had our advance points out.

Just as we got to the top of the hill, which was thickly wooded on one side, one of the points tore back to say the Germans were in ambush for us in the wood. Well, if we didn't cross the bridge we should be cut off, so we made a gallop for it.

It was a steep hill and at the bottom was a sharp corner. When we got to the corner the pace we were going and the dust we kicked up prevented us from getting round. We all smashed into one another—a great kicking, struggling mass, with the bullets buzzing round us like bees. It was awful. I lost my horse and all my arms, so made a run for it. I was blinded with dust, couldn't see where I was going, so I stumbled on till I fell down a deep ditch and there I lay in about six inches of mud and water. In a few minutes four of my mates fell in the same ditch as me and they had all lost their arms, too. So we lay there with no means of defence save one lance and my jack-knife and another pocket-knife—and our good British fists.

We were right among the Germans. Their shots were singing over our heads, so to move would have meant death for us; and presently they came to search for us. They walked over the top of the ditch and then they couldn't find us. After about an hour we crawled out of it safe again.

THE SHELLED BATTERY WAGON.

Bombardier Williams (Royal Field Artillery). —I was in charge of a firing battery wagon which consisted of six horses, three drivers, four gunners, and the coverer. I was that one. I was just thinking we were safe when they opened fire. A shell dropped which cut the wagon in two, cut the wheel horses in half and the driver to pieces, and one gunner was shattered and blown everywhere. My horse was shot under me and all I had was a big piece across my leg.

Lieutenant A. H. Selwyn (Royal Engineers). —My sub-lieutenant was talking to a slightly wounded man from the trenches. The latter said, "Oh, yes, sir, we have small bets on where the next shell is going to land and who will be knocked out next."

The British Tommy is really a marvel; his conversation is interlarded with scraps of French. The way he gets on with the inhabitants is wonderful. He has a knack of strolling into a cottage, cadging a terrific meal, nursing the baby, and making himself thoroughly at home.

15 October 1914

An officer of Guards—One of our men did a splendid thing three days ago. There was a thick fog and a group of three men was out in front as a patrol.

The fog lifted very suddenly and before they had time to get back into the trenches they were fired on. One was killed, one slightly wounded, and managed to crawl back, and the third badly wounded.

A man volunteered to go out and help him in. So he started off and crawled out with bullets striking close all round him (one took the heel off his boot), got to the wounded man, and crawled in again. Then he and another man crawled out again with a stretcher.

Having once got the man in the stretcher they stood up and walked in with him, as, of course they would not then be fired at. The whole thing took an hour. The one man has been recommended for a "V.C" the other for a "D.C.M."

Captain A. F. G. Kilby (2nd South Staffordshire Regiment). — The Germans have got a huge gun in position somewhere near here which we call "Black Maria," and she leaves her card on us at "frequent and uncertain intervals," but without doing any damage. She dropped an unburst shell yesterday, which measured 32in. long by 8½ in. in diameter—quite a little cough drop.

HOW CAPTAIN TANNER DIED.

Private W. B. Algar (1st King's Liverpool Regiment). —Our battalion was put into a wood (during the Battle of the Rivers) right in front of our guns, which were peppering the Allemands for all they were worth. We are two miles away from headquarters.

We tried to find the German infantry, but no, they stuck well down behind their guns and they would not budge. We were walking along in file through this wood (which was very thick), headed by Captain R. E. Tanner, when all of a sudden we were confronted by German infantry. Captain Tanner was shot in two places and two or three men were also shot. As soon as we opened fire they took to their heels for all they were worth. We managed to get three officers and fifty eight men as captives.

By this time two stretcher-bearers came along to carry Captain Tanner away, but they were struck by a shell and Captain Tanner was again wounded in the leg, so I assisted to carry him away. We were now being shelled in this wood, "Jack Johnsons" and "Coal Boxes" were everywhere. At last we came to the edge of the wood, but found we could not go any further owing to the deadly fire.

There we stopped until dark, when the fire slackened a lot. God knows how we escaped from being hit. They were dropping all around us; poor Captain Tanner's moans were terrible to hear. We could not do anything, only bandage him with our field dressings. He handed me 500 franc notes (£20) which was money belonging to the company. They were soaked with blood. I handed them on to the Provost Marshal. We made our way to the village about two miles and took Captain Tanner to a temporary hospital. He thanked us with what little breath he had, but I am sure we would gladly have carried him another two miles if needed. He was a good officer. I saw by yesterday's paper he died, poor Tanner. (Captain Tanner was officially reported on September 29 to have died of wounds.)

14 October 1914

Left: An all too familiar scene on the British Western Front showing the everyday aspects of war. Beside a broken railway crosses mark soldiers' graves; shell cases are strewn about and a transport wagon is heading to the front line.

FIGHT IN THE AVENUE

*(Private Gibson,
of the 1st Lincolnshire Regiment, writes.)*

Away we went up the town (Mons) and to the avenue. Off with our gear and started felling the trees across the road for a barricade to get behind on that beautiful Sunday afternoon.

We waited patiently for them to come. "Get loaded," our captain cries, and we did like one man. "Here they come!" cries the flag. "Don't fire yet, lads, let them come a bit nearer." The range from them was 350yds. "Get ready, fire," and didn't we blaze away at them. Just fresh from home, and a new thing in our life, no blank there, but live rounds. It was war—life for life.

"Cease fire." was ordered. Now you should have seen down that avenue. What a sight! Not an English soldier killed, but bags of Germans. Then came the next order. "You have got to retire." "All right," shouts the flag. "Leave three men behind." They wanted the best runners to stop behind. I am not a runner nor yet a sprinter, but I'll give you my word I never ran so fast in my life before as I did when I had a chance to nip.

Fancy three of us lying to crush two army corps of Germans. It couldn't be done (not then). Now this is where I saw a sight that I shall not forget. The Germans, the blackguards, came up the street pushing women and little children in front of them to get up the avenue. Now what could we do but fire on them, because it was very hard to hit the Germans without hitting the latter. Our good old flag says: "Stop firing! It's heartrending." So it was, I can tell you.

He says to me: "Let's retire out of it," and away we went, ran up a street, across a garden, and fell over some barbed wire.

5 November 1914

THE BULLET'S CAREER

*Sergeant E W Turner
(Royal West Kent Regiment)
writing to his fiancée.*

The bullet that wounded me went into one breast pocket and come out of the other and passed through your photo making a hole in the breast. What a strange coincidence. It then passed through my watch and struck a large clasp knife, smashing it to pieces and driving it though my finger.

14 September 1914

Above right: **Infantry in the trenches protect themselves from the dangers of poisonous gas.**

Below: **At the Second Battle of Ypres in 1915, 168 tons of chlorine gas was released over a 4-mile line. Nearly 6,000 French and colonial troops were killed instantly, with many more blinded and 2,000 captured as prisoners of war.**

GASSED!

AGONIES OF OUR BRAVE MEN.

(Extract)

Next morning early they reached the hospital, and one man was dead by 5 a.m.—ten hours. They did better in the open air, and did less well in the ambulances. At the time we have been looking at them, about thirty-three hours after exposure to the gas, the worse ones are in a process of slow drowning, for this reason, as you will have guessed.

SUFFOCATION.

The effect of the intense irritation of the bronchial mucous membrane is to produce quantities of clear fluid which fills the tubes and cannot be expelled. Death is from suffocation with almost full consciousness; you may see one man signing to a nurse by turning his head vigorously from side to side. I am told, but have not myself seen it, that one post mortem showed the mucosa and more to be destroyed by the corrosive action of the gas. Very little coughing is heard, hardly any.

Can nothing be done for them? Yes, something can. They are being given quantities of salt and water to drink to make them sick. Even if they only retch, quantities of clear frothy liquid are then expelled from the lungs. When the tubes are empty, oxygen is given if possible, and heart stimulants. Patients are best laid on their sides. Artificial breathing is done.

8 May 1915

MEN WHO NEVER WAVER.
Leading Companies' Officers all Killed.

When I think of their heroic death it seems to me, so tenacious were they until the end, that in distant days the peasants who cross these barren plains at night will see their pale shades in the moonlight, still hacking at the barbed wire, stabbing, smashing, falling—yes, falling all the time before the inferno of fire belched at them by the German machine guns.

If you would hear the manner of their death then follow me first to the extreme right of the line to that sinister group of ruined houses known as Port Arthur. We are with the 1st 39th Garhwalis, a tough regiment that showed its worth in Burma and in the Tirah campaign.

Whistles blow, the men leave their trenches. Instantly they are withered by a fearful blast of fire. The German trench is untouched. So is the barbed wire, 200 yards of it. The Garhwalis never waver. All the officers of the leading companies are killed right ahead of their men. The battalion staggers under the blast of fire, loses its direction, swings to the right, and captures, after fierce in-fighting with bayonet and knife, a section of trench there, only to be cut off in the upshot by the Germans in the intact trench.

On their left the Leicesters have gone through with a rush. Handy men with the bayonet, hardly a man in the battalion, the 2nd, that does not do his work. So gallantly, indeed, did the Tigers bear themselves this day that after the fight the Divisional General visited them in their billets to congratulate them on the good showing they made. The Leicesters come in for fire from the German trench which has been left intact. It is a bad gap in our attacking line and it must be closed.

Five of the Garhwalis' officers are dead now, killed in the first line after prodigies of bravery. In this fight the battalion is to lose 20 officers and 350 men killed and wounded. The Germans have started to shell the Garhwali trenches. But the men, though without officers, are steady. These stout little hillmen have seen their officers fall, fearlessly exposing themselves. They remember that and it keeps them firm.

Now the Leicesters are going to effect a junction with the marooned Garhwalis. A bombing party is creeping down the communication trench to pelt the Germans into the open. Cricket is good training for bomb-throwing, and the Tigers fling their bombs into the crowded German trenches as fast and true as though they were throwing down a wicket. As the Germans are driven out into the open they are shot or bayoneted or slashed with the kukri. The captain lays out five Germans with his revolver.

18 April 1915

WHY DON'T THEY TELL YOU AT HOME?
(A lieutenant in the A.S.C. to his mother.)

It's marvellous how the British Tommy manages to keep clean but quite resigned. They accepted food and drink and shelter in the most phlegmatic manner and seemed too exhausted to talk even among themselves. An ambulance train just in! We brought two R.A.M.C. officers along with us from a base hospital and they told us some tales! Some of the sights are awful. The Germans have suffered appallingly, but our losses aren't far behind, I fear. As one major put it to us, "What can you expect when all we could spare for reserves was a company to each battalion? Heaps of our fellows were lost through sheer inability to keep awake and thus take necessary cover."

One has to be here to realise the deadly seriousness of it all. Every able man in England ought to be training, and yet we read in the papers we get that recruiting is bad. We're all as cheery as the days (and nights) are long, but I guess most of us pray for conscription in England! And if I, only out a fortnight, have my eyes so opened, what must be the feelings of those who have suffered the strain at the front for so long?

I've just been talking to an officer in——division. They were sent originally to relieve Antwerp, but only got part way (on land, of course) when Antwerp fell. They had to put up another "Mons" retreat on their own. Eventually they reached —— and were ordered to hold it (a line of eight miles) till the main line of troops turned up. Well, they did so—but there are very few left to tell the tale! The fellow told me he had got into such a state that he wanted to shriek whenever he heard a shell explode—and he looked pretty tough! Why don't they tell you at home these stories? If people only realised what the average Tommy is going through there would be no need for conscription. Well, I'll close now; there's an aroma of something cooking, and an emptiness in my little inside that draws me to it.

24 November 1914

Above: **Exhausted troops grasp the opportunity to get some sleep in this German dug-out on the Vimy Ridge.**

Below: **Shell craters and abandoned trenches litter the landscape of the battlefield.**

AN OFFICER'S LIFE IN THE TRENCHES.

(Extract from an Officer's diary-letter.)

You think of them all at home and you feel angry with the papers showing you comfortable and warm dug-outs and showing pictures of us on machine guns. All is rot and unlike the real thing, and thankful we are that, those who love us do not know just what being in the trenches means. I will not further or more minutely describe it. Our candles give us light stuck in the top of a bottle, and you walk about with your shoulders stooped as the roof is generally 5ft. 5 in. in height only. Still there is the feeling about it all that the others are doing the same and the men are worse off than we are, and you just go on, inwardly mutinous and outwardly, well, wondering what the next day will bring forth.

Somehow you get into the habit of living each day as a separate little life of its own, and in the darkness you hear the crack of a rifle from the German trenches and the singing and speeding of the bullet, then ping, as it strikes your mud parapet. Then sleep will come along and you dream you are at home and it is warm and happy and no worries such as these; yet they are not worries exactly, but duties gladly undertaken, and after all, carried out with all the energy of your mind and body.

Saturday, January 2. —The floods here during the last few days have been terrific, hundreds of acres being swamped and submerged, and unless the rain stops things are going to be bad. Once you get wet it is almost impossible to get dry again. We never undress, of course, or take off a boot or sock; there is no time to, and you are liable to be called at any moment night or day. We try to get some sleep during the day as well.

We have been comfortable in these billets though four of us are packed into a little room. We all sleep on our valises on the floor. I have a good servant, though, and he has kept me fairly comfortable. In our last place he tore a piece of curtain and put it in front of the table I used as a washing stand, and it made it look clean. Here we shave sitting on the floor, and I hold my little pocket mirror between my knees at the same time and a candle for light stuck in its own wax on the edge of a chair. We have no tables, there is room for none, and our chief and only luxury is very hot water in the morning, as we have got on to the good side of the worthy French couple who own the estaminet.

4 February 1915

Below: **A soldier from the Cheshire Regiment is posted on look out duty while his comrades rest in a captured German trench in Ovillers-la-Boiselle.**

Above: Men lie on stretchers at a field dressing station. Although conditions were usually very basic, the medical care given was frequently a life-saver for many soldiers.

Below: The Wiltshire Regiment cross a piece of open ground.

We arrived by train at a place called ——, and from there we started a long march, which unfortunately ended in a downpour of rain. We were wet to the skin, but in these times if you do feel miserable it is as well to disguise your feelings.

After a long march we arrived at ——, and camped for the night. Early the next morning we were having breakfast (about 5.30), when everybody was startled by the crackle of a machine gun.

We harnessed up, and after a mad gallop of 2,000 yards or so we came into our first action. We opened fire immediately. It was just like our practice camp, except that I think everybody realised that we were firing at targets composed of flesh and blood instead of canvas, but having to concentrate our minds on the working of the guns it soon passed off.

Presently the German shells began to whistle over us, or rather scream. It was comical at first to see everybody's head duck down as the shells came over, but we soon got hardened to that.

After a battle lasting all day we were forced to retire from a very hot corner, but thanks to our officers it was carried out very successfully.

During the day our wounded were continually coming past our guns, away to the rear. Contrary to expectations, we did not seem to feel so very horrified at seeing wounded men.

12 October 1914

ALIVE AFTER FIVE BULLETS.

(Letter from a Private in the Royal Warwickshire Regiment to Lord Norton.)

I can hardly say how grateful I am to you for your kind and welcome letter. I rather think you are making too much of my doings at the front, although I did my little bit with the Maxim gun before I was wounded.

I was dressing a comrade at the time of my accident. I got five bullets, one through the back which came out under my left arm; three through the left upper arm, and I have still one in my left hand with which I have to undergo an operation. I rather think I am one of the luckiest fellows alive to have had five bullets and none proved fatal.

I heard there were two more Saltley boys of my regiment wounded but I cannot confirm this statement. We were in that battle at ——, which is about four miles N. E. of Ypres. The battle had been raging fiercely for three continuous days and nights when I came away and it is still going on. We were forced to retire once on account of overwhelming numbers, but we made up for it the next day. We drove the Germans back four miles, both sides losing heavily, but Germany, by far, lost the most men.

All the Belgians and French are marvelling at the pluck and endurance of the British soldier.

16 November 1914

CLOTHES FOR THE WOUNDED.

FROM FIELD-MARSHAL LORD GRENFELL

Sir,—May I appeal to the possessors of well-stocked wardrobes to remember the wounded and otherwise disabled soldiers? Greatcoats, mackintoshes, and rugs are of great service during the passage across the Channel, and flannel shirts, woollen socks, and underwear, especially woven, are invaluable everywhere. Lounge suits and stout boots are a blessing to those invalided out of the Army and obliged to make a fresh start in civil life.

The above-mentioned articles, or the money to buy them, will be gratefully and promptly acknowledged at 3, Grafton Street, Piccadilly, W1, which Mrs. Arthur James has placed at the service of the fund. Mrs. Arthur James will superintend the distribution of the articles under the direction of the St. John Ambulance Department.

GRENFELL, F.M.

29 October 1914

LIFTED 20 FEET BY A SHELL.

BLACK WATCH CORPORAL'S ESCAPE.

ARMY.

A Corporal in the Black Watch. —To tell you the truth I am the luckiest man alive in the British Army. Last Monday week I never thought I should be alive to tell the tale. The whole of my section got killed. We were lying behind a thick hedge. We could not move our heads. I believe the Germans fired 200 shells at us the time we were there.

The officer got shot and we got an order to go forward from the right. I had the right section. We rushed down into a wood about fifty yards away. We were only about ten seconds there when a shell landed right into the bank. I was lying behind and it lifted me about 20ft. in the air. I was the only one of the section that escaped, but I got knocked stone deaf. I am getting my hearing back all right.

26 September 1914

THE EVENING NEWS. WEDNESDAY. NOVEMBER

THE BRITISH SOLDIER AT THE FRONT.

OUR FIGHTING MEN'S LETTERS. | NEWS OF BRITISH WOUNDED.

FRENCH GUNS FALL in mud. We are being well clothed. Life "EVENING NEWS" LIST FROM VERSAILLES
INTO in the Army is the finest man can have HOSPITAL

FEARLESS GUNNER.

"THE SOONER THROUGH THE SOONER HOME."

SOLDIER'S LETTER TO CHUM'S FATHER.

ARMY.

Gunner Batey (Royal Garrison Artillery) to Mr. Robert Mann, of Kimblesworth, near Gateshead: You will be surprised to hear from me. I have just come back from the front, and I met your son, Gunner F. Spencer Mann, out there. If it had not been for him I would not be here to tell the tale.

I got severely wounded in the severe fighting we had for three days across the Meuse. We had our heavy siege guns in action, and I was hit with shrapnel. When I fell our men drove off, but your son and I had been fighting side by side and he missed me.

It was like the fires of hell, and your noble lad came back and carried me to safety, although he was wounded himself, but not dangerously. He gave me two letters, one for you and one for his brother Jim; but I lost them, and then I thought of your address. So I thought I would write and tell you. He said that if God spared him he would never come back until the war was finished. It is a cruel war, but our lads will win, and you can be proud of your son, as we were all proud of him. He dropped them like sheep in hundreds.

Your son was the lad for them. When he laid the gun it played hell with the Germans. He seemed in his glory, and with such men as him England must win. He fears nothing. He is always cheering, always shouting, "Into them lads; the sooner we get through the sooner we will get home." The captain is proud of him.

19 September 1914

RACE AFTER A GERMAN.

Private Frederick Beech (Northamptonshire Regiment).— Referring to a charge of the regiment mentioned in despatches: I got through the charge all right and on looking round for anything in the shape of a German, an officer of theirs rose to his feet and bolted for all he was worth. A race ensued and I was quickly overhauling him when he turned round and fired his revolver, one bullet passing through my arm just above the wrist. I managed to get back to the rear by rolling and crawling. I spent two days in caves where wounded were attended.

22 October 1914

ARMY.

Private Ernest Waters: There's one chap in our company has got a ripping cure for neuralgia, but he isn't going to take out a patent for it, because it's too risky, and might kill the patient. He was lying in the trenches the other day nearly mad with pain in his face when a German shell burst close by. He wasn't hit, but the explosion knocked him senseless for a time, and when he came round his neuralgia had gone! His name was Palmer, and so we all call the German shells now "Palmer's neuralgia cure."

"THE EMERGENCY RATION."

An Officer in the Army Service Corps.—I have a pet rabbit which I found in a deserted farm, so we are taking it along with us. It travels in one of our cars and sleeps with us at night. I call him the emergency ration. He is a mixture of white and yellow, and quite a sporting little chap.

23 September 1914

Below: **Exhausted soldiers enjoy a brief respite leaning against a shattered wooden barrier.**

Above: **A British officer watches as German trenches near Leuze Wood are shelled in 1916. Troops soon renamed it "Lousy Wood".**

GERMAN TOYS IN BRITISH SHOPS.

To the Editor of *The Daily Mail.*

Sir,—Can you explain the following? In the window of a local shop the most prominent toy is an automatic cruiser flying the German flag at stern and mast and with "Emden" painted on her bows. Near by are mounted despatch riders with spiked German helmets and field-grey uniforms. Are these toys to cater for the custom of our 22,000 enemy aliens still at large here and the vast number of naturalised Huns?

No self-respecting Briton would give the Emden to his boy, knowing well that after telling its story it would soon be at the bottom of the nearest pond. Would one find in any German shop window a model, say, of Admiral Sturdee's flagship? The Hun is out to sell his goods, not to have his windows broken.

M. MEREDITH BEAUMONT.
8, Castello-avenue, Putney, S.W. 15.

RATIONS FOR VEGETARIANS.

To the Editor of *The Daily Mail.*

Sir,—Sir Arthur Yapp has suggested a certain scale of rations for meat eaters. Why has he not suggested rations for non-flesh eaters? What are we to substitute? We require more fat in some form. Are we allowed more bread?

D. D. BENNETT, Rector of Gislingham.
Eye, Suffolk.

BICYCLING IN LONDON.

To the Editor of *The Daily Mail.*

Sir,—Now that the petrol restrictions have still further decreased the motor traffic, the London streets are comparatively empty, and cycling is no longer a dangerous pursuit. There are bicycle and tricycle boys and girls delivering parcels, but one seldom sees a man, and still more rarely a woman, using a bicycle as a means of transit.

If every man, woman, and child who can ride a bicycle in London would do so it would improve the conditions for those who must travel by omnibus or tube.

For many weeks I have cycled daily when shopping and going to and from war work, and I can say that it is infinitely less fatiguing than struggling to enter crowded omnibuses and trains.

CHARLOTTE R. HILLIARD.
30, Wilton-place, Knightsbridge, S.W. 1.

WELL-FED "CONCHIES."

To the Editor of *The Daily Mail.*

Sir,—Why, in the name of reason, should the conscientious objector be allowed to exist in England? There are no "Conchies" in France or in Italy or in America, and few, I should imagine, in Germany.

The "Conchy" was the creation of "Wait and See," but "Wait and See" has departed never to return, so why not send the "Conchy" after him? A short Act of Parliament is necessary, and then the conscientious objector could be employed behind the lines. We might trust the military authorities to see that he rendered a good account of himself. HORACE BLEACKLEY.
19, Cornwall-terrace, N.W. 1.

22 November 1917

HUN PRISONERS' TOBACCO.

To the Editor of *The Daily Mail.*

Sir,—I notice a suggestion that English women shall give up smoking. I believe I am correct in saying that in *The Daily Mail* recently you published the fact that German prisoners of war and interned Germans in this country are allowed to purchase, should they so desire, 200 cigarettes, 100 cigars, and 2lb. of tobacco a week.

O. F. W. JAMESON.
72a, Sinclair-road, Kensington, W. 14.

24 November 1917

BELGIUM IS STILL ALIVE.

(A soldier writes home:)

The other day several men of my company saw a big placard placed about 200 yards in front of the German trenches and which did not seem to have been there before. They made the remark to one of my lieutenants, who, in spite of very good glasses, could not read what was on it.

A few plucky men decided to go at night to see what it was. They went, and brought back a big placard, in a corner of which was a German flag and in the centre in large letters, "Anvers has fallen. Hurrah!" And then the date of the fall of Antwerp.

We decided to reply in German and immediately prepared another placard, in the corners of which we put the four flags of the Allies and in the centre in German, "Thank you, we have known it for six days, but we also know that Belgium is still alive," and last night we went to put it in the place of the one they had put for us.

For ten days we have been occupying the village of —. For several hours a day the Germans shelled the village, at the beginning, without even hitting one of us. The other day they resumed their fighting with more energy than ever, and succeeded in wounding one soldier—a German.

This is how they did it. A shell burst in the house where our major was, and passing through the roof fell in the barn full of straw. There were in that barn a few soldiers who were not hurt, but who suddenly saw a man falling from the roof, as from the sky... It was a German... His regiment had left him behind ten days before, and he had carefully hidden himself in the straw, and spent ten days there without eating anything.

He was of the reserve, father of nine children, and had been wounded in the arm by that German shell. Falling like Cyrano from the moon, he found himself to his terror among a group of French soldiers and prayed them not to kill him. He was taken to the major, who gave him some brandy, and then to the doctor, who nursed him.

10 November 1914

NOT A LEG TO STAND ON.

(A soldier at the front sends home the following anecdotes from the trenches.)

During the battle of the Aisne River a man was bringing the mail up to the men. A sergeant had just put his hand up to receive a parcel from home containing some cigarettes when a kind German friend sent a souvenir across in the shape of a bullet. The sergeant readily accepted it and received both parcel and bullet in the same hand together.

Two chums were discussing the relative values of their birthplaces. The Cockney was evidently having the best of the argument, when a shrapnel shell burst above them and the Londoner received a bullet in each leg, while the Birmingham man escaped unhurt.

"I should think you'll give way now!" said the man from Birmingham.

"Why?" asked the Cockney.

"Well, you haven't a leg to stand on," was the reply.

10 September 1914

Right: **French troops defend their position at Verdun.**

Below: **Troops use the camouflage of a smokescreen to launch another attack.**

BOTHA ADDS TO THE EMPIRE.

GERMAN S.W. AFRICAN ARMY SURRENDERS.

322,450 SQUARE MILES WON.

AN ULTIMATUM TO THE DOOMED FORCES.

THE GOVERNMENT AND COMPULSION.

" OU

able
that
was

£21,000,000

The London
subscribed for
Loan

SIR ARTHUR CONAN DOYLE
BOER WAR LESSONS.
WHAT OUR ARMY LEARNED IN SOUTH AFRICA.

LETTER FROM BRITISH EAST AFRICA.

From a Motor-Cycle Despatch Rider in British East Africa. —The other night, when it was just getting dark, the captain had to send someone to the next camp, and I was asked to go. It was twenty-three miles away and there is only one road or track to it running right through jungle all the way. Off I went on the most exciting ride I have ever undertaken.

I was fully armed with a service rifle and revolver, hunting knife, water-bottle, haversack, and ammunition. All that was on my back, including a bandolier, the whole lot weighing about 50lb. The first thing I ran into was a pack of baboons, some of them as tall as 5ft. They ran in front of my light for about a mile. The brutes would not shift; you ought to have heard them bark. I rode behind one big brute within three yards of him. I would not have got into his clutches for all the money in the world. However, they at last turned off into the bush.

The stray game that were hanging about that road—well, it is impossible to mention. I swore I would shoot some the next morning. I saw two fine leopards. One brute did not attempt to move until I was within three yards of him. I suppose he thought it wiser to get out of the road of the bright light and the roar of the engine. He opened his mouth and snarled, then sprang to one side, and I did not half go when I had passed him in case he took it into his head to follow me.

Everyone was up ready when I got there. They had heard me coming. I delivered my message to the captain. Then he asked me into his tent and gave me something to eat and drink. I told him about the leopards I had seen, and he was very interested and said that just before I came in, two of their sentries had been driven away from their posts by lions.

When I was lying out under my blanket that night we could hear their roaring about a quarter of a mile away, and despite the wild beasts I slept as sound as if I were in my old bed at home.

8 October 1914

Sir Arthur Conan Doyle, in The War Illustrated writes on "How the Boer war Prepared Us for the Great War." "The continental military critics," he says, "never understood the importance of the Boer War because, as in the case of the North and South struggle in America, they looked upon it as a scrambling, amateurish business which bore no relation to the clash of disciplined legions. Hence those solid infantry formations and gigantic cavalry charges which amazed our representatives at the various Kaiser manoeuvres.

"Two things we learned in Africa—the importance of good shooting and the necessity for using cover. Our excellence at both was a revelation to the Germans at Mons, as has been admitted by many of their officers. They were the two factors which saved us during that perilous business, for, outnumbered as we were, and faced by a far stronger artillery, we could not possibly have saved the army had we not some make-weights upon our side. Those were the all-important make-weights— that we could inflict the maximum and receive the minimum of punishment with the rifle. They saved us— and we owe them both directly to the South African War. Before that lesson we were no better than the Germans.

"It is in the cavalry that the Boer War left its mark most deeply, though it will always be a fair ground for argument whether it left it deeply enough. Certainly our cavalry have been splendid. They have adapted themselves to everything, and been the general utility men of the Army. I have notes of one regiment which executed a famous 'arme blanche' charge in the morning, fought as dismounted riflemen in the afternoon, and formed themselves into a gun-team to pull off deserted guns in the evening.

"Since then they have spent a good deal of their time making and holding trenches. Such men cannot be improved upon, and if they, in their nimble suppleness, present a contrast to armour-plated, top-booted Continental types, it is once again to South Africa that we owe it."

14 January 1915

GERMANY'S "PLACE IN THE SHADE."

Below: **Togolese men in traditional dress are recruited into the army in German-controlled Togoland at the start of the conflict.**

9 July 1915

THE A.S.C.'S WORK.

GERMAN AWE OF FRENCH 75'S.

LOOTING THE FOES' TRENCH.

(A Private in the A.S.C. writes.)

We generally deliver our load to our different regiments and then go to the railhead and unload. Of course, it all depends where our regiments are as to where we unload. Often we have gone right up to the firing line and dumped our stuff at the trenches. I can assure you a very warm job too, and such jobs better appreciated at a distance. Other times we dump it down on the road and leave it there to be picked up by the transport of the regiment, as every regiment has its own horse transport. Our load consists of anything, sometimes hay, oats, foodstuffs for the troops, and ordnance stores. Lately our load has been tin rations and fresh meat. Our usual day's work consists of about twenty miles, what with going to our regiment and then to railhead and back again where we are stopping, although some days I can remember we have often done 80 to 100 miles.

When we have gone to the trenches to deliver we generally wait until it gets dark and then make a dash for it with all our lights out, and then the fun starts.

28 January 1915

Below: **Once the signal is given, troops leave their trenches at Morval.**

Opposite: **Lancashire Fusiliers fix their bayonets prior to assault.**

15 July 1916

SOLDIERS' LETTERS.
A CONTRAST.

By J. M. N. JEFFRIES.

ROME, July 15

One misses the soldiers' letters in our English papers. I suppose they died suddenly on a dark night, strangled by military exigencies, and we shall never see their like again till after the war, when everything is going to be published and so little, I fear, is going to be read. They were wonderful letters, plucky, anomalous, witty things, telling of bright incidents from the field of gore, homely trench struggles, neighbourly grenade throwings, exclusive little hand-to-hands, and they certainly illuminated the school-report style of the official news.

Here in Italy the newspapers remain full of soldiers' letters. One letter from the field stirred the whole of Italy. It was the letter sent on his deathbed by Lieutenant-Colonel Negrotto, commander of a Bersaglieri regiment (who fell mortally wounded when leading his men on the banks of the Isonzo); to his little son. "To you," it runs, "Enzo, my son, at the moment of his quitting this life for ever, this is the message and legacy your father bequeaths you: Be ever obedient and dutiful to your mother. She who will now be alone in the world clinging to the name and to the memories of your father has a right to find her consolation in you, her sure defender in you, our dear son. Be always and in all places honest, hard-working, and brave, and proud of the name of an Italian. See that all you do helps to increase the power and glory of our people and tends to honour the unspotted name which I leave you as an heirloom. A great big kiss from your old papa who has been so fond of you always."

20 July 1915

9 SOLDIER BROTHERS.

EIGHT KILLED OR MISSING ; ONE WOUNDED.

Nine brothers in the Army and eight killed or missing and one wounded is the war record of the Restorick family, of Birmingham.

The youngest brother, Private Thomas Restorick, of the Cameronians, fought at Mons and Neuve Chapelle, and was so badly wounded by shrapnel on July 15 that he has been invalided out of the Service.

All the Restoricks were in different regiments, and it is from other soldiers who have been in contact with his brothers that Private Thomas Restorick has learned of their fate. The father and mother of this family of soldier sons are dead, but there are four sisters living.

Private Restorick is at present in Berwick, staying with his father-in-law. He is thirty years of age, a fitter by trade, and his injuries have left him unfit for the performance of any but very light duties.

TWO BROTHERS KILLED.

News has reached Belfast that the brothers Joseph and James Murray, privates in the Inniskilling Fusiliers, have died.

They were in the same battalion, fought together in the Dardanelles, were sent together to another front, gassed at the same time, taken to the same hospital, and died on the same day.

9 September 1916

GOING INTO THE BATTLE.

Before the battle the "back area" is a hive of industry, making ready for the attack. Rifles and guns are cleaned, bombs detonated, gas masks tested, water bottles filled, and battle gear put into order.

No soldier cares to go into an attack with "excess luggage," and all unnecessary equipment is left behind in his pack. His haversack contains just those personal properties which he considers it right and proper should go with him—a pair of socks, a razor (the clean-faced Tommy is proverbial), a tooth brush, towel and soap, a waterproof sheet, biscuits, a tin of bully, some sugar and tea.

Before the attack he destroys his correspondence—a wise precaution—and, perhaps, writes home—just ordinary letters to say that he is well. He packs his treasures—with the exception of his photographs, which never leave his possession—into a small parcel and addresses them home in case—well, in case, as he says, that he may be unable to deliver them personally.

And then there is the will. Simple, yet fine human documents some of them are, scribbled roughly in pencil on the last sheet of the pay-book.

A final shave, a good "tuck in," and another glance at his arms to see that they are in order. The bolt of the rifle works well; the ammunition is clean; the eyes of his respirator are whole; his bayonet is sharp and clean; his water-bottle does not leak; his field dressing is intact. All is ready, then.

The warrior stuffs his pocket with bombs and cigarettes, slings his rifle and moves on his journey of adventure. Past the barking batteries to the reserve trenches, then to the point of assembly to wait through the long hours until the tempest of shell hurls him howling into the flood of humanity which goes on and on.

A. W.

24 September 1918

WITH THE IRISH FUSILIERS.

(Notes by an Officer)

We attacked and carried a position on the afternoon of October 13. It was raining heavily and very misty; difficult for us to see and also for the enemy. Our brigade was disposed—Seaforths on the right, Irish Fusiliers (Faugh-a-Ballagh) next, and Dublin Fusiliers on the left, with Warwicks in reserve. It was a splendid attack carried right through, ending with a charge and final occupation of enemy's trenches.

The Seaforths, I think, did the best; anyway they had the heaviest casualties. Our own attack was excellent, no fault to be found with it. One man was killed and 23 were wounded. The enemy had no artillery on this occasion.

Last night we billeted in this village, which had been part of the enemy's position the night before. I slept in the house of the priest, a charming old gentleman, a scholarly, courteous old fellow, so unfeignedly glad to see us. Five hundred men slept in the church. He was so distressed lest they should feel it cold. Another 500 odd were in schools and other places round the church. The clergy are unusually glad to see us, because we are Irish and so of their faith.

2 November 1914

FINE WORK WITH ARTILLERY.

(Second Lieutenant T. J. Moss, R.F.A., a quartermaster-sergeant, who told his wife on saying "good-bye," that he would return with a commission, writes to his family at Teddington.)

On two occasions I have taken our gun right up to within 500 yards of the German trenches, and the last time I blew up a German gun they had put in the trench over-night, and also killed fifteen German infantry as they were about to attack our infantry with fixed bayonets. With this all the others went back to their trenches, and didn't try it on again.

They often have "night attacks" to try to get through, but they won't come near our boys' bayonets; when they see them they turn round and run away. We are having our biggest battle near the coast. I am writing this in a "six-foot dug-out," with shot and shell falling quickly all round. The Kaiser has taken command of his troops and is trying to get through, but we simply say, "Let 'em all come." The other day one of our bombardiers, unarmed, caught four armed Germans; in fact, all the Germans are "fed up" with it and don't want to fight.

MINES IN FISHING NETS.

(From the skipper of a Lowestoft trawler, writing to his sister at Patricroft, Manchester.) We were coming in with £72 worth of herrings on Tuesday morning, and about seven o'clock we were about four miles off Lowestoft and about a mile below the Corton Float, when we saw the gunboat Halcyon put up her flags.

The next second I saw a shell burst alongside her, and looking out to sea I saw eight German ships. For about a quarter of an hour the lot of them were just like lightning leaving their sides. How the Halcyon lived through it I don't know. Shells were exploding all round her in the air and others fell in the sea and sent up the water like a fountain. Three more of our torpedo-boats joined her, but the Germans were too big for them, and they only steamed about in a zigzag fashion as fast as they could.

After the Germans left off firing they steamed into the S.E., and presently altered their course to N.E., laying mines as they went.

Some of our boats had narrow escapes from mines. One had just steamed over a mine when it blew up and blew the log-line off the boat's stern but didn't hurt the boat. Another mine exploded alongside the John and Norah. Pieces of the mine flew aboard, as well as a splendid codfish, which is now in one of the fish-shops at Lowestoft, with some bits of the mine alongside.

Our brother Dudley had a narrow escape. When they shot their nets they got full with mines which fouled the nets. Just before dark a mine exploded six nets away from the boat and blew all the nets out of the water, and he said that after it cleared away dead herring lay on the water like a sheet. They dared not haul in their nets, so they slacked away and let them be till next morning at daylight. He said there were 34 mines exploded round them in the night. When it got daylight they started to haul in their nets, and they had hauled in 13 when a mine came out, and one went under the boat and tipped it but didn't explode. Thereupon they cut away from their other 80 nets and came in and left them. There were several boats that left their nets at sea full of mines.

I don't think the Germans are so bad in some things. They might have sunk every boat of us there was at sea on Tuesday morning and there was nobody to stop them, but they did not fire a single shot at one of our fishing boats. They might have blown up Lowestoft and Yarmouth if they had liked. There was no one to stop them. What they will do another time I don't know. It is all very fine for people to say they cannot do this and that. What I have told you in this letter I have seen with my own eyes, so I know you will believe it.

Don't think I am running our own Navy down, but I think we have a rum foe to fight against. Anyhow they have messed our fishing up. They say the Spanker exploded 160 mines off Lowestoft. We could hear firing all day.

14 November 1914

Left: **Highlanders at the front line march to the accompaniment of bagpipes.**

Above left: **Red Cross transport is on hand to assist wounded soldiers.**

Opposite: **Men from the 8th East Yorkshires move up to the front-line during the Battle of Broodseinde in October 1917.**

OUR DEATHLESS INFANTRY.

We were told that this was a "war of machinery," an "airman's war," a "tank war," and a "war of artillery," but the infantryman has won it. Flesh and blood might have conquered machinery: man has proved mightier than his weapons. The axiom of Napoleon's General Morand, "L'infanterie c'est l'armée" has again been vindicated.

The Lee-Enfield of the British soldier has proved as deadly as the long-bow his forebears wielded at Crecy, his marksmanship as effective as that of his great-grandfather at Waterloo.

The infantry is the queen of our arms. The airman battling in the clouds is superb, the gunner slamming shells into the reeking gun breech is magnificent; the tank man voyages into Hunland in his death-spitting travelling fort, the supply services bring up their convoys to the very tick of time no matter how hellish the shell fire; but it is to the man in the trench that the palm of victory must be given.

From those dark days when with bleeding feet he limped from Mons his spirit has been indomitable. He has never failed the Empire. His courage has transfigured that theatre of the politicians' folly, Gallipoli, into a shrine of Fame. The bones of many bleach in the desert sun, the bodies of others rot in the mire of the Salient, but, as they fell, their comrades caught and held aloft the flaming torch of their unquenchable valour.

In the beginning we lacked aeroplanes, machine guns, and artillery, but we were not deficient in heroes. When the Germans descended in overwhelming hordes the infantry stood firm and slew them until the swamps of Flanders stank with their corpses.

The Boche made hand-grenades and tossed them into the British trenches, but the infantry caught them and tossed them sizzling back to burst and blow the luckless throwers to pieces.

There were bad days when the Hun swamped the trenches with his Devil's gas, but the British soldier clapped wet rags upon his mouth and nostrils and killed his man before he rolled back frothing blood.

The infantry waited while an unready Empire forged its weapons. The time came and they rose from the trenches and stormed by frontal attack the greatest fortifications that man has ever made. They paid a heavy price, but they broke the field-grey's moral.

The tide of battle has ebbed and flowed, but in triumph and adversity the British soldier has never lost his head. He has fought in trenches and without them; he has endured tortures more excruciating than ever Torquemada devised; he has fought parched with thirst and with limbs rotting from frostbite. He has suffered an iron discipline without complaint; his has been the worst paid of any branch of the service, his casualties the most grievous.

But he has endured and won.

SIDNEY HOWARD.

12 November 1918

A NEW SOLDIERS' CHORUS

(Sergeant S. King, 2nd Battalion, the Border Regiment, writes:)

I have enclosed a little chorus which may be very interesting, as a lot of our fellows are singing it at present. It is a song to the tune of "Hold your hand out, Naughty Boy":

Hold your hands up, Germany,
Hold your hands up Germany,
The boys in khaki and the boys in blue,
They have caught yer,
They have caught yer,
With your Zeppelins in the air
You were thinking of Leicester Square.
And it won't be very long
Before the Kaiser hears your song.
Hold your hands up, Germany.

5 November 1914

COMPULSORY NOTIFICATION.

Sir,—We have received such an overwhelming response in letters and offers of help from both men and women to the appeal in our letter on venereal diseases that we strongly feel the necessity of further and prompt action.

Many of our correspondents, chiefly wives and mothers, express the deepest thankfulness for the demand of protection for themselves and their children, and painful regret at the past absence of it. We wish to associate ourselves very strongly with the letter in Tuesday's newspapers from the National Council demanding adequate provision for free treatment, the prohibition of quack treatment, and the granting of certain privileged communications.

But we feel that without compulsory notification and treatment efforts to cope with the disease will fail. All our correspondents, with one exception, join in demanding compulsion. We feel that we owe it to them to press for it with all our power.

EVA GRAHAM-MURRAY; ELLEN ASKWITH.

25 October 1916

Above: Australians make their way to the trenches in December 1916.

Opposite: Troops and guns pass through a French village in the battle zone.

DETACH THE TURKS.
To the Editor of *The Daily Mail.*

Sir,—May I endorse Mr. Arnold Hills' suggestion, in a letter to *The Daily Mail*, that England should detach Turkey by kindness? We know that our pre-war diplomacy alienated the Turks. They should be fighting with us against the Huns.

I am convinced that if we made friends with the Turks it would arouse great enthusiasm among Moslems in India. DOUGLAS FOX PITT.
25, Russell-square, Brighton.

21 March 1917

To the Editor of *The Daily Mail.*

Sir,—One has only to go into almost any restaurant to see bread worse than wasted.

Almost all men, the fat ones without exception, have bread and pats of butter beside their plates, and after every mouthful of meat and vegetables they butter a piece of bread and eat it.

The meat and vegetables are, presumably, meant to satisfy hunger, but here is a double quantity of food taken, more than necessary. It only makes men fat and diseased to gorge bread and butter as well as meat.

Either have a meat and vegetable meal, or else a bread and butter meal, not two meals simultaneously.

If bread were charged as an extra, like hors-d'œuvres or fruit, it would at once settle the difficulty. Let a man, if he wants to eat a double meal, pay half a crown for his bread and butter. HYGIENE.

24 April 1917

NAME THE REGIMENTS.

Sir,—A few weeks ago we people in the county of Durham were somewhat startled to see the Durhams mentioned in The Daily Mail in connection with the fighting in France. I need not say how we read it over and over again.

Again, in Friday's Daily Mail Mr. Beach Thomas actually says that he "may report the great fighting reputation made by some of the Durhams."

The war has been raging for three years, and our men of Durham have been, and still are, in the bloodiest part of it. We at home continue to shoulder our griefs and awful losses, trying strongly, as befits us, to bear them without complaining. Need I say how thousands in the north have watched the reports of the fighting, absolutely longing to see our dear lads at least mentioned, but no, months are rolling into years, until "hope deferred" is not only making north country hearts sick but angry also.

N.N.E.

8 August 1917

THE WHIP HAND.

Kaiser: Answer to the reins and I won't use the whip. No man could speak fairer than that.

(The German Note to America magnanimously tells her if she does just as she's told she will suffer no hurt).

12 July 1915

74

WAR SERVICE FOR WOMEN.

By CHRISTABEL PANKHURST,
Editor of the "Suffragette".

Women's help in this war is enough to make the difference between defeat and victory. Therefore women welcome the announcement made in the House of Commons on Tuesday by Mr. Walter Long that the National Register is to include women as well as men.

Some of us have been urging, appealing, for ten months past that women should be admitted to war service. The appeal is to-day made more insistently and more passionately than ever.

The belief that women ought to be mobilised for war service, that such service should be universal and compulsory for men and women both, was born in the tragic days preceding the battle of the Marne. It was born of the realisation that the Germans' attack on Europe is the most deadly attack that civilisation has ever sustained at the hands of barbarism, scientific or otherwise. Besides, to see the magnificent working of universal war service in France was to understand that this system, self-imposed by a free people, is as far from Prussianism as is the voluntary system. And obviously it is far better defence against Prussianism! Universal service is, moreover, far more democratic in practice than voluntaryism is. It is also the most effective means of keeping in check the selfishness of employers, workers, or any other class.

Universal war service necessarily involves war service for women. The women of France are not obliged, as British women are, to beg and pray to be allowed to protect their husbands or sons at the front and to defend their homes, their honour, their country by working in munition factories. As Mr. Lloyd George tells us:

In France a vast amount of work in the way of turning out shells, and especially the delicate work of fuse-making, is done by female labour.

We are further assured by Mr. Lloyd George that shell-making is not highly skilled work and can be very quickly learnt by a fairly intelligent person. And in the same breath we are told that there is a serious shortage of munitions!

It is agony to think what women could have done and have not been allowed to do since the beginning of the war. We are devoured by anxiety when we think of women's hands still idle while precious time is slipping by.

1 July 1915

TRADITION FOR ALL FAMILIES.

Now that the best blood of the aristocracy has been sacrificed it would be wise to ensure that the great tradition of "Noblesse oblige" shall be preserved.

The heir to an ancient title, who deemed it an honour to fight in the ranks, expounded a theory that is worth considering.

He had been wounded and sent to England to recuperate. He had then refused a "safe job" and voluntarily returned to France. He had been fighting since 1914 and had earned a rest; therefore his decision evoked my admiration, for he knew to what he was returning. I asked him his reason.

"In my family," he said, " We have traditions. Each member of it is taught our history, just as he is taught our history of the Empire. If I accepted a 'safe job' when I was fit to come out again I should not be worthy of my ancestors. It is just a point: if every man knew his family history he would hesitate to do anything that was not in keeping with it."

His point was that although John Smith, the yeoman, has a family history as stirring as that of any noble family, it has been allowed to pass into oblivion, and therefore he is the poorer by its loss.

Formerly many families kept a large bible wherein were inscribed the births and marriages of several generations, but the family bible has long since fallen into disuse.

War has taught us the value of tradition. Lectures on regimental history have had a great moral value; men in whom no one suspected the inspiration of sentiment have died rather than "let the regiment down."

Never in history has our Empire contained so many heroes, and the record of their deeds should be preserved to inspire their direct descendants. To have fought at Mons, Loos, the Somme, Arras, Messines, and Valenciennes is as worthy of remembrance as having fought at Hastings, Agincourt, or Barnet.

If every family compiled a brief record of the war history of each soldier member—the name of his unit, the places he visited, the actions in which he fought, with such amplifications as they might care to make— the foundations would be laid of family traditions as noble as any that had their origin in the valour of mediæval knights.

SIDNEY HOWARD.

21 November 1918

HUTS FOR OFFICERS' WIVES.

To the Editor of *The Daily Mail*.

Sir,—Your article in Monday's *Daily Mail* on " Huts for Officers' Wives " is excellent. May I point out that we are separated from our wives and families even while convalescent from wounds?

On discharge from hospital one is sent to a convalescent hospital where everything is done for one's comfort. But at a time when one is often run down and depressed, and when one is only waiting to become fit enough to return to the front, it is hard to be deprived of the society of wife and youngsters. If they are brought to an hotel near the hospital the expense is great, and they can only be visited when one is allowed out. Surely married officers might be more considered.

A Convalescent Officer.

To the Editor of *The Daily Mail*.

Sir,—As an officer's wife and the mother of two babies, may I be permitted to say how glad I should be to see some plan come into force for housing officers' wives and families?

Not only do the landladies of furnished rooms overcharge excessively, but refuse accommodation altogether as soon as they find we have children.

I have tramped miles searching for rooms, only to meet with this apparently insuperable difficulty.

The same condition prevails with regard to renting furnished houses—I have been obliged to go into the country and furnish a small cottage, the only one I could obtain. It is too far for my husband to " sleep out," and most of his spare time is spent in riding to and fro on a "push bike." This is only one of many similar cases.

An Englishwoman.

Near Shoreham Camp.

18 July 1917

OUR COOL MEN.

BACON AND EGGS AND A GOOD VIEW OF THE BATTLE.

An officer writes:

I am sitting on the battlefield, with a good view of the battle, eating bacon and eggs! Nothing perturbs us. Even in the midst of our consolidating the enemy trenches the postman arrived with the day's letters!

Extract from a Scottish officer's letter:

For coolness in action our Scottish troops are unbeatable.

One great act of gallantry was recorded yesterday when our trench mortar battery was in action. The mortar shells, which are packed in cases, were being handed from man to man to the man working the gun, and as the shells were being passed one of the men heard the fuse burning inside a shell. Knowing that the shell would explode in a few seconds, he coolly walked with it in his hands to a trench, into which he threw it. The shell exploded immediately afterwards, and by this wonderful act of bravery he saved the lives of the whole of his section.

A private of the Scottish Borderers was wounded in the knee just after capturing two Germans. One of the Germans gave the Borderer a cigar, which the Scot began to smoke. Just afterwards he saw a stretcher lying on the ground near by; this he made the Germans bring along, and, seating himself on it, he directed them to our dressing station.

13 July 1916

Then our own artillery burst forth. It was a stupendous salvo. It rumbled overhead like gigantic engines thundering through the air.

OFFICER AT 16.

M.P.'s SON WHO ENLISTED AS PRIVATE AT 15.

Second-Lieutenant Richard J. Sheehan, of the Royal Munster Fusiliers, one of three sons of Captain D. D. Sheehan, M.P., who are serving with the colours, has been wounded at the front. He joined the 7th Leinsters as a private when 15½ years of age, and got his commission last September, when he was 16 years old.

He has sent a message describing how he received his wounds, stating:

" I volunteered to take a raiding party into the German front line. I did it two nights in succession. They were, however, prepared for us the second night. Immediately we got up to throw our bombs they threw theirs. Two bombs landed quite close to me, and I lay in a shell hole stunned for some time.

" When I came to I was alone, and as it was getting rather light I got up and made a race for it. The Huns turned on a machine gun, and one bullet just grazed my arm. I got two wounds from the bombs—one in the jaw and another in the left arm, below the elbow."

Lieutenant Sheehan's wounds are not serious, and he hopes to be in the firing line soon again.

2 June 1916

"THE FINAL WILL BE ON IN THREE WEEKS."

(Private E. Attrill, Hants Regiment, writing home from hospital on November 23, says.)

I have got rheumatics in the legs after standing in trenches half full of water, and the frost and snow helped it on. It is hard luck after being in the semi-final, but I hope to get in the final, which will be in about a fortnight or three weeks' time, and then we will sweep them off the map. You think of the empty bed at home just for a few seconds when you are soaking wet through in the trenches, but you are soon reminded of where you are when you hear the joyful words whispered from man to man, "Here they come." We let the Germans get close up and then the band plays and the kinematograph commences, but you don't pay at the door for these picture shows. I had a couple of narrow squeaks, one from a shell-burst, which injured my mate, and snipers had a go at me when I was making for the trench.

1 December 1914

Top: **A group of soldiers, complete with a pet dog, are home on leave from France.**

Above: **A soldier tries to protect himself from the sun in Gallipoli.**

Below: **Men from the Machine Gun Corps make a dash for their outposts.**

BOMBERS.

HOW THEY PLAY WITH SUDDEN DEATH.

Bombers really carry their lives in their hands. The Mills bomb, with its pineapple-like exterior, is a dangerous weapon. To use it successfully against an enemy, and at the same time guard against mishaps, requires special knowledge and training.

The British soldier takes naturally to bombing— that is, the offensive part, of attacking and hurling the missiles. At first, however, when he joins a bombing school, he evinces considerable shyness of these little, waspish weapons of war. This shyness is prompted by ignorance, and quickly gives place to enthusiastic keenness when once he has learned how to manipulate the by no means intricate weapon.

It can easily be understood that from the nature of their work bombers run a considerable amount of daily risk before they are fitted to get on business terms with the enemy. Far behind the lines, and out of danger of hostile shells, many incidents of heroic self-sacrifice are recorded.

What could be finer than the action of one young hero who flung himself on to a bomb which had fused prematurely in a crowded trench, thus saving the lives of his comrades while cheerfully yielding up his own?

The Mills bomb is fused by releasing a spring, after which it takes a certain number of seconds to explode. It would, therefore, obviously be useless to release the spring and hurl it into the midst of an onrushing foe if it bursts some seconds later. To get the best results it is necessary to retain the bomb in the hand for as many seconds as will allow it to explode just as it reaches its objective. This, needless to say, requires cool judgement, practice, and iron nerves.

An officer in charge of a bombing school in France insisted on his pupils being thoroughly impressed with the fact that the bombs could be retained safely in the hand for several seconds. To demonstrate this practically, and at the same time inspire confidence in the beginner, it was his custom to stand about twenty yards away and allow a pupil to release the spring and throw the bomb at him. A good cricketer, he caught the bomb, and, in turn, threw it some distance where it would burst. Hundreds of times he performed this nerve-testing feat till a defective bomb made a premature burst just as he caught it. The result was, of course, fatal, but his life was not sacrificed in vain. Those pupils who had passed through his hands learnt a lesson in coolness and confidence with which later they were able to inspire others.

6 September 1917

ADVANCING WAVES.

For the next half-hour my eyes were glued to my periscope. I shall never forget that half-hour of vivid expectancy. I prayed for something to happen that would break the spell. My heart was thudding in my throat.

Should I be able to keep my legs firm when they came over? How would it feel when the bayonet was pushed into my body? And, above all, what would happen if I lost the line? What would the men say, and the captain and the colonel and the general? These were the thoughts that coursed through my excited brain.

Then the first wave of the expected counter-attack scrambled over the enemy's parapet. A thread snapped in my brain. I rapped out a fire order.

A movement rippled down our line. My men were manning the parapet. I dropped my periscope and stood up on the fire-step. I felt no sensation of fear; only a vast and consuming curiosity as to whether the Huns would reach our trench.

The first wave advanced fully thirty yards before one of them dropped.

A machine gun crackled its staccato rat-tat-tat-tat… rat-tat-tat… rat-tat; and several others picked up the crisp chorus. The leading wave still ran towards us. But in their centre a wide gap suddenly yawned. In this gap the ground was strewn with figures; some of them squirmed and wriggled, others lay placid in death… the wave of men still rushed on. A second wave poured over the parapet of the enemy's trench.

Then our own artillery burst forth. It was a stupendous salvo. It rumbled overhead like gigantic engines thundering through the air. In front of us the attackers wavered. The detonation of bombs sounded farther down the trench.

I turned my periscope sideways. Hun bodies were being flung over our parapet… My sergeant appeared. "Cleared 'em out with bombs, sir," he remarked. "Look, sir!" He pointed to our front.

"Cease fire," I ordered. For the attackers had disappeared. What was left of them had retired.

"That's the end, sir!" chuckled my sergeant.

I thrust my hands into my breeches pockets, I did not want him to see they were trembling.

DRYSDALE SMITH

6 August 1917

Above: **Weary men return from the battlefield.**

Below: **Canadian troops successfully captured about 4,000 German soldiers at Vimy.**

> *A German officer climbed up from the trench and, removing his own Iron Cross, pinned it on our hero.*

SEARCHLIGHT ATTACK

Private J. Eustace (Royal Irish Rifles)

"At Mons, on August 23 ... they outnumbered us about ten to one, but after the first onslaught our forces forgot everything but the Germans in front. For three hours their shells were terrific, but towards evening our artillery checked their murderous fire ... Darkness fell at last, and the fire slackened but not altogether, for the Germans brought a powerful searchlight into operation and harassed us through the night. About two o'clock we got orders to retire .. and daybreak found us out of danger, but only for a while as the Germans could not be kept back ... Some of the time we were firing at three hundred yards' range and with fixed bayonets ready to charge, but the Germany infantry didn't want any ... On the Monday we had a little respite ... Tuesday we were into it again, and they made it hot for us towards midday ... As evening came the Germans seemed to have the best of it, so we had to make a hasty retirement and had some difficulty in getting the gus safely out of action.

They beat us back into the town, and her we got mixed up and I found myself with a few men of different corps forming a rearguard to protect the guns. ...Wednesday at daybreak we started over again and here the Germans gave us what ho!"

12 September 1914

From Corporal Sam Haslett - 5 September 1914

The other day I stopped to assist a young lad of the West Kents who had been badly hit by a piece of shell. He hadn't long to live, and he knew it. I asked him if there was any message I could take to someone at home. The poor lad's eyes filled with tears as he answered, "I ran away from home and enlisted a year ago. Mother and dad don't know I'm here; but you tell them from me I'm not sorry I did it."

'When I told our boys this later they cried like babies. But, mind you, that's the spirit that's going to pull England through this war, and there isn't a man of us that doesn't think of that poor boy and his example every time we go into fight.

At daybreak the morning after we had repelled an attack, we saw that the Germans had collected their wounded, with the exception of one man who lay groaning in agony half way between the trenches. Our captain jumped forward from his trench. The Germans fired and he was hit. He staggered but with a magnificent effort kept his feet rushed on towards the wounded German. Then, although badly wounded himself, he picked him up and carried him direct to the German trenches. We heard the roar of cheers as he gently laid the body down and saluted. A German officer climbed up from the trench and, removing his own Iron Cross, pinned it on our hero. Sadly back in our lines, the captain died from his wounds and I am broken-hearted that his cross is a wooden one rather than the VC he deserved.

11 November 1914

ADVICE FROM AN OFFICER ON WHAT TO SEND MEN AT THE FRONT.

We can't receive too many socks. In this dampness, they get so muddy they have to be thrown away and cannot be repaired. We also need indelible pencils, paper and envelopes. A very good gift is a bottle of quinine pills, which can avert a coming chill and cure rheumatism or stiffness in the bones. An occasional bar of soap can always be disposed of with great ease and should be carbolic or disinfectant. Very few of the men have any tooth powder or tooth brushes left. A towel is generally a useful present. I can't insist too much on chocolate, as Tommy loves sweet things and gets very few out here. Send him a mouth-organ or a football, and you will help him forget the monotony of his days.

1 February 1915

DEATH PRESENTS THE BILL TO THE KAISER -
"The assaulting forces in the end grew tired of climbing over the bodies of their fallen comrades, and the assault spent itself before the horror of those mountains of corpses. They number thousands - those whose madness the Kaiser has sent to their deaths" - A powerful cartoon by Louis Raemaekers on the slaughter round Verdun.

PUTTING DEATH IN ITS PLACE.

This war has put death in its place. It has tumbled it down from that fearsome pinnacle it perched on before the war, that pinnacle supported by heartrending wailings and gnashings of teeth, and it has made it—if one may use the words—homelier, commoner, more of a consummation and less of a cutting off of the human life.

"If I should die, think only this of me—that there's some corner of a foreign field that is for ever England," and again: "The dead will not hurt the spring"—were written by soldiers who had sensed already, maybe, the death that was to be the radiant crown of a great life.

I remember when one read as a boy of the everyday duellings of two generations before how splendid it seemed—that running a foeman through and hearing the choking cough that spelt his death; and how terrible an affair that same adventure was for us grown up shopkeeper English folk of 1913 to contemplate.

"We have become too civilised—too soft," a man of the world used to say to me before the war, and I used to shake my head and laugh. He was right. We had magnified death till it was all mortuary and no romance, all horror and no glory. Well, the war has taken us back to the duelling days, when honour counted more than life and rightness more than ease.

The innate love of adventure, the ingrown patriotism, the inbred spirit of England that long had lain dormant awaiting the trumpet call brought the change quickly to our young men; the sorrow and pride in their valiant dead have brought it to those that stayed behind. I count it a great privilege to have received letters written to me in France by the relatives of "mates" of mine who had been killed. One father immediately on receipt of the news could so put his grief aside as at once to send each man in the battalion a present. Another wrote bravely: "The news came as a great shock but not as a surprise," and another lady who had lost both her gifted sons wrote: "I do not begrudge them the honour of soldiers' graves. I know that is how they wished to die."

Death must hide his head for very shame before conquering words as these.

Who dies now, dies in noble company. Think of them that are with the gallant dead—Charles Lister, Raymond Asquith, William Redmond, A. F. Wilding, A. G. Poulton, Ivan Heald, Julian Grenfell, Rupert Brooke, Dixon Scott, and Harold Chapin. Who can question that these men have made dying easier?

One of my dearest friends said to me before we went to France: "Dying for England would be the best thing I have done—my trump card." Well, he has died, leaving his thoughts for us. He is of

"Them that died that we might live
And, living, learn to plan
A life like theirs, and then to give
The earth an Englishman."

This war has made dying an Englishman a glorious consummation; and death—as 1913 understood it—is no more.

JAMES HODSON.

1 August 1917

The innate love of adventure, the ingrown patriotism, the inbred spirit of England that long had lain dormant awaiting the trumpet call brought the change quickly to our young men.

UP GUARDS AND AT 'EM

"You thought it was a big crowd that streamed out of the Crystal Palace when we went to see the Cup Final. Well, outside Compiegne it was just as if that crowd came at us. You could not miss them. Our bullets ploughed into them, but still they came for us.

I was well-entrenched, and my rifle got so hot I could hardly hold it. I was wondering if I should have enough bullets when I pal shouted "Up Guards and at 'em!" The next he was rolled over with a nasty knock on the shoulder. He jumped up and roared, "Let mc get at them!". They sill came on. When we really did get the order to get at them we made no mistakes I can tell you.

They cringed at the bayonet, but those on our left tried to get round out. We yelled like demons, and after racing as hard as we could for quite 500 yards, cut up nearly very German who had not run away. You have heard of the Charge of the Light Brigade. It was nowt to our chaps. They went at them yelling, and cut them up again and again."

Private Whitaker of The Coldstream Guards.

9 September 1914

Opposite: **Troops undertake trench maintenance during a lull in the fighting. Ladders were fixed to the sides of the banks to allow soldiers to scale them quickly when launching an attack.**

Above: **British soldiers return from front-line duty after the Battle of Loos.**

Right: **Camaraderie among the troops helped keep the horrors of war at bay.**

A GREAT WEEK.

HAIG'S NEW SUCCESSES TO CROWN IT.

Sir Douglas Haig's reports which we publish today crown the successes of one of the most important weeks in military history. Indeed, the victory won by the British Army in the Battle of Arras is in every way the greatest gained in the west since the Battle of the Marne. Its results throw into the shade those of the first week of the Somme.

Our troops have gained greatly in efficiency. The management of our curtain-fire is now superior to that of the enemy. The tactical handling has markedly improved. That the capture of the strongest portion of the enemy's line in the north-west, with 166 guns and over 13,000 prisoners, should have been accomplished with moderate loss on our side is a very remarkable feat of generalship.

Hindenburg may boast as he likes, but our army has now the ascendancy over the enemy. The "impregnable" Vimy Ridge was taken on Tuesday. On a front twelve miles wide, between Monday and Wednesday, the enemy was most severely punished and pushed back at points to a distance of 5 miles. The snowstorms hampered our advance, but Sir Douglas Haig was able yesterday to report a great series of gains bringing him astride the Hindenburg line. Of special importance is his thrust beyond Lens and his movement to turn Havrincourt Wood, one of the strongest German positions south-west of Cambrai.

14 April 1917

Above: **Troops march through Shrapnel Valley in Gallipoli. It was often called Death Valley by the men as it was the main path from the beach to the Anzac front, receiving constant shelling from the Turks based high up in the hills. Traverses were built into the sides enabling troops to dash from one to the other and take cover.**

Below: **Reserves move up to support the advance on Morval.**

FURIOUS FIGHTING.

From W. BEACH THOMAS.
War Correspondents' Headquarters, France,
Tuesday.

Encounters as magnificent as terrible were engaged in yesterday evening across the bare but undulating country beyond Arras. In the open soldiers marched and charged and fell and retreated. From the wake of a charge groups or masses of prisoners were herded back, so obvious to the naked eye that their own guns could spare them.

I should doubt if ever the Germans have counter-attacked in greater volume or thrown in fresh troops in a more determined manner from the north to the south of the front of attack. Monchy was the centre of the storm system. Yesterday afternoon 3,000 fresh German troops gathered in the Sart Wood and as many in the Vert Wood. In the Sart they were seen as they entered and so broken by concentration of our heavy artillery, whose shells are today exploding with more power and regularity than ever before. That force was shattered, and the miserable remnant dared not debouch. The force in the Vert Wood was luckier. They massed without much disturbance and charged the lines we had captured earlier in the morning south east of Monchy, and in spite of great losses drove us back a few hundred yards. A handful of our prisoners could be seen among the green coats on the way back to Vert Wood.

Two hours later we again attacked and forced back the German storming party from most important places. All the while the enemy emptied shells into Monchy, which went up in red brickdust till nothing but a few skeleton houses were left. The smoke and dust quite obscured the hill, in spite of the strong wind, for half-hours at a time. A non-combatant in one of the trenches on the hill was continually sprinkled with earth and bits for four continuous hours, and when he finally escaped he saw, to his disgust, that shells were bursting over the country three miles behind him, and what are called "Whistling Percies" were sprinkled farther back still. This counter-charge of the Germans was repeated in various degrees all along the front.

25 April 1917

20 December 1917

ARMY.

Lieutenant O. P. Edgcumbe (to his father, Sir Robert Edgcume, of Newquay):

For the last week or ten days we have been fighting hard, and are now for one day resting. Altogether during five days and five nights I got six hours' sleep, and so am rather weary. However, bullets and a real enemy are a wonderful stimulant, and I feel as fit as anything. All our men are somewhat fatigued but are very keen and full of fight.

My regiment has had a bad time, and I am dreadfully afraid they have been badly cut up, although I can as yet get no details. They were caught in a village by Germans, in the houses, who had managed to get there by wearing our uniforms. Never again shall I respect the Germans. They have no code of honour, and there have been several cases of their wearing French and British uniforms, which is of course, against the Geneva Convention.

THE ORDERLY RETREAT.

Private Martin O'Keefe (Royal Irish Rifles):

Our part in the fighting was limited almost entirely to covering the retreat by a steady rifle fire from hastily prepared trenches. We were thrown out along an extended front and instructed to hold out ground until the retiring troops were signalled safe in the next position allotted them. When this was done our turn came, and we retired to a new position, our place being taken by the light cavalry, who kept the Germans in check as long as they could and then fell back in their turn.

AVENGING THE COLONEL.

Sergeant W. Holmes:

After four days to get fit we are off again, this time with some of the French, and it's enough to give you fits to hear the Frenchmen trying to pick up the words of "Cheer, Boys, Cheer," which we sing with a great go on the march. They haven't any notion of what the words mean, but they can tell from our manner that they mean we're in great heart, and that's infectious here. We lost our colonel and four other officers in our fight on Tuesday. The colonel was struck down when he was giving us the last word of advice before throwing ourselves on the enemy. We avenged him in fine style. His loss was a great blow to us, for he was very popular. It's always the best officers, somehow, that get hit the first...

The German officers are a rum lot. They don't seem to be in too great a hurry to expose their precious carcases and so they lead from the rear all the time. We see to it that they don't benefit much by that, you may be sure... They seem terribly keen on pushing their men forward into posts of danger but they are not so keen on leading the way except in retreat, when they are well to the fore. Our cavalry are up to this little dodge, and when riding out to intercept retreating Germans give special attention to the officers.

11 September 1914

5 August 1917

Above: **Troops outside their dugouts near Bazentin-le-Petit after the village and neighbouring Bazentin-le-Grand were taken.**

A Soldier's Letter to His Little Son.

Explaining the War to a Child. What a Battlefield is Like.

THE following interesting letter was written by an Army officer in France to his nine-year-old son who had asked his father what a real battle line was like. The rough drawings in the text appeared in the original letter.

My dear Brian,—You would like to know for your drawings what a real battle line is like, so look at these drawings.

In the distance you see a hill and on the right some woods. Some farmhouses, one or two still intact, and others mere heaps

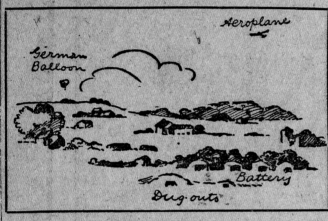

Near the trenches.

of brick, lie dotted about. Near you on the right is a battery hidden under bushes and earthworks. Nearer you still are the dug-outs in which the men live underground.

In the distance is a German anchored balloon watching the country. On the right and overhead is an aeroplane.

HOW THE GUNS ARE AIMED.

Beyond the hill and the woods are the trenches in which the infantry face the German infantry, also in trenches. Somewhere near the trenches and where he can see them well and the country on the German side are the artillery observation officers, who telephone directions to the batteries and direct their fire where they want. All this is done very accurately on a special system called registration, by which having once hit a target you can always go on hitting it or anything near it.

For instance, yesterday when I was directing the battery at one of these places a German put up a tin on a pole and waved it about in the air in his trench. I saw this, told one gun what angle to lay at and the range, and the next moment the shell arrived and the tin went up in the air. What happened in the trench I don't know, but the shell burst in it. One burst in ours this morning and killed one man and wounded two others So they can do damage.

LIVELY TRENCHES.

The trenches are very lively places at night when a lot of rifle fire is always going on, and one side or the other sends out patrols or snipers to peep over the other's trenches and shoot men; and the trench mortars get busy and send over high explosive bombs, or someone more daring than others crawls out and throws hand grenades into the trench.

Behind these front trenches are other trenches, which lead in a zig-zag way to the front, or hold more men ready to help if the front trench is attacked. This is really the nastiest place to be in because the German artillery are always ready to shoot at them, and do shoot at them when there is any excitement.

Hidden all along the trenches are machine-guns which fire flankwise and are very destructive. Then come the artillery, and behind them again the big guns—the very big ones of which drop shells a tremendous distance and blow blocks of houses to bits. They say one of ours not long ago dropped a big shell into the middle of an infantry regiment—a German one—and blew 500 of them into little bits. Dotted about around the country where they are most needed are the anti-aircraft guns, whose shooting at

Anti-aircraft guns shooting at an aeroplane.

"birds," as they call the aeroplanes, is very pretty — and very bad.

One sees an aeroplane in the middle of a lot of white blobs of smoke—of bursting shells—but although I have seen two fall from the machine-gun fire of another aeroplane, I have not yet seen any good shooting of the guns, either our own or German.

Away back behind all these are the aerodromes and captive balloons of our own watching the front, where all the roads are busy with motor transport feeding the firing line with grub and ammunition. You would never think how many men and how much transport are necessary to do all this properly

BEHIND THE BATTLE LINE.

That is the curious thing in war. Up in this firing line where we are there are mud and shells and rifle fire and discomfort; and a little way back where the shells rarely, if ever, go, and certainly not very far back, the Army lives in comfort, the officers in nice warm houses with fires looked after by soldier servants, and all the table and living arrangements one gets at home.

Farther back still, of course, so far as danger is concerned, I think it is safer than London since Zeppelins took to bombing it.

A battle starts with terrific artillery bombardment, sometimes for days, and when the enemy's trenches are absolutely destroyed and their men dazed with the rain of high explosives and gas and bombs the infantry charge across.

Sometimes the machine guns have not been knocked out and they take a big toll of life, and always there are plenty of men

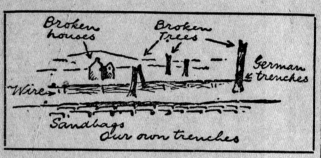

All one can see of a battlefield.

whom the bombardment fails to knock out. The drawing shows all you can see of a battlefield.

THE INVISIBLE ARMIES.

There is never a soul to be seen. There is only a terrific roar of guns and explosions, and the perpetual snapping of rifles and rattle of machine guns. There is a view of some broken walls, trees without leaves or branches, and trenches everywhere

You would think there was no life anywhere if it were not for the row, and yet one knows that if you put up a head a thousand eyes will see it and half a thousand fingers pull a trigger.

A DUMMY AND ITS FATE.

Some men near me the other day put up a dummy on the parapet and before you could say Jack Robinson two shells and heaven knows how many bullets had been fired at it. Men are always being killed and yet they will put up their heads and look over the parapets instead of using a periscope.

It is all very destructive, very costly, and very useless, war, but it brings out all that is best in men, and sometimes, like with the Germans, all that is bad. No doubt it is for a good purpose which we do not realise at present, when we only see the ruin and the killing and the waste.

Sometimes the world wants cleaning like the pistons of a motor to make it run smoothly, and this is the way it comes about. You boys later on will reap the benefit of it all.

THE BOY WHO DIED.

HIS LAST LETTER.

"BUT WE SHALL LIVE FOR EVER!"

We have received from Mr. W. L. Townsend, of 2, 3, and 4, New Basinghall Street, E. C., the following copy of a letter from his son, 2nd Lieut. E. L. Townsend, London Regiment, who was killed in France on September 15, leading the first wave against the German position. The letter was enclosed in the gallant boy's will, to be opened only in the event of his death.

"I send it to you," writes the father, "because I think it contains some fine thoughts which may, perhaps, bring comfort to other families."

Eric Townsend was one of the leading boys of the City of London School, where he was captain of the shooting team.

8 September 1916

Dearest Mother and Father,
You are reading this letter because I have gone under.

Of course I know you will be terrible cut up, and that it will be a long time before you get over it, but get over it you must. You must be imbued with the spirit of the Navy and the Army to "carry on." You will still have dear little Donald, who is safe at any rate for some while. If he should ever have to go on active service I somehow feel that his invariable good luck will bring him through.

You must console yourselves with the thought that I am happy, whereas if I had lived—who knows?

Remember the saying attributed to Solon, "Call no man happy till he is dead." Thanks to your self-sacrificing love and devotion I have had a happy time all my life. Death will have delivered me from experiencing unhappiness.

It has always seemed to me a very pitiful thing what little difference the disappearance of a man makes to any institution, even though he may have played a very important role. A moment's regret, a moment's pause for readjustment, and another man steps forward to carry on, and the machine clanks onward with scarce a check. The death of a leader of the nation is less even than a seven days' wonder. To a very small number it is given to live in history; their number is scarcely one in ten millions. To the rest it is only granted to live in their united achievements. But for this war I and all the others would have passed into oblivion like the countless myriads before us. We should have gone about our trifling business, eating, drinking, sleeping, hoping, marrying, giving in marriage, and finally dying with no more achieved than when we were born, with the world no different for our lives. Even the cattle in the field fare no worse than this. They, too, eat, drink, sleep, bring forth young, and die leaving the world no different from what they found it.

But we shall live for ever in the results of our efforts.

We shall live as those who by their sacrifice won the Great War. Our spirits and our memories shall endure in the proud position Britain shall hold in the future. The measure of life is not its span but the use made of it. I did not make much use of my life before the war, but I think I have done so now.

One sometimes hears people say, when a young man is killed, "Poor fellow, cut off so early, without ever having had a chance of knowing and enjoying life." But for myself, thanks to all that both of you have done, I have crowded into twenty years enough pleasures, sensations, and experiences for an ordinary lifetime. Never brilliant; sometimes almost a failure in anything I undertook; my sympathies and my interests somehow or other—why, I cannot tell—were so wide that there was scarcely an amusement, an occupation, a feeling which I could not appreciate. And as I have said, of most of these I had tasted. I don't suppose I ever met anybody who was not my superior in knowledge or achievement in one particular subject; but there his knowledge and his interest ended, whereas my interests comprised nearly the whole field of human affairs and activities. And that is why it is no hardship for me to leave the world so young.

Well, I have talked a lot of rot which must have given you great pain to read and which will not bring you much comfort. I had intended to try and say words of comfort, but that scarcely being possible, it has drifted into a sort of confession of faith.

To me has been given the easier task; to you is given the more difficult—that of living in sorrow. Be of good courage that at the end you may give a good account.

Kiss Donald for me.

Adieu, best of parents,—Your loving son, ERIC.

27 October 1916

THE "GHOST" GUN.

Now that the whole battlefront is more or less on the move, the machine-gunner comes into his own.

The text-books inform you that the great object of the machine gunner is to support the infantry, and that important ways of doing so are by concealment and surprise effect. They add that the machine gun should be "the ghost of the battlefield." This is perhaps not a very happy way of suggesting that the machine gun should be mysterious and silent in its movements, appearing unexpectedly and after doing its deadly work disappearing, like a phantom. Certainly machine guns in open fighting are used with uncanny and terrifying effect.

The trained gunner, given a suitable piece of ground, can so mount a Vickers gun that it is invisible a hundred yards away. But to do this requires some skill and an eye for background, and there are several things to be guarded against. For instance, all parts of gun and gunner will harmonise with a suitable dark background except the gunner's face and hands.

Another "giving-away" factor is unnecessary movement by the gunner. You may lie with your gun in the middle of a turnip field and kill Boches wholesale, while all their observing officers search for you in vain—if you keep still. But an awkward or careless movement in reloading or "immediate action" will mean a prompt dose of Boche shell.

Another point is a smoky gun. But this should not bother you unless you have been foolish enough to over-lubricate.

Steam from the water jacket is not a difficulty. After firing "rapid" for a little while the water in a Vickers gun boils, and it boils hard. It doesn't just simmer—it emits a dense white cloud of steam. This would, of course, be fatal; but every gun carries a condenser-tube by means of which the steam is condensed by passing it into a bucket of cold water. The machine gunner who forgets to fix his condenser would deserve what he would certainly get.

The one real trouble about concealing a machine gun is its noise. There is no camouflaging that. You can't pretend it is a nightingale gone hoarse or a cuckoo off colour. It is a nasty noise, and it attracts attention and high explosive.

Fortunately there is a bright side even to this trouble, as although the noise of firing infallibly gives away the presence of a machine gun it doesn't give away its exact position; for the sound is most deceptive, and often, owing to echo and what the French call "claquement," it is entirely misleading as to the actual position of the gun.

CHARLES H. STUART.

1 October 1918

After firing "rapid" for a little while the water in a Vickers gun boils, and it boils hard.

BEHIND THE GUNS.

There is a general impression among civilians that the "man behind the gun" is safer than the infantryman who goes "over the top." Let us take a peep at "No. 2" behind those long lines of guns on the western front.

Night and day he stands by his gun, ears aching, eyes bloodshot, hands bleeding. Standing close to the breech when others leap aside, he "pulls the lanyard" and sends the projectile hurtling on its mission of destruction. Grimed and almost choked by the spent gases which follow upon the discharge of the gun, it is he who bears the brunt of the deafening explosion.

Shell after shell is rammed in, the cartridge follows, and "No. 2" closes the breech. The muzzle slowly rises to its elevation, the "friction-tube" is inserted, the lanyard is "hooked in." This is all the work of "No. 2." Holding the lanyard across his chest, with a curious turn of the shoulders he tautens it. The gun is fired....

For an instant the darkness of the night is cleft by a blinding flash; for an instant the shock of the discharge numbs the senses of the gunner; yet even while the "piece" recovering from the recoil, slides slowly back to its normal position, there is a figure working automatically on the right of the breech. Blindly his hand seeks the "friction-tube," and, ere the "piece" finally comes to rest, his thumb, with pressure to the left, has ejected the now-spent tube. "No. 2" has completed the operation.

"Fire!"

"No. 2" throws his weight upon the lanyard, the "Friction-tube" sends its spark to the cartridge, a spurt of smoke is emitted from the "vent," the gunners wait with tautened nerves, but there is no shock ofdischarge. "No. 2" pauses; then, with infinite caution, he removes the "tube" and another is inserted. Again the "Fire!" is given, and again the cartridge fails to do its work.

Now there is a longer pause. A stream of smoke is pouring from the "vent"; the cambric containing the cordite is smouldering; at any moment the gun may fire. "No. 2" is impatient; he will try just one more "tube," his hand reaches to the back of the breech. Crash! ... He's flung violently to the ground, a moan escapes his lips. Two of his team bend over him in the darkness; hurriedly they bandage his hand and arm, now smashed to a bloody pulp; and even as he is being helped to the dressing station the gun thunders.

Another "No. 2" has stepped to the breech.

R. STODDART LONGCROFT.

6 November 1918

Opposite: **A lone soldier keeps watch through a trench periscope.**

Below: **Despite the heavy shellfire, the 29th Canadian Infantry battalion trudges across no-man's land towards the German lines.**

Above: **Much of the time in the trenches could be spent playing the waiting game. In between battles, officers drew up rotas to ensure a balance of duties, sleep and rest time, but this inevitably led to boredom as soldiers waited for orders.**

"DOWN THE LINE."
By JAMES HODSON.

There is always some gossip-loving soul in a company who, a day or two before the time for relief is due, will go dodging round the traverses in the front line telling everybody—sometimes with his tongue in his cheek, more often hoping it is true, but always with a great air of secrecy—that "We are going down the line for about three months to A——."

The time always runs into months and the place is always A——. It is a sort of standing joke, an evergreen companion that enlivens the life.

The lads go "down the line" with the same sort of champagne feeling that people who visit the seaside once a year take their holiday. They talk about nothing else for days; every company "knows"; every platoon has its pet rumour. You are going to Vimy, Ypres, Arras, Mesopotamia, Egypt, Salonica.

Every sector has its backers, every battle-front its admirers. You are going in omnibuses, in trains, you are going to the —th Corps as storm troops; pioneers; on lines of communication; guards at G.H.Q.; fatigues at the base. You pick your tale, or if you don't like any of them you invent one of your own.

8 June 1918

WIRE TWO-FINGERS THICK.

WHAT WE FOUND IN THE HINDENBURG LINE.

From W. L. McAlpin, Paris, Thursday

The German losses are estimated here at 28 per cent. in the past few days' fighting on the Scarpe of the troops engaged. A Pomeranian division of at least 10,000 men was almost annihilated and a regiment of a Prussian division, say 2,000 bayonets, was mown down almost to the last man. When the Bavarian divisions were exhausted they were replaced by the Prussian Guard.

One of the most gratifying features of the furious conflict is that most of the British wounds were comparatively slight.

The Matin says:

The tanks did wonders. Three were engaged without a stop for eight hours. Besides their customary good work they exercised a salutary impression on the enemy. The new German anti-tank guns do not seem to have sensibly interfered with their operations.

Near Fontaine-lez-Croisilles the British carried at the end of the day a portion of the Hindenburg line. Here the first belt of barbed wire was 20 yards deep and the wire was two-fingers thick. Behind this was a series of ditches wired at the bottom. Then came reinforced concrete trenches perforated at regular intervals and provided with loopholes. The machine-gun emplacements communicated every 20 or 30 yards with connecting and supporting trenches. Lastly, tunnel shelters linked up the first and second lines of defence.

Great things were expected from this formidable system of obstacles, but the British were equal to them.

27 April 1917

A BOMBARDMENT: WHAT IT FEELS LIKE.

By James Hodson.

You are in support, and you get into your little "cubby-holes"—shallow pits dug into the parapet just a couple of feet of earth above you. If you are lucky you are sharing the hole with a pal. It is comforting.

The hole is a close fit for two, and you are squeezed together as you sit, and your knees and feet are poking out in the trench. You light a cigarette and wait. You do not wait long. The whistle comes, and then the tearing, rending crash. Shrapnel, heavy and black and bursting low—you can tell by the crash of it. Bits patter like heavy hail on the trench outside and overhead. You nestle comfortably. Your tin hat is pressing into the earth above; your vision sees but the clayey side of the trench opposite. You feel rather safe. You know it is foolish and that any decent sized piece would come through the earth above you, but you do feel rather safe. You cannot help it.

The whistles are getting more frequent; now they are a chorus; now the whistles and bangs and kr-r-umps are hopelessly intermingled. The shrapnel is still tearing overhead, but the kr-r-umps and the crashes, with a peculiar metallic clan-n-g, and the rocking and trembling of the earth tell you that H. E.s are dropping all around. You venture a look at your pal, who grins at you in the gloom. You pull yourself together. You press your back into the soil and your tin hat into the roof. Doing that seems to help a bit.

The trench outside is full of smoke and fumes and they drift in and make you cough. Your knees and feet are covered with bits of dirt, and pieces of earth from the roof are beginning to drop on to you. The crashings, the earth-shakings, are still going on. How your little hole contrives to be missed you do not know. Shells are dropping all round, within yards. You speak, but you cannot hear your voice. There is a sort of splashing noise outside and you know part of the trench has fallen in.

The crashes are fewer; the smoke outside begins to blow away. The bombardment stops. It is as if weights were lifted from your head. You are fearfully thirsty and you drink from your bottle and pass it to your pal. Slowly, painfully, you crawl out. You are stiff and you ache. The quiet is profound, and you hesitate for a moment before breaking it with your speech. You look at your watch; an hour and a half since it began! Five yards away is a lad with a broken leg. Another one is killed…

You can get used to some extent to shell-fire for a few days, but not for a period that will include rests out of the line. Every turn "up" the line is like beginning all over again your apprenticeship to shells. But you take far less notice of shells on your journey out of trenches than on your journey in. Exhaustion kills fear.

11 April 1918

Left: **A wounded soldier receives a welcome helping hand.**

MARRIAGES WITH THE B.E.F.

"Our sergeant is marrying a little Frenchie today! Wonder what his folks in Blighty will say?" exclaimed the orderly of a Church Army hut in France.

Are the girls of Britain aware that many a French wife will preside over our Tommies' households after the war?

I peeped in at the wooden church adjoining just in time to see a well-set-up young soldier standing at the altar with a smart, dainty little French mam'selle by his side. Two stripes, more especially three, have a great attraction!

Coached well in her part, the bride answered, without a trace of nervousness, with a pretty French accent.

A good number of French relatives were present. Marriage is a serious business in France. Every French girl has her dot, small or large as the case may be.

In England a funeral is far better attended by the working classes than a wedding. In villages especially the country folk come in crowds to speed some poor soul out of the world into the Great Beyond, but stay at home when they ought to wish couples "God-speed" on their marriage. In France it is different. There are the bride's dot and other family affairs to be discussed.

Again, the bride's parents will not give their consent to the union before learning the man's character. How do they manage about the character and antecedents of our Tommies? They will find out from the vicar of the parish or village where Tommy resides or write to the mayor or even to the police.

If the report be favourable, then little Lisette is embraced, kissed, and loaded with offerings of lingerie and things dainty and chic for her trousseau. Yet Lisette's troubles are not over. M. le Curé is announced.

"What! Our sweet Lisette is going to marry a heretic!" he exclaims. "Ah! le bon Dieu knows these English soldiers are admirable, but consider! They are not sons of Holy Mother Church."

Lisette and her parents are adamant. Mother Church has lost much of her influence. Still, poor Lisette promises after the civil marriage at the mairie to have a religious ceremony at her own church, while her fiancé insists on being really married by his own C.F. The result is that at the end of her wedding day poor Lisette is in a fainting condition and her sergeant "hubby" bored to death and very grumpy.

Are these mixed marriages a success? It depends on the mother-in-law's reception and many other things at home in Blighty!

COUNTRY PARSON.

22 July 1918

The whistle comes, and then the tearing, rending crash. Shrapnel, heavy and black and bursting low.

ARMY

An officer of an Infantry Regiment:
The men have played up beyond our wildest expectations and we are jolly proud of them. There's the devil of a lot of heavy gun fire on now, but all is serene where I am writing under an apple tree with a clump of mistletoe growing on it.

Top: **Troops pass the saluting point in front of the French General Henri Berthelot.**

Above: **A soldier inspects a portable wire entanglement. These posed a formidable obstruction but could also be moved from place to place with ease.**

Below: **Injured men from the Middlesex Regiment are wheeled to makeshift hospitals to receive treatment.**

THE SINKING OF THE HERMES.

(Private J. H. Carpenter, Royal Marine Light Infantry, writes.)

I should like to give my experience in H.M.S Hermes when struck by a torpedo from a German submarine.

I had come off watch of the 12-pound gun (it is our duty to look out for submarines), and I went to the paintshop to have a talk with the painter. As I got there the first explosion came; all our pots of paint came tumbling down, and I was flung across a hatchway, and am still suffering from the injury.

I went out to the upper deck and found the men getting the boats out. I tried to help out with the second cutter, which we found had got jammed. I was in for a quarter of an hour and then thought it best to get out. Heard afterwards that the foremost falls gave way and the boat hung by the stern. I don't know if any of the men were drowned in it. We got struck about 8.20 a.m., and it was 8.50 when I left the ship, as my watch, which I had in my trouser pocket, stopped at that time. I was in the water about an hour. I had found two petrol cans on the upper-deck which somebody must have discarded, and I tied them with a piece of rope over my shoulders.

There was a very heavy swell running at the time. Just before I was picked up by H.M.S. Lucifer my cans got washed off me. My arms were numbed with the cold. I went under twice. The third time I came up I had a fight for my life. My thoughts came at random, and I could plainly see the vision of my wife and three little children in front of me. It all occurred in a few seconds. I must have had supernatural strength given me; made a plunge for my cans, and managed to catch the rope tied to them and pulled them to me. My mouth was just going underwater again, but I held my breath and got the cans under each arm, the rope across my chest. I was picked up soon after—I couldn't have stuck it much longer as I was getting exhausted. I must praise the officers and crew of the Lucifer, as they were very good to us, and we ought also to be very thankful for the petrol cans, as I think nearly a hundred men had them.

18 November 1914

BURIED IN A TRENCH DESTROYED BY A SHELL.

(Private G. Fennell, 2nd Battalion Wilts Regiment, writes to his wife from a Greenwich hospital.)

Do not trouble about me. I am mending as quick as possible. I am not going to tell you much now. Still, I am a lucky fellow to be here at all.

Last Thursday week our trench was blown in with lyddite from the Germans. Four of us were buried in some tons of earth. Many of our men ran away at the moment. I was in a position something like a trussed chicken, with my hands pointing up. Thus by scratching upwards a few inches I pulled the earth down until I had made a small hole big enough to breathe.

I shouted for all I was worth, and although the trench was badly blown in, one plucky fellow came with a spade to dig me out. While so doing, another shell came in almost the same place and filled up the small hole I had made; also my mouth and eyes. Still, he worked and soon cleared me.

Next day, Friday, I was shot by a sniper on leaving the trenches. I rolled toward the trench, only a couple of yards or so. Then my mates pulled me in very quickly. I have three men to thank I am here.

I had 2½ miles to walk after I was shot, but the same fellows that pulled me into the trench supported me on either side. In fact, they attempted to carry me, but I could not stand the weight of my legs dangling.

So far, so good. Still, I think I promised you to be back before Christmas.

We have lost a lot already. We had fifty casualties in ten minutes. Many of the men who were at Lyndhurst camp with me are beneath the Belgian soil. If you could have seen the battlefield after six days and nights of ceaseless murder, and our enemies strewing the ground in heaps, you would be surprised at the few wounded we got.

17 November 1914

I was shot by a sniper on leaving the trenches. I rolled toward the trench, only a couple of yards or so. Then my mates pulled me in very quickly.

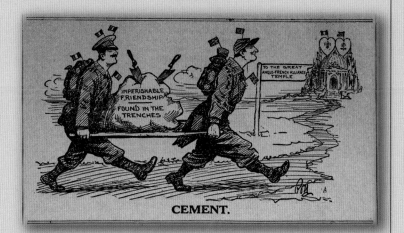

CEMENT.

(FROM A CAPTAIN IN THE 2ND EAST LANCASHIRE REGIMENT.)

We officers live exactly the same as the men, and if we want any extras we have to carry them ourselves. T----(one of my subalterns) and I generally work together. He is a splendid fellow and a great pal of mine. Always cheery and bright and on for anything. We cook together and often share blankets at night for warmth.

It is wonderful what you can make in an ordinary Tommy's mess tin. The rations are plentiful and good, but not much variety. We are both of us champion foragers, and often go on expeditions at night. We found a pig bowled over by a shell in a field, and had a fine supper of pork stew. You can generally get potatoes and vegetables in the fields, and sometimes a chicken meets with an accident. There are lots of them to be found around the deserted houses, for along the trenches the country is almost destitute of population. They make a pleasant variation to the endless round of "Bully" and biscuit which is the staple food of the Army. We get a good issue of bacon, and when we have fried it we keep the fat to spread over bread (or biscuit). It is quite a good substitute for butter, especially when it is so perishingly cold.

19 December 1914

TOO TALL FOR THE TRENCH.

It was soon discovered that there was a big difference in the height of the Americans and the French. The former are so much taller than their French Allies that it will be necessary to dig the trenches deeper so that the men will not have to maintain a continual stooping posture.

Opposite above: **Men from the Argyll and Sutherland Highlanders in their quarters near the Broodseinde battleground.**

Below: **A panoramic view of the devastation of the battlefield at Passchendaele in November 1917.**

THE HEROISM OF SERGT. BROWN.

(From Sergt. W. Shaw, 2nd Bedfordshire Regiment, who was in Belgium and is now home wounded.)

On Friday, the 23rd (my Waterloo), we left the trenches as soon as it was light and moved out to get nearer to the Germans and if possible dig another trench. As soon as we left the trenches we had a hail of bullets over our heads and down we all dropped, taking cover. The order was given to advance and we ran ahead, the bullets flying over us. A few men dropped with a cry, but I, being impenetrable, never expected to be touched.

Well, we searched all round with glasses and couldn't see a German. We knew they were Uhlan snipers and had heard of their tricks. We passed a wood and reached a long ditch in which we took cover from the buzzing bullets. Here we spotted a machine gun firing from the top room of a house and we fired a volley into it. We never heard anything more from that quarter, so I think we must have done a bit of good.

We were ordered to retire back to the trenches, so went back one at a time. Each man ran back and lay down. I ran with an officer to a wood. It was a ridiculous thing. Four men (the asses) joined us and immediately we got a shower of bullets into the wood. I got a terrific blow in the left hand, my rifle being sent yards. My hand was bleeding, although I felt hardly any pain. A bullet had gone through the fleshy part of my left hand. I picked up my rifle and we all crawled out of the wood in a ditch full of water. We reached the trenches all right.

I saw here a case where Sergeant Brown, of my company, really deserved the V.C. or at least the D.C.M. There was no officer to see him, so the deed was unnoticed. Sergeant Brown carried a man, wounded through the chest, for 300 yards while the bullets were flying all round. He reached the trenches without being hit and laid the wounded chap behind the trench. He jumped in the trench and asked some fellows to help him get the man in the trench.

They went to help, so Brown jumped out to lower the man down. Mind you, he was exposed all the time. Just as he was about to lower the man he was shot through the thigh and bowled over. He crawled in and lay down, but no officer saw the act to get him the due reward.

20 November 1914

Murdered Officer.

[Letter from — Weeding, of the Surrey County Council staff, now at the front.]

Poor Captain Horne, of the Cameron Highlanders, was practically murdered. He was shot in both legs and was carried to a ditch slightly in the rear of the firing line and left with a sergeant.

Then the regiment had to retire. They made a red cross on a handkerchief with his own blood and hoisted it on a stick. They advanced again later and found Captain Horne with his head knocked in by rifle butts, and shot.

A Lucky Escape.

[Letter, dated October 3, from Trooper W. G. Fish, 9th Lancers, to his parents at Chingford.]

We are having very bad luck lately with the German shells. One day we came in from the trenches and got the order to groom our horses. When we had finished we were all talking together when we heard a whistling noise in the air.

Some of us scattered and some stood still; then all of a sudden there was a terrific report. A German shell had dropped right in the middle of our troop, and when the smoke cleared away the sight which met our eyes was something shocking. There were arms and legs all over the place, and two horses were blown to pieces.

Altogether that day we lost eleven killed and forty-eight wounded, besides horses which had to be shot because of their injuries.

I had a little splinter each side of my neck and one beside the nose, and I think I was lucky indeed, because the sergeant I was standing beside was killed on the spot.

"Our Troops More Confident Every Day."

[Letter, dated Oct. 11, from Pte. P. Young, R.A.M.C., to his brother at Brighton.]

We had a narrow escape the other day. We had all been called out of the barn where we sleep to attend a service in the hospital (which is a mansion belonging to a French admiral). We have got a parson here, so we have two services a week and Holy Communion on Sunday morning.

Ten minutes after we had left the barn a German "coal-box" crashed through the roof and through one side of the wall and dropped into the garden in front of the hospital, but luckily it did not explode.

We have not been getting so many wounded during the last few weeks. We go about as if we were at home. We have even played football in the garden, although there was a German aeroplane hovering over our heads, and a few shells bursting not far away. Our troops are doing well, and getting more confident every day.

There is an interesting cave underneath the hospital. It runs down a long way. There are dates which were marked on the wall by Germans in the war of 1870. I obliged by putting my name on also.

22 October 1914

STAFF OFFICER'S LETTERS.

Dearest Mother, — This is the first moment's breathing-space I have had during this awful week. From five in the morning till eleven at night we have been at it hard. When I got to the War Office on Monday I was told I was accepted and was from then under orders.... I am a lieutenant without commission and my pay is £250 per annum as interpreter, but I won't see that for months....

Your affectionate son,

FRONTIER, AUGUST 27

Dear Mother—I am writing you this on scraps of paper because they are the only things I can get hold of. "Rough and ready" in everything is the motto for active service, and we eat, sleep, and work how we can. I have left the Intelligence Corps pro tem, and am attached to the General Staff, a great honour for a new soldier like myself. With the General Staff there are only majors, colonels, and generals, picked men from every regiment, who are much pleasanter to work with than some of the conceited young lieutenants in the Intelligence Corps.

I am doing cipher work now, but the first qualification of such a worker is discretion, and so I can say no more about it except that we of course know everything that is going on even before the big people get the information.

The Staff officers have the rottenest time of all. Ceaseless worry and responsibility and very little sleep indeed. For us fellows in the Intelligence attached to the General Staff it is hard, because we have no orderlies to help pack our kit or keep our uniform clean or do our washing. We are only lieutenants in theory. Some of our fellows in the Intelligence Corps were wounded yesterday, but as I am attached to the G. S. I don't suppose I shall see much action, as we are always some miles away from the actual fighting....

Love to all,

25 September 1914

THE GERMANS IN GHENT

(The following is from a man in Ghent.)

I am sure you will be glad to receive some news from Ghent. A friend of mine is going to Holland on foot and will post my letter there. Here no trains, no postal service, no newspapers! On Monday, October 12, the Germans, coming from Antwerp, were at the entrance of the town; all was calm. At nine o'clock in the morning they came to the town hall. No one expected them so soon.

The main body of troops came about twelve o'clock and walked through the whole town; about 80,000 of them. They took the money chest in the presence of our mayor. Up to now they have not asked for an indemnity but only for provisions, which they receive daily. This army corps only passed through, and now there are only about 5,000 to 10,000 of them here. Some are billeted on the wealthy inhabitants. Happily I have not been obliged to receive any. Several houses which had been forsaken the Germans burst open and despoiled.

I suppose that the occupation of Ghent will soon finish. They had placed on the square of St. Pierre a high pole for wireless telegraphy, but they have now taken it away, and yesterday they also removed all the wires they had placed in numerous streets for telephones and telegraphs. They are occupying the whole Palais de Justice, and no one is admitted, not even the high officials. It is the same in the other public buildings. They have taken all the carriages and all the horses of any value.

On the second day of occupation the mayor was arrested by a German captain. He had been asking for petrol, but there was no more, so the mayor was brought before the governor—von Yung. After explanations the mayor was released and the captain was obliged to apologise and was told to go to the front in half an hour. This last week four Germans have committed suicide; two of them were officers.

This is the proclamation posted up in Brussels by von der Goltz:

I inform the population of Brussels that the arrival of troops coming from France is imminent. Our army is coming back from motives of humanity in order not to propagate in the ranks the cholera epidemic now raging among the French soldiers. I invite the population to supply willingly all the requisitions demanded of them.

2 November 1914

DYING HERO'S LAST CIGARETTE.

Pathetic Incident on the Battlefield.

"When our stretcher-bearers returned they found the man dead, with a half-smoked cigarette in his fingers."

This little incident was the tragic climax of a story of British heroism, only one of the scores that are told every day. It concerned a brave Tommy, mortally wounded, who declined to be carried to the base until all his wounded comrades had been taken away. "I'm done for," he said cheerily; "they can be patched up to make good soldiers." A cigarette was all he needed to ease his pain during the time of his passing to eternity.

The incident serves to show the place occupied by tobacco in the life of the soldier. In the cheerless nights spent in sodden trenches it is his comfort. Even in the shadow of death it is his close friend. Surely then it is the duty of every British man and woman at home to see that none of our fighting men want for cigarettes and tobacco. Mere lip admiration for the men who are pouring out their life blood on the plains of Northern France and Belgium in order that we may sleep securely in our beds is of little use. There is a good deal of it about just now, too. What is wanted is practical gratitude.

22 October 1914

A cigarette was all he needed to ease his pain during the time of his passing to eternity.

Opposite: **The wreck of an artillery limber and its dead mules lie beside the road at Pilckem while two pack-horses continue their journey.**

Right: **German Red Cross workers pick up the dead and wounded after an engagement near the Argonne Woods.**

Top: **Troops in the trenches at St Quentin.**

Middle: **Stretcher bearers carry a wounded British soldier to safety.**

THE GREAT WAR OF 1938.

By EUGENE P. LYLE, Jun.

Nothing could more clearly show the nature of the German reply than the following article from the American " Everybody's Magazine" of September :

"IF WE HAD ONLY SEEN THE THING THROUGH IN 1918!"

These are wo ds that with inexorable certainty will be wrung from our agonised lips twenty years from now—if, in these tremendous moments of the world-struggle, we falter, relax, and in weariness fall short of finishing our task now and for all time.

What is written here is not a prophecy; it is not a dream. It is a thought that even now sears the souls of fathers and mothers everywhere and steels them to the ultimate sacrifice NOW, that they and their grandchildren may not face in 1938 the death and downfall Mr. Lyle pictures in this article.

Being nearly fifty, I was too old to fight in the last war—*the* war, as we have always called it since—yet here I am in the trenches twenty years after, and already I have held home the trigger of an obsolete, rusted automatic rifle and blindly let the stream play on an incoming wave of massed grey human bodies. But my being here is nothing worthy of note. The notable thing, and the significant thing, as gruesome as despair, is that among the million civilians in this sector trying to relieve Dover and save London—vain hope, and we know it!—are hundreds, thousands, who like myself were too old to fight in 1914-1918 and who, like myself, gave their sons instead.

Why, then, are we in it, we grandfathers of grown men, and this scourge of a new war not yet a month old?

That the trenches are dug in the soil of old England only partly answers the question, although the frantic rush to stem the invasion caught up all ages, even women and children and the stranger within the gates.

Nor is the ghastly thought that we failed to back those boys of ours in 1918, that we let their blood flow for naught, that their children must now face what they did, what they fought to save us from for ever—not even is this grisly spectre of remorse wholly the thing that harried us here. It was enough, God knows, and I would to God it were all. But the real reason lies deeper yet. It lies like lead on the heart of mankind and may not be denied, yet the pain of dying is easier than the pain of acknowledging so hideous a certainty. So we are here to die, we old men and our children and their children, three generations of men bearing arms, or what antiquated weapons we can lay hand to.

We intend to die. We are resolved to. Men make this decision when life ceases to be endurable, and we know that life cannot hereafter be endurable. Our cause is lost already. It was lost in 1918. The time has passed when we might have kept those things that we hold dearer than life. The hour of opportunity, when we might have secured them for all time, is gone We cannot, because the day is fading out now, so we have come to die with them.

* * * *

Back in 1918 peace as an actual fact astounded the world hardly less than the outbreak of the war.

In these dark days twenty years later, in this hopeless present agony of mankind, that capitulation on the eve of triumph seems the most monstrously incredible thing in history. We see clearly now. It was the forsaking—the betrayal of humanity.

Still, we to-day of the passing generation were the generation of affairs then, and all had our part, our blame, in it. Twenty years is a short time. We have but to go back to our state of mind in that drear November of 1918 to understand how we lost heart at last and were duped by our crafty foe.

mad pack, pouncing ravenously on the world's depleted stocks of raw material!

"RECONSTRUCTION."

As a matter of fact, while the war was yet

THE DISARMAMENT BAIT.

In the matter of armament she proved as tractable, and for as good a reason. Disarmed, she had naught to fear from democracies disarmed in the same proportion. And for ten years at least she did not want the burden of keeping up armaments. Her people would have revolted, or in any case could never have recovered economically. Like an exhausted prize-fighter, the bully of Europe asked nothing better than to break training in order to build up a shattered constitution. So the world was reassured. I remember personally the deep breath of relief I drew. At last Militarism had come to its senses. And we turned away impatiently when certain men of clear vision exclaimed that the safety of the world would be better served by imposing on Germany the necessity of maintaining vast Armies and Navies. But instead we gave her every facility to recover strength, since we agreed to the principles of no discriminatory tariff and no embargoes.

And so Peace came. And when our soldiers, climbing out of the trenches, said, " God help you if you haven't let us finish our work!" we told them that their work *was* finished—that they had saved Civilisation.

The world, indeed, did feel safe; and all the evidence went to justify our comforting sense of security. Yet I recall the flare of impotent anger that swept over the Allied peoples when the curtain was lifted from interior Germany and we beheld the nation of palsied, starving, stinking scarecrows on the verge of bloody revolution to whom we had submitted in a negotiated peace. How much more just, and to these wretched victims most of all, had we let the war go on to a finish! Then, in honest reality, we could have had the voice of the German people in the matter, and our hand would have been held out to them—to help and lift them up.

But, to ease our chagrin for the manner in which we had been tricked, we said to ourselves that these noisome cadavers that still breathed would dream no more dreams of supermen and *Kultur* and *Deutschland über Alles*. The reasoning was plausible and did console us.

And then we said, too, that it was better that the war should end in a tie. Had there been a victory, we said, no matter by which side, the world would remember that a victory was possible, and be about the hideous business again sometime.

During those first years after the war, while the Allied nations bound up their wounds and, with the hope of lasting peace that was itself a healing balm, looked forward to an early convalescence, Germany herself did most to fortify that hope. The grim cauterising, to all appearances, had done its work, and the sore was clean. Much there was to admire in the way the German people set bravely and patiently to work to make, once again, homes and shops and farms out of what had become a vast desolation, with their apparently repentant Government rendering loyal aid.

It's hard to realise, as we read the daily papers to-day, that the starting-point of the newer Prussian World-Dominion was almost stark destitution, and that only a short twenty years ago. We know now, when it is too late, that the German way, out and up, was over the economic bars that our peace commissioners let down to them. How they surged through, that famine-

asked ourselves, done wrong in not letting those boys of 1918 finish the job according to their own idea of a finish? We were beginning to realise as we did not at

the stewardship of posterity, of civilisation in 1918, and we all to an accounting and the conceptions

dishonoured prophets the wild-fire spread man gun clubs. Ex ksmanship had be from the Baltic to attterned after the in Switzerland

14 October 1918

Can the blow be parried? No one thinks so; no one may hope so. The thing was decided back in 1918, with the war that failed of a decision. But there will be a decision this time, and a decisive war decides a thing for centuries. The Turks waged a decisive war, and for centuries superior white races were their slaves, and some of these are their slaves to this day.

Now the Germans are waging *their* decisive war. Centuries and centuries we, with a clear-visioned consciousness that they are an inferior breed, will be their slaves. After centuries we may, perhaps, creep back into the light of day. But no brave man will consent to live the first year of these centuries in prospect, nor leave behind him his children to do so. When these shall have chosen their manner of death, those left by the awful elimination will be only those of slave stuff, and deserving to become slaves.

In all the wretched lexicon of regret there is no word more futile than the ghastly word " if." It avails nothing, ever, and yet to-night the word is branded deep on the aching heart of humanity—

" IF *we had only seen the thing through in 1918!* "

THE GREAT WAR OF 1938.

To the Editor of *The Daily Mail.*

Sir,—I feel it is a duty to compliment you on the foresight exercised in publishing Mr. Lyle's story "The Great War of 1938" in Monday's *Daily Mail.* [This article, reprinted from the American *Everybody's Magazine,* described the unavailing regret of a grandfather in the trenches in 1938 because we did not finish the war in 1918.]

It would be a blessing if this story could be printed in pamphlet form so that its lessons may be brought home to everyone. You deserve the thanks of the nation for publishing it.

A SOLDIER'S FATHER.

To the Editor of *The Daily Mail.*

Sir,—Your issue to-day (Monday) is a real patriotic effort to show your readers that for Britain their "Day" is *now.*

"The Great War of 1938" should be reprinted in millions and distributed in every city, town, and village in Great Britain.

If the Great War of 1918 is not finished as only it ought to be finished, by the complete and utter defeat in the field of the unspeakable Hun and all his *confrères,* then nothing is so certain as that the Great War of 1938 will be a reality.

FRANK H. A. GRIGG.

The Constitutional Club, Exeter.

17 October 1918

93

OUR AIRMEN PAYING BACK THE HUNS.

OUS RAIDS IN RMANY.

FRENCH ATTACK.
DEEP INTO HUN LINES.
OVER 400 PRISONERS.

MORE PIGS AND

12 BIG SHIPS SUNK.

HUN BOOTY IN RSSIA.

DS OF GUNS.

HELPLESS FEELING UNDER AEROPLANES.

(From an Officer in the Royal Field Artillery to a Friend.)

Here we are, after much weary marching and very little sleep, all quite cheerful, sheltered from aeroplanes we hope, in a field under trees. We are within sound of heavy firing and hope to be in action ourselves fairly soon now. We have been billeted almost every night, and it is extraordinary how good the inhabitants of the villages and towns are; and on two or three occasions we five officers have been billeted in private houses; the people have ransacked their rooms to give us all beds or mattresses on the floor and all their best wines have been produced. One man especially has been overwhelmingly kind and seen to a hot bath for each of us himself. His wife and family are in England out of harm's way. I was meaning to send you his name and address so that you might send him some little thing as a souvenir, but, of course, I can't tell you the town he lives in.

A German aeroplane was brought down quite near us yesterday. It landed easily. The men were captured, the engine removed, and the rest burnt. We've seen a good few German planes, but many more of the Allies' ones. It is a helpless feeling to see a plane a great height up observing you and know he can't be touched except with a lucky shot from a special gun. The weather has been really kind to us except for one bad thunderstorm and two days' rain, but not all the cold and rain and wind I expected in October—that is to come.

Don't like to make my letter too long as the Censor might get fed up reading it and burn it. I find our mess cook can talk French quite well and gets us, and himself I've no doubt, lots of things. I saw a village the Germans had been in the other day and it was mostly in ruins. I expect as we push on we shan't find many roofs left to sleep under. Seen two or three Uhlan helmets brought in as trophies and some alleged spies. That is all.

2 November 1914

"FORCED DOWN."—A Hun 'plane photographed just as it struck the ground when forced down by French airmen.

THE WAR WILL BE WON IN THE AIR.

Admirable in every respect, vigorous, true to life, specially timely in view of Lord Rothermere's declaration in favour of reprisals, and splendidly fresh is the story of "An Airman's Outings" (Blackwood, 5s. net), by "Contact," a flying man of renown.

None is more convinced than he that the war will be won in the air:

Towards the end of the war hostilities in the air will become as decisive as hostilities on land or sea . . . By the end of 1918 aircraft numbered in tens of thousands and with extraordinary capacity for speed, climb, and attack will make life a burden to ground troops, compromise lines of communication, cause repeated havoc to factories and strongholds, and promote loss of balance among whatever civilian populations come within range of their activity.

Those pundits who once disbelieved in air warfare are having its importance impressed on them in very painful wise, so that they will hardly question "Contact's" verdict. In another passage, precious for the very superior people who will hear nothing of bombing the Hun at home, he remarks that the damage done by aircraft at the front is "as much moral as material since nothing unnerves war-weary men more than to realise that they are never safe from aircraft."

　　　＊　　　＊　　　＊　　　＊　　　＊

18 March 1916

Top: **A German plane is photographed minutes after French airmen force it to the ground.**

Above: **A cavalryman aims a Hotchkiss gun at an enemy airman. These machine guns, predominantly used by the French and the Americans, were very sturdy and reliable, weighed 24kg and had a range of over two miles.**

Below right: **Initially, bombs were released by hand over the side of the aircraft and aimed in the general direction of the target, without any real accuracy.**

Below left: **Life expectancy for pilots was low but many of the accidents occured during training rather than in combat situations.**

Opposite below: **Infantry exposed to enemy fire on the open ground of the battlefield.**

Opposite right: **A young German soldier in full kit.**

FRENCH LAD'S ELEVEN GERMANS.

(A French lad, aged eighteen. 6ft. 2in. in height, writes to a friend in England.)

Please excuse me if I did not answer before to your kind card, but as I left the front because of a bad wound on my right leg by a German shrapnel I received your card yesterday only. I went to a Red Cross hospital during one month and I was soon better.

I have had a fortnight's holiday and am now ready to start again with much pleasure. Just like you, I trust also a decisive victory will be given to our splendid armies. Eleven Germans are already killed by my hand, and I hope to make out the dozen in a few days. I am now at the depot of my regiment near Angoulême, and I hope I will remain no longer here, where I feel miserable.

4 November 1914

OVEN FROM BISCUIT TIN.

(From a member of the Royal Field Artillery to his uncle.)

Yesterday we all got a hot bath, the first since we left Harrow, in the laundry of a château. There was no water in the house as a shell had destroyed the tank. While here we are getting our washing done in the village, and the woman mends our socks too.

We get up at 5 a.m. every day and go down to the stream by the village to wash and get water. Then over to the horse lines (where drivers and the captain live with them); and water and feed horses and get back to the guns to breakfast at seven. After that as a rule one of us takes the horses to exercise, and the other two are generally employed either going over to the French lines or along our own trenches seeing what progress is being made and trying to locate German trenches and batteries. It is after dusk before we get back to our woodland home, when we get dinner and go to bed about 8.30 or 9.

I have made an oven out of a biscuit tin and we are getting to be first-class cooks. The major makes clear soup and I make apple charlottes. We have built a thatched mess hut and each a little hut to sleep in.

4 November 1914

GERMAN BAND'S MUSIC STOPPED WITH SHELLS.

(An officer writes home.)

There has been the h—l of a battle going on for the last two days; guns banging all over the place, and many aeroplanes of both nationalities overhead. I have not seen one of ours hit yet, though fired at frequently. They are doing very good work. We hope to get another mailbag tonight if not moved. I am sleeping on a motor-lorry at present; our food supply continues excellent, and cigarettes are arriving for the men. The fellows in the trenches must appreciate them immensely.

Affairs are very interesting out here now and very fierce fighting. I hate to see our good fellows brought in wounded, and am only happy in the knowledge that they give back with interest, which I know for a fact to be the case. We had lots of German prisoners here yesterday—poor miserable devils; very young most of them.

The doctors have had to work very hard indeed, but we don't leave our wounded lying about like the Germans. They have many more to deal with, of course. Our ambulance wagons are very fine and beautifully organised. They run backwards and forwards day and night to the firing line. They are very speedy 30-horse-power motor wagons.

Our food supply, too, is marvellous. How the roads stand the traffic I know not. My nearest escape has been a shell bursting about five feet away, and it's not a pleasant experience, the noise being perfectly damnable.

On the Aisne rather an amusing incident occurred. The Germans had the insolence to start a band playing the "Wacht am Rhein" in their trenches one night. The Irish Guards, who were in trenches not far away, did not like this, so asked us if we could stop it. We fired four rounds, when we got the following from them: "Many thanks. Music stopped. Meeting hurriedly dispersed." No more bands after that.

I've got some bits of "Black Maria" for you which did not miss me by very much.

4 November 1914

We had lots of German prisoners here yesterday— poor miserable devils; very young most of them.

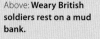

Above: Weary British soldiers rest on a mud bank.

Below: The delight on this Tommy's face is evident as he collects a pile of letters and parcels from home.

Below right: American troops advance through a gap in the enemy's barbed wire.

Opposite: The Grand Fleet, pictured shortly before war was declared. At the beginning of the conflict most of the Navy's larger ships were stationed at Scapa Flow or Rosyth in Scotland, with smaller ships grouped around the British coast.

"THREE MILLIONS OF THOSE CHAPS."

John Bull: Just fancy, some fifteen months ago they were still in their cradle.

CHAIRS IN THE ROYAL PARKS.

To the Editor of *The Daily Mail.*

Sir,—The anonymous writer of a letter from the National Liberal Club which appeared in *The Daily Mail* a few days ago is entirely misinformed.

Wounded soldiers have the privilege of sitting free on any chair or seat in Hyde Park and in all the other royal parks; also they are admitted to the band enclosure and given programmes free of charge. A notice board to this effect is displayed.

This rule has been in force from the beginning of the war.

The last time that 2d. was charged for a chair in the parks was over 20 years ago.

M. W. SHANLY,
Chair Licensee, Royal Parks.

COUNTRY DISREGARD OF RATIONS.

To the Editor of *The Daily Mail.*

Sir,—Unless the rationing of food is made compulsory I fear it will become impossible to keep to the limits. Since I received from Government the printed notice asking me to exercise economy in my household I have been endeavouring to do so, but find that I cannot get servants, as I am described in the village as "the meanest woman on earth."

I have been making inquiries and find that locally little or no economy is being exercised, and the village hotels and inns do not ration their visitors in any way. What am I to do—exceed the limit of rations and get a "good character" for generosity as other mistresses here are doing, or do without servants and be considered mean? From a selfish point of view, I would prefer to do the former. BEWILDERED.
Northumberland.

THE CHANNEL TUNNEL.

To the Editor of *The Daily Mail.*

Sir,—Let us unflinchingly get on with the war and leave the Channel Tunnel, the public war monuments to the fallen, and, above all, the War Museum until we are the victors and have peace.

The British Government is to-day wise strategically by not promoting the construction of the Channel Tunnel now that our enemies are on Belgian and French soil. Had the tunnel been in existence in 1914 Germany might not have taken Antwerp, but to-day the Germans are quite near to Calais.

When the war is over, possibly a newly designed subterranean and submarine tunnel may be jointly constructed by the Governments of France and Britain.

It is at the present time the duty of the Government to employ all available labour preferably on our canals instead of on the Channel Tunnel, as was done long years ago on the fens.

ALFRED FRAMPTON, Architect.
King's Bench Walk, E.C. 4.

13 September 1917

NATIONAL MARRIAGE AGENCIES.

To the Editor of *The Daily Mail.*

Sir,—It has been a matter of wonder to me that the question of marrying our surplus girls has been given so little attention.

Only last week a letter in your paper from an overseas officer pointed out how impossible it was for a stranger like himself and hundreds of others to make the acquaintance when on leave in a legitimate manner of our good-class, desirable, nice English girls, much as they longed to do so and keen as the girls are themselves to make friends— a tantalising position for both sexes.

Before the war the mothers of Great Britain were wondering how on earth they were to get husbands for their attractive, domesticated, surplus daughters. Here, but for silly, senseless social laws and customs, the solution is at hand, and yet no steps have been taken to bring together, either by a matrimonial bureau or society, these men and women with a view to making happy homes in our Dominions after the war. Time and opportunity are passing. The men from overseas will not be with us always. Let there be no delay in encouraging our charming maids and our splendid overseas sons to meet one another in a pleasant, natural manner.

A MOTHER OF GIRLS.

"SWINGING THE LEAD."

To the Editor of *The Daily Mail.*

Sir,—When a naval ship is at sea the "chains" are always kept going for practice and also because "Nelson did it." "Chains" means taking sounding for depth.

To do this a seaman stands on a small platform well clear of the side of the ship and about in line with the bridge. He leans well out on a rope supported on each side with chains. He uses a 14lb. lead weight attached to a 25-fathom line which is marked at certain places.

The ship is travelling and the lead towing astern. He has to haul in the line and coil it up in his hand; then he leaves about 2 to 2½ fathoms (6ft. to a fathom), and the lead hangs down from the hand which is nearest the stern. He now proceeds to swing the lead backwards and forwards until he can, with a sudden jerk, swing or "heave" it over his head in a complete circle, which if not done properly will nearly pull the arm out or bring the lead on to his head. After allowing the lead to make three complete circles he lets it fly forward to the bows; the lead sinks and allows him to "feel" for soundings. When well out to sea the seaman will, if the officer cannot see him or if it is dark, simply "swing" the lead and not "heave" it properly, trusting to the splash as the lead hits the water to make the officer of the watch believe that he is carrying on. We used to use that term of "swinging the lead" to mark any way of "dodging."

A. E. JORDAN, late R.N.
Newport, Salop.

23 August 1917

"SWINGING THE LEG."

To the Editor of *The Daily Mail.*

Sir,—With regard to the article in *The Daily Mail* on "Swinging the Leg," as far as my experience goes this phrase is usually understood to mean one who "dodges the column" or feigns sickness, and so gets off parades.

This type of man is known as a "leg-swinger," and is the thorn in the side of his officers and "N.C.O.s" alike. LIEUTENANT.

To the Editor of *The Daily Mail.*

Sir,—"Swinging the lead" is the phrase we use rather than "swinging the leg." It probably comes to the Army from the Senior Service, and means plumbing the depths to see how far you can go—in fact it is "bluff."

ONE WHO HAS SWUNG IT.

11 August 1916

THROUGH THE GERMAN LINES.

A PASSPORT DRAMA.

SEA OF MINES.

(Private A. E. Bryant, the Queen's Royal West Surrey Regiment, writes home.)

Trust you received my last letter and postcard safely. Since I wrote those I've been through a time such as I hope and trust I shall never go through again.

To start at the beginning. I was sent with three other chaps to reconnoitre a piece of ground which was believed to be infested by the enemy and told to report their position and strength. We set off, the four of us, and everything was going splendidly. As a matter of fact we could just discern the Germans through the trees, when one of the fellows accidently let off a round from out his rifle. We all knew it was a case of U P if we stopped where we were, so we "cut" for it as hard as we could go over a field, followed by a score or so of the enemy. Well, we got over the field all right, and on the other side of the hedge was a lovely deep ditch which formed an ideal trench, so there we anchored and let them have a few very nice, tasty pieces of lead.

We kept this up for about half an hour and I should think we shoved half their lights out, when up came quite a company of Germans as reinforcements. Very nice, wasn't it? Just think of it—over two hundred of them against four! Of course it would have been nothing else but suicide to have stopped there, so we made another sprint for it and this time they must have fired enough shots to wipe out a whole battalion, much less four men. But luck seemed to be on our side and we managed to get into a large wood, where we climbed up the trees. You could hear them coming along, but we knew we were safe because they wouldn't climb up every tree. So we kept quiet and they passed right underneath us, and a more murderous-looking lot of cannibals I've never seen. We stopped up the trees until dusk, when we got down, or rather fell down and made our way out of the wood.

And luck must have been shining on us, for we struck a road directly we got out from under the trees. However, we thought it advisable not to go too far away, so we decided that we should sleep just on the verge of the wood. We woke just before dawn, had a piece of "bully" and biscuit, and if I'd only known what we had got to go through I'd have been still stuck up the tree.

Nothing happened until we got to a place called ——. We were just entering it when a Belgian peasant woman who could speak a little English beckoned us to go into her house. We did, and what she told us fairly made me nervous. I'm not a coward, but honestly I was never so frightened before in all my life. She said that the place was occupied by the Germans and that even at the minute there were a dozen of them sleeping in the house two doors away. They had been looting and pillaging and doing things which I am sure would shock the most uncivilised mortal in creation. She told us they had found two of our chaps in the town wearing civilian clothes and had first of all made them dig their own graves, cut their hands off, and then cut their throats. Of course I can't vouch for the truth of that, but it didn't tend to make us any the happier.

Well, we were absolutely at a loss to know what to do until one of our chaps proposed that we should bury our clothes and get the old girl to rig us out in civilians',

which she did when we had asked her nicely. Heavens! but I would rather have been captured by the enemy than you to have seen me as I was made up. To top the blessed lot, I had to wear a pair of their wooden clogs with the toes turned up, and they were the cause of a good many uncomplimentary words being said. However, it wasn't a time to study comfort, so I made the best of it.

The old girl told us they were using passports, so that was another delightful bit of news that had to be overcome somehow or another. However, she said the Germans only just glanced at the passports, so we collared hers and the next door neighbour's. But here another difficulty presented itself—there were four of us and we only had two passports. At last we decided to toss up for them. The two who lost would have to get out of it the best way they could. We spun the coin up and I was one of the lucky ones. So off we went up the main street, which was crowded with Germans, like two Sexton Blakes. We were a bit hungry, so we went into a café and got the chap to understand we were English soldiers. Directly he knew he took us upstairs and gave us such a glorious feed—eggs and bacon, coffee galore—and let us have a wash and a brush up in general.

After thanking him as best we could we made our way along the street until we came to the place where the Germans were inspecting the passports. Didn't I feel shaky! Still, it was a case of now or never, so we shoved on and went straight up to the fellow in charge. He looked at us, then at the passports; then he said something, and I humped my shoulders up like the French do, signifying that I didn't understand. All the time I thought he had tumbled to the fact who we were, and expected every second to feel myself being collared. But he had one more look at us, gave us our passports and pointed down the road, and you can bet, as the old song runs: "It wasn't very long before we shifted lower down." Still, our troubles were not over yet, for every 500 yards or so we were stopped by cycling patrols and made to show the passports. It was wonderful we got away, because both our passports bore a woman's name.

When we at last lost sight of that town you can bet we were glad. Well, we trudged for about four miles, and then we heard that the English and French troops were some twenty miles north of where we were. So we decided to rest in a barn which we could see until morning, and then make our way towards them. After that decision the first item on the programme was to throw those wooden clogs as far as I could, for they had very nearly crippled me. The next day we came across a French cavalry patrol, and when we told them we were English soldiers they nearly burst themselves with laughter. And one couldn't help it, for we must have looked two beautiful boys. However; they took us to their headquarters, gave us a good feed, a box of cigarettes each, and then motored us here, where I have been four days now. I don't know how the other two chaps got on. I hope they got out all right. You have that coin to thank for my being here now.

Personally, I am as happy as the King of England. One thing is certain, I am a jolly sight happier than Kaiser Wilhelm II. is. Now must close.

14 November 1914

AFTER-THE-WAR SOLDIERS.

The number of officers and men who wish to remain in the Army after the war is quite amazing.

For four years the cry has been, "Give me my ticket." "When peace comes you won't see my heels for dust," has been another favourite expression.

The man desirous of remaining in the Army has hitherto been much in the shade. It has always been fashionable to regard the Army as an institution in which you have only one interest—to get out of it. Anyone seriously wishing to adopt it as a vocation has been regarded as a bit of a curiosity.

The "curiosity" still hides his candle beneath a bushel. Even though he knows much of the common talk about the Army to be mere cant, he does not like being looked upon as something between a hero and a fool.

But the prospect of early peace has served to throw the limelight on him. When conversation turns on civil life he does not say, "I am going to stop in the Army," but his eloquent silence makes you feel that this is what he means.

And when a rumour went round an officers' mess the other day that volunteers were to be asked for in the event of an Army of occupation in Germany being required, the great majority expressed themselves glad to volunteer.

When one recalls how ardently men have prayed to be released from the Army this seems not a little strange, but a few other considerations make the fact quite understandable.

Every soldier who has been where shells, bombs, bullets, "minnies," mines, and gas play a large part in life has said horrid things about the Army and has longed from his soul to be quit of it. But thousands of soldiers have survived these conditions or have never known them, and in the kindlier environment of home service or lines of communication they are more generally disposed towards the Army and in a mood to appreciate its advantages.

We have got so used to a mental attitude of sympathy towards the man in khaki that we forget that in peacetime the soldier's life is an astonishingly easy one. But many thousands of men to-day, having threaded themselves in the groove of Army ways and disinclined to change, do not forget this. They have learnt enough of the Army to know that for a quiet life, free from worry, they can do much worse than wear the King's uniform.

Thus there will be no lack of volunteers for the after-war Army.

L. S. M.

8 November 1918

OUR FINE ARTILLERY.

(Extracts from letters sent by Seargent H. C. Hughes (R.A.M.C.) to his family.)

September 30.... The Germans have a huge siege gun which our troops have named "Black Maria," and they say it fires "coal scuttles." It only fires once every half-hour, but men say they can see the "coal scuttle" coming. There is no mistake about the effect of our artillery, by the looks of some of the Germans we have had to attend to. One man I saw had a lance wound on the head, a shrapnel wound on the back, and both legs broken by a shell, but he said he was glad to be wounded as he knew we should look after him and feed him.

All along the line, wherever we stop, the French women ask us if we have any "Allegman soldats" (German soldiers), but we have to keep the blinds down as they are very demonstrative. The French people are awfully good to our wounded, as every little place we stop at they give us hot milk, coffee, fruit, chocolate, etc. We are just waiting now, to go off to the front again, but there are three or four trains waiting so there cannot be many wounded to shift which is a good sign.

October 5.... A wounded chap was telling me the other day how his regiment charged some trenches with the —. They hung on to the stirrup-leathers until they got into the thick of it, but the Germans simply would not face our men. As soon as they see our bayonets, down go their heads, and up go their hands... I saw another German aeroplane brought down yesterday, and the airman won't fly again as his machine and himself were blown to bits. He came a little too low and paid the penalty. Our troops are doing grand, but getting impatient, as it is mostly artillery duels, with a bayonet charge now and again but it means death if a head appears above the trenches.

October 10.... We have been up to the front for nearly a week picking up wounded, but leave to-morrow morning with a train load. I am quite well, and, although I feel the cold a little, I mustn't complain of anything. I have plenty of warm clothing, and as I live on the train I am fairly comfortable. Talk about a Cook's tour; I reckon since I landed in France I have travelled over 4,000 miles.

October 29.... I saw a fine air duel the other day between a German and five of our aeroplanes, but the German was too high and got away. He came back later and one of our guns finished him.

We picked up a German boy recently, he was only fifteen and I asked him why he joined the army and he said that he was at school only five days beforehand, so Germany must be in a pretty bad way when she sends boys to the firing line. We have just come from Ypres in Belgium and are going back there again to-night.

5 November 1914

IT'S AN HONOUR.

(An Officer in the Bedfordshire Regiment writes to his aunt.)

In the trenches, Oct 19—
Our men are a good lot, and were delighted at the chance we had the other day of getting at the Germans with the rifle. It has generally been the big gun fire, and of course this destruction of villages talked so much about is quite necessary when they happen to be held by the opposition.

The Germans treat our wounded quite well—in fact, tie them up as soon as they can.

Please don't be upset in any way if I happen to get the wrong side of a bullet. It's an honour; don't you think so? At the same time I shall be very much annoyed to have to come home before the work is over, having been here from the beginning because—well, perhaps one can do some good here after all.

Be brave, as I know you are. No doubt we shall be spending Christmas together. What fun, eh?

My watch was smashed the other day. We are now in the trenches, and it is amusing to hear the men arguing hard as to which would be the best company at football. The Germans—quite a secondary matter!

13 November 1914

Above: **A fellow soldier tends Canadian graves.**

Below: **Gordon Highlanders on the march with a wounded German soldier on a makeshift stretcher.**

Please don't be upset in any way if I happen to get the wrong side of a bullet. It's an honour; don't you think so?

ARMY

An Officer in the King's Own Yorkshire Light Infantry. —The houses have really strong cellars, and when the German big siege gun is turned on, as it is every day, we get into them and are as safe as at ——. We call the gun "Calamity Jane," and she lives on a huge motor-wagon about seven miles away.

Fortunately you can hear the shell coming quite distinctly and generally have time to go to ground.

"ARCHIBALD AND CUTHBERT."

An Army Airman. — We are sitting down opposite the old Germans, who are on the far side of the Aisne. We have been out a lot directing our gunners' fire and ordinary tactical reconnaissance. They dig their guns in alternative positions for each battery. It is very hard to spot what battery is doing our people harm, as they are cute enough to cease fire as soon as they see an aeroplane is up.

They have a topsides gun we call "Archibald." He shoots extraordinarily well on some days and damn badly on others. They always get our height correct, but so far have brought nobody down. Several machines have been hit by his shrapnel, bullets and bits of his shell.

He also flies a sort of parachute which he uses to range on. The other day we pulled his leg properly by getting between him and a bright sun so that he could not see us properly. He sent up his parachute, height exactly correct, fuse well timed, and proceeded to pepper it no end, all about half a mile away from us.

Once I heard his beastly shells whistling above the noise of the engine when we came out of the clouds, so he must have been jolly near.

He has a big brother named "Cuthbert," who is a large howitzer. His first shot is good, but the remainder always miles behind. Chasing German machines is quite the order of the day, but they are not over-busy as I believe they are short of petrol.

"Archibald" certainly is a drawback, as one has to be rather careful to circumvent him as the blighter's shooting has improved wonderfully.

13 October 1914

FETCHING HIS FRIENDS.

Private Jas. Bonner Smith. — Some of the prisoners declare that they will be in Paris in a week, London in two weeks. Some are not so sure. The prisoners are generally very willing to give themselves up. One corporal, whom I was talking to, said three Germans gave in to him when he had no rifle, and one went back to the wood and fetched six more of his pals. He said that once, when he was driving along, two ran into the road, but he was not taking them that journey, so he passed them; so they ran and jumped into his lorry.

Private C. Rutley. — We had a lorry which had been going pretty badly for several days, and we kept it going until we could give it a good overhauling. We got to a place where we had to stop for a couple of days and gave her a good tuning up.

Towards evening a couple of fitters, an officer, and three other chaps got in her to give her a bit of a run and see how she was going. They hadn't got but just down the road when out of a wood came a party of Germans. One of our chaps said ——, and they were just about to reverse and try to get out of it when the German officer in charge tied his handkerchief to his sword, and when they came up they all surrendered, over thirty of them, fully equipped and with enough ammunition on them to sink a Dreadnought. They did look a God-forsaken lot, plastered with mud. They had only had carrots for four days. Our chaps hadn't got a rifle between them.

BOER WAS A "JOLLY BEANFEAST."

Jack Hesselop (Essex Regiment). — I was in South Africa and that was a jolly beanfeast to what this is. I have been all day soaked to the skin standing knee deep in water. Sometimes all is quiet, then shot and shell come down like rain and men drop out all around one, but we English Tommies know how to shoot and that is more than the Uhlan does. We came to fists with them once and we know more about that also. I downed three with my fist and I believe I stuck four with my bayonet before I got shot. Our officers are simply grand. They work with us, and one pulled me out of the trench when I was wounded and carried me a little way back.

13 October 1914

Three Germans gave in to him when he had no rifle, and one went back to the wood and fetched six more of his pals.

Above: **Mairi Chisholm (left) and Elsie Knocker, nicknamed the "Madonnas of Pervyse" by the press, nurse a wounded Belgian soldier.**

Below: **British troops march to the front past their French allies.**

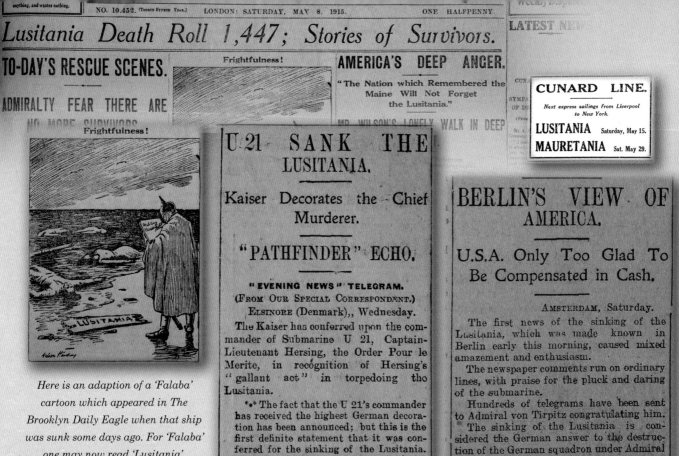

Lusitania Death Roll 1,447; Stories of Survivors.

TO-DAY'S RESCUE SCENES.

Frightfulness!

AMERICA'S DEEP ANGER.

ADMIRALTY FEAR THERE ARE NO MORE SURVIVORS.

"The Nation which Remembered the Maine Will Not Forget the Lusitania."

MR. WILSON'S LONELY WALK IN DEEP

LATEST NEW

Frightfulness!

Here is an adaption of a 'Falaba' cartoon which appeared in The Brooklyn Daily Eagle when that ship was sunk some days ago. For 'Falaba' one may now read 'Lusitania'.

U 21 SANK THE LUSITANIA.

Kaiser Decorates the Chief Murderer.

"PATHFINDER" ECHO.

"EVENING NEWS" TELEGRAM.
(FROM OUR SPECIAL CORRESPONDENT.)
ELSINORE (Denmark),, Wednesday.

The Kaiser has conferred upon the commander of Submarine U 21, Captain-Lieutenant Hersing, the Order Pour le Merite, in recognition of Hersing's "gallant act" in torpedoing the Lusitania.

*** The fact that the U 21's commander has received the highest German decoration has been announced; but this is the first definite statement that it was conferred for the sinking of the Lusitania. The only other man upon whom the Order has been bestowed who is not either a Prince or a general was the submarine captain Weddigen, a German national hero.

It was the U 21 that sank the Pathfinder in the early days of the war. We have the authority of Herr Olton von Gottberg, a German writer, who saw this inscription on a torpedo-tube: "Through a shot from this tube on September 5, 1914, the captain sank the English cruiser Pathfinder."

For this feat Hersing received the Iron Cross—and many offers of marriage from patriotic Fräulein.

He has (again according to Herr Olton von Gottberg) sunk a number of merchant vessels in the Irish Sea.

BERLIN'S VIEW OF AMERICA.

U.S.A. Only Too Glad To Be Compensated in Cash.

AMSTERDAM, Saturday.

The first news of the sinking of the Lusitania, which was made known in Berlin early this morning, caused mixed amazement and enthusiasm.

The newspaper comments run on ordinary lines, with praise for the pluck and daring of the submarine.

Hundreds of telegrams have been sent to Admiral von Tirpitz congratulating him.

The sinking of the Lusitania is considered the German answer to the destruction of the German squadron under Admiral von Spee.

The papers say nothing so far about the consequences. Some hint that if American lives had been lost America would only be too glad to be compensated in cash.

The Copenhagen correspondent of the same news agency says:—

I have received a telegram from Berlin stating that the papers have printed in colossal type the news of the sinking of the Lusitania.

The torpedo is regarded as a new triumph for Germany's naval policy.

The general impression is that England "has got what she deserves."

8 May 1915

PASSENGERS ON THE LUSITANIA.

MISS MARTHA ALLAN.   LADY MACKWORTH.   LADY ALLAN.

8 May 1915

Below left: Scenes at the Cunard London office as friends and relatives read the latest lists of those missing and the fortunate survivors. On 1 May, 1915 the British liner RMS *Lusitania* (bottom) sailed from New York, destined for Liverpool. Six days later a German U-boat torpedoed the ship just off the coast of southern Ireland. This, combined with a resulting internal explosion, led to her sinking within 20 minutes, with the loss of almost 1,200 lives. The disaster caused outrage on both sides of the Atlantic; although Britain urged the United States to enter the conflict, President Wilson maintained neutrality for another two years.

Above left: One of the lucky 764 survivors from the *Lusitania* arrives home. The ship sank so quickly there was not enough time to launch all the lifeboats, even though there were sufficient for everyone on board.

Top: A Cunard Line advertisement, placed in the Daily Mail, for the trip on the Lusitania.

NO GARBLED HISTORY.

Nothing is more surprising in what should be an age of historical accuracy than the average man's tendency to garble history. Already sensational episodes are distorting facts. When a man grows enthusiastic over the exploit of a ship or a regiment he should take the trouble to recall the whole story, not half of it.

An example is the Vindictive. She will always be remembered in connection with the St. George's Day raid on Zeebrugge, but her subsequent exploit at Ostend must not be forgotten.

"Where is she now?" I asked a friend who was talking about her the other day.

"At Zeebrugge," he answered.

"No; she was sunk at Ostend," I said.

"You are wrong," he returned. "If you do not believe me, look at that kinema poster."

Surely enough there was the kinema poster headed "Vindictive at Zeebrugge." To satisfy my curiosity I went into the kinema and saw, projected on to the screen, photographs of the hull of the Vindictive at Ostend, but the scene was described on the film as being at Zeebrugge.

The newspapers, a few days before, had correctly described the salving operations as taking place at Ostend, but through the carelessness of the title-writer of the film and of the poster some millions of people must have been wrongly informed on this one point during the course of the week.

The St. George's day celebrations emphasised the error. The Vindictive is now remembered only in connection with Zeebrugge—yet her hull is even now in Ostend harbour!

Surely the attack on Ostend on Thursday, May 9, 1918, is worth remembering? Is it fair to forget the great exploit there of the gallant men some of whom had previously taken the Vindictive alongside Zeebrugge Mole?

We have short memories, but there is no need to garble history.

SIDNEY HOWARD.

30 April 1919

NAVAL FEAT AT ZEEBRUGGE.

OLD CRUISERS DASH IN.

BLOWN UP TO BOTTLE THE BASE.

MOLE SUBMARINED.

OUR MEN LAND AND FIGHT.

VOLUNTEERS FOR CERTAIN DEATH.

The Admiralty at midday yesterday issued a brief announcement of a British naval operation against Ostend and Zeebrugge, in the course of which five obsolete British cruisers and an old submarine were deliberately sunk to block the harbour exits. This first report was made in anticipation of the Germans wirelessing that they had sunk these cruisers by gunfire.

At 4 p.m. Sir Eric Geddes, First Lord of the Admiralty, gave the House of Commons the story, so far as it is known at

25 April 1918

I respond with great pleasure to the request to supplement the first communiqué issued to-day and give the House such further information as has so far

THE KING'S MESSAGE.

SPLENDID GALLANTRY.

The King to Vice-Admiral, Dover:

I most heartily congratulate you and the forces under your command who carried out last night's operations with such marked success.

The splendid gallantry displayed by all under exceptionally hazardous circumstances fills me with pride and admiration. GEORGE, R.I.

plosives, were to be blown up, destroying and damaging the pile-work connection.

"At Ostend the operation was simpler. Two of the block-ships were to be grounded and blown up at the entrance

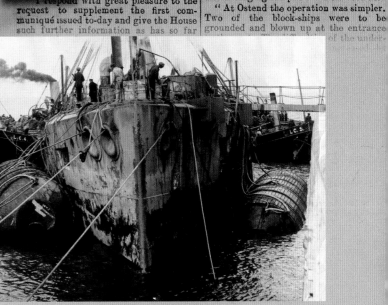

The Imperial Germany Navy was using the Belgian port of Zebrugge for U-boats and light shipping which were a threat to Allied shipping. The Zeebrugge Raid launched by the Royal Navy on 23 April 1918 planned to block the port by sinking obsolete ships in the entrance of the canal, thereby blocking the passage of German vessels. Casualty figures were high but it was delared a victory and eight Victoria Crosses were awarded.

Above: **HMS *Vindictive*,** returns home battered by gunfire. The following month she was sunk in Ostend Harbour during an attempt to block another port. The operation was not totally successful but did stop larger vessels from getting through.

Below left: **The engine crew of the *Vindictive*** who gallantly stayed at their posts during the raid.

Below right: **A few of the 200 Royal Marines** who leapt upon the Zeebrugge Mole to try to destroy the German gun positions. Many were equipped with flame-throwers.

"CONSCIENCE" MEN.

CONFESSION OF A PACIFIST.

The War that Turns Loafers Into Heroes.

Confessing himself a pacifist, Professor Patrick Geddes made a speech at King's College to-day which may be read with profit by the peace-at-any-price party.

Professor Geddes, addressing the opening of the Summer School for the study of the social tasks and problems of the war, said:

"The peace from which we have departed was only a war peace, thinly disguised and potentialising war.

"It was no such high state as we thought, and to do justice to the war we must recognise its manifold superiorities over the world of peace we have left.

"While I make no scruple of confessing myself a pacifist, and with all my loyalty to peace, I want all the more to do justice to war, because we must confess that the pacifist cause has lost immeasurably by insisting so much on the good side of peace and the bad side of war, and have failed to do justice to the other.

WHAT DISCIPLINE DOES.

"We must recognise what we owe to war. Observe its effect on the youth who fill our streets in khaki. They are better set up, manlier, than they were, they are restrained, vitalised, and disciplined as peace did not vitalise or discipline.

"The slackness of the youth at the street corner has gone, and this dramatic change is before us all.

"*Most dramatic of all to me in my own everyday life and experience in Edinburgh between the squalid old High-street and the Old Castle has been the rapid change of the deteriorating loafer into that cutting edge of desperate battle which they call the Black Watch. This is an educational process.*"

Professor Patrick Geddes is professor of botany at University College, Dundee, and senior president of University Hall, Edinburgh. He has travelled widely in the east and west, and is a scientific writer of note.

12 July 1915

There were an estimated 16,000 conscientious objectors during the war who objected to enlisting, usually on the grounds of religion or pacifism. These 'conchies', as they became known, were summoned to tribunals once conscription was introduced; if granted exemption, many were asked to perform non-combat roles to assist those who were fighting. Others who refused to support the war effort in any way were imprisoned.

The public often perceived these men as shirkers. They were frequently shunned or ridiculed and had white feathers handed to them to shame them.

Above and opposite: **The Dartmoor conscientious objectors were housed at Dartmoor Prison where they were given relative freedom but required to work throughout the war.**

Below: **This "Conchy", formerly a Sunday school superintendent, has converted his "broad arrow" spade into a manifesto.**

"CONSCIENCE" MEN.

PRINCETOWN FARCE.

"WORK-SHIES" WITH MOTOR-BICYCLES.

The irritation of members of the House of Commons over the preferential treatment given to "conscientious" objectors was manifest again yesterday.

Answering various questioners, Mr. Brace, for the Home Office, said the "conscientious" objectors have no right to commandeer football fields. Discipline at Princetown is improving.

Mr. Shirley Benn: Are not these the men who went before their local tribunals claiming to be "conscientious" objectors but were found to be only faked "conscientious" objectors who were not exempt from military service? (Cheers.)

"SOME ARE SHIRKERS."

Mr. Brace: I think the facts are as stated, but they were afterwards held by a central tribunal to be "conscientious" objectors, and hence they came under this scheme.

Mr. Butcher: Is there any chance of these shirkers being brought under military service?

Mr. Brace: Well, that is a matter of policy for the Government.

Mr. Outhwaite (indignantly): Does the right hon. gentleman accept the description of these men as shirkers?

Mr. Brace (emphatically): It is quite true as regards some of them. (Cheers and laughter.)

Mr. Brace also said the Committee were meeting that day to consider the facilities now given "conscientious" objectors for getting leave and free railway travel. On March 20 instructions were given that "conscientious" objectors were to be put on the Food Controller's rations for civilians. Complaints have been received that extra supplies are bought in Princetown, and the committee are in consultation with the Food Controller on this matter.

24 April 1917

NO PENSION FOR SHIRKERS.
To the Editor of *The Daily Mail.*

Sir,—Why should not "'conscientious' shirkers" be disqualified for the old-age pension when their time comes to claim it?

M. NORRIS LEE.

Hatfield Vicarage, Harlow.

9 May 1917

HAPPY "CONSCIENTIOUS" OBJECTORS
To the Editor of *The Daily Mail.*

Sir,—Is it not about time that the protection afforded to the so-called "conscientious" objector should be withdrawn?

Men are returned to the fighting line with as many as four and five wound stripes, and now even the discharged men who bore the brunt of the fighting at Mons and elsewhere are to be re-examined, while these "C.O" skulkers are kept under a glass case.

We all recognise that as long as we are able to fight our job is not finished, but there is a strong feeling in the Army that it is time these pampered objectors should be made to do their share.

THREE TIMES INVALIDED.

10 April 1917

WEEKLY PARCELS FOR SOLDIERS

Sir,—It has occurred to me that there are many girls with ample dress allowances who might like to help individually by sending a parcel each week direct to the troops.

I and several of my friends are doing it. This is, roughly speaking, what we send:-

6 pipes, 6d. each, wooden, with covers
6 threepenny wooden boxes of boracic ointment for sore feet.
6 twopenny tins of Vaseline to soften the insides of boots.
½ lb. of coarse cut tobacco.
3 or 4 packets of unsweetened chocolate in a tin.
1 tin of acid drops
6 pencils, with covers.

I usually also enclose three or four newspapers, I send the parcel direct to the sergeant major in charge, and add the name of the regiment, etc. Each parcel only costs between eight and nine shillings and gives great pleasure to both soldiers and senders.

ROSALIE NASH, 5 CRESSWELL GDNS, S.W.

19 September 1914

COBBLERS AT THE FRONT.

Sir,—The winter is approaching. Is "Tommy" to suffer in the matter of footwear? What a scandal!

Here is a suggestion which might be usefully developed. We have at the front of our farriers and our smiths. Why not our boot-repairers? No doubt there are many qualified boot repairers serving with the colours. Withdraw them for this useful work. At the same time, offer inducements to practical men to join a field boot-repairing corps. There would surely be many volunteers.

It is undoubtedly true that campaigning is "hell for leather" on the boots. Yet it will be found that this almost invariably applies to the soles only. Then why discard the uppers which are sound and capable of carrying two or three resolings? Large quantities of cut soles might be easily packed and cheaply conveyed to the front for this purpose. Set the field cobblers to work at the base, and Tommy need never be ill shod. I think it can be taken for granted that he would prefer the old boots and comfort to a new pair of possible corn-twisters. Comfort is a valuable asset in his trying circumstances.

I offer the suggestion to the powers that be in the public interest and the comfort of our gallant little Army.

A. E. SIEDLE, SWANSEA.

1 October 1914

"MY CHUM'S" LAST REQUEST

Touching Story of Comrade.

"At about twelve o'clock we were in the thick of the fight. My best chum was lying by my side and we were firing shot after shot. Soon after dusk, when the firing was not so brisk, my chum asked me for a drink of water—and I had none. I asked, 'why, what's the matter?' He replied, I think I am dying.' I bound him up, but a quarter of an hour later he had gone."— Private Jack Pemberton.

"You mustn't run away with the notion that we all stand shivering or cowering under shell fire, for we don't. We just go about our business in the usual way. If it's potting at the Germans is to the fore we keep at it as though nothing were happening, and if we're just having a wee bit chat among ourselves we keep at it all the same.

"Last week when I got this wound in my leg it was because I got excited in an argument with wee Geordie Ferris, of our company, about Queen's Park Rangers and their chances this season. One of my chums was hit when he stood up to light a cigarette while Germans were blazing away at us."—A Wounded Gordon Highlander now in the Royal Victoria Hospital, Netley.

"Keep your eyes wide open and you will have a big surprise sooner than you think. We're all right, and the Germans will find that out sooner than you at home."—Private J Willis.

14 September 1914

THE ARMING OF OUR OFFICERS

Sir,—In view of the large percentage of officers already killed and wounded in this war, would it not be advisable for the War Office to reinstate the practice inaugurated during the Boer War—viz., that of dispensing with the sword and arming the officers with revolvers.

It is, I believe, the general opinion in military circles that the sword is a useless weapon in modern warfare, and therefore should never be used except for parade purposes.

A brandished sword on a sunny day undoubtedly forms a good target for a marksman, and there is no doubt that the enemy takes full advantage of this fact in directing the fire towards our officers.

VICTOR E. WARD.

25 September 1914

2 April 1917

NO VOTES FOR OUR FIGHTING MEN.

To the Editor of *The Daily Mail*.

Sir,—If anything were needed to prove the crying need for women's franchise it is the inexpressible, unbelievable meanness and ingratitude of women's present rulers towards our fighting men.

Does anyone suppose that in a country where women were citizens the meanest hound that bites would dare to propose a general election which ignored every man who had given his life and all that makes life worth living to his country's service? Such sheer brazenness of ingratitude leaves one with little wonder to spare for the exquisite baseness which ignores also all the young women who have worked so enthusiastically and given their lovers to their country so bravely. When once we elder women have the franchise we will never rest till our brave girls have been given what they have so well earned.

But if the average male stay-at-home voter acquiesces in this infamous proposition to ignore our fighting men's existence and steal their rights, he will have proved himself more abject than any Suffragette ever dreamed he could be, and it is up to the women of Great Britain to treat him accordingly. ALICE COBBETT.

Lyceum Club, W. 1

SHELLS, LANCES, THEN BULLETS.

(Corporal Roffey, 12th Lancers, writing to a friend.)

I am writing this not exactly under ideal conditions. We are at present halted, don't know how long for, while our guns are shelling the Germans out of position. They really give them the gruel, then they let us loose to stir it up with our lances, and if that cannot be done we give them bullets, and they want some digesting.

It is a cold, dull day. Aeroplanes are flying about and I am sitting in a turnip field. Nearly every day we have been under shell and rifle fire, and as the enemy believe in shell fire I can assure you they do stick them in; without their artillery the German army could pack up tomorrow. There seems to be a never-lacking number of them. Their losses are enormous compared with ours; the superiority of our rifle fire stood us in good stead.

My first baptism of fire was on August 20, and it was shell from their big, dirty, greasy, black smoke siege guns. The shell hit a house 300 yards from where I was and laid it in ruins. Then followed Mons and the retirement, almost into Paris, and only those who went through it can realise. Then, when our pursuer thought we were smack up we set about him in fine style. Yes, we have got right among them with our lances, and to tell what it is like with a square-headed German at the end of it I will leave until I come home.

I have a revolver at present, Government pattern, which I took off an officer with which he stood up and took deliberate aim at me not more than ten yards away. But he missed me, and as I drove the lance through him at stretched gallop I cannot remember now what I said.

I thank Heaven for getting away. Three horses shot out of seven and then have to run across ploughed fields to get away out of range is not nice. I expected capture at least, but the majority are cowards and only bet when they are on certs. This last three nights, had one on guard and two in the trenches; honestly, no sleep for at least sixty hours. Yesterday we lost a man killed and one officer badly wounded while on patrol. My section some days ago got in it while crossing a pontoon bridge; one severely wounded, one shot in the knee, bullet came out the other side, into the saddle and lodged in the horses back, and the third struck side of breast, grazing arm, but not severe, and I myself nil. It's the hardships that tell on us. We possess only what we stand up in. Had a week's rain only recently. Of course, it dried on us. A bath, change of washing, and a shave is what I want, to say nothing about a decent bed and cooked meals. Bully beef and biscuits. Oh my! Fried fish is my first dish when I come back—soles for preference.

2 November 1914

Below: **American troops advance through a gap in the enemy's barbed wire.**

Opposite above: **The jubilant Northumberland Fusiliers after their victory at St Eloi in 1916.**

Opposite below: **Staff cars, mule limbers, lorries, an ambulance, infantrymen and their officers crowd the roads at Fricourt.**

GERMANY'S YOUNG SOLDIERS.

"A SHAME TO SHOOT DOWN BOYS."

(Lance-Corporal William McGillicuddy, of the Irish Guards, writes to his brother from a hospital in France.)

I sleep in a bed now, as you may see by the above address, and I am well—wounded slightly.

I've copped two small bullet holes in the left hand; one in the finger and the other in the palm.

We had devilish hard fighting during the day of the 22nd, and advanced during the night. We were fired on frequently by the enemy, and, naturally, we returned the compliment at regular intervals. As we were getting uncomfortably close to them they opened a very hot fire, with the result that I was struck rather too forcibly, as above recorded. I had to leave the gun and retire because I could no longer hold a rifle.

The Germans are by now properly fed up with fighting. Still, what they gain on the roundabouts they lose on the swings, as that seems to be the only proper feeding the poor devils get.

One poor German who voluntarily gave himself up seemed properly disgusted with the war and things in general. When we got him he had no food of any kind in his bag, not even a sausage.

One of our chaps gave him a tin of meat and some bread, and when he had despatched that he asked for some more. He seemed very pleased to think that for him at least the war was at an end. Perhaps when you treat him well in England for some time he may come back to the firing line—on our side.

In my opinion the Germans will soon have to give in. They are now sending boys of fifteen and sixteen to the front, but this, to my mind, is only adding another disgrace to the German programme of "culture."

It seems a shame to shoot down boys who should be at school, but they and theirs have only to blame the horrible German system.

Here in hospital I scarcely dare to dwell on the many sights I have seen. God grant that our native soil may never know the horrors of war. It is too terrible to think of—the fate of Belgium and a large part of France.

One day we came on a large country gentleman-farmer's place. The Germans had shelled the place, and it was all burned to the ground. In a large fattening shed we found forty-three stall-fed bullocks chained around the neck and burned to death. Still, that meat didn't go to waste, as we took it away and used it instead of our own supplies.

It makes one's heart bleed to see splendid houses that were once happy homes burned to the ground.

I've been in a few hot corners, but it is fairly comfortable sometimes in the trenches. When the command "Fix bayonets! Charge!" rings out, then you see some sport. We have had several, but we usually see the backs of the Germans at such times.

Hoping to hear from you before I again leave for the firing line.

2 November 1914

LATE WAR NEWS.

CANADIAN DASH AT YPRES.

RECAPTURE OF LOST POSITIONS.

1500 YARDS OF TRENCH.

WAR AFTER THE WAR

MR. HUGHES & GERMAN
TRADE VAMPIRE.

FROM OUR OWN CORRESPONDENT.

Paris, Tuesday.

Sixty delegates, representing the eight Allied Powers, will meet in secret at...

GREAT RUSSIAN STRIDES.

RAPID ADVANCE ON KOVEL.

DNIESTER FORTRESS CAPTURED.

DUBLIN MYSTERY.

SERGEANT ACQUITTED.

HIS SUSPICION OF AN
OFFICER.

THE LITTLE CROSSES AT THE FOOT OF THE HILL.

(An Officer of the R.F.A. writes.)

My observing station is at the cross-roads of a little village, through which the troops must pass every evening in relief, for duty in the trenches, which are some distance on down the road towards the enemy's position. So I meet many of the regiments in turn—Highlanders, Irish Fusiliers, Rifles, Canadians—all going down silently at dusk to the mud ditches. Every day they come back to the cross-roads, not so many as passed through the previous evening.

The number of pathetic little crosses under the willows at the bottom of the hill increases. They are not the worst off. Those who have to be dug out with spades, frozen in liquid mud, endure hardships which they would gladly exchange for merciful bullet. And the bad cases have eventually to be amputated. One regiment which went into the trenches 900 strong three weeks ago now numbers 233. There is never a word of grumbling. The conditions are accepted as quite ordinary. It is for King and country.

10 February 1915

SOLDIER WITH A CHARMED LIFE.

(Lance-Corporal P. Aubrey, Machine Gun Section, 1st Queen's (Royal West Surrey) Regiment, writes.)

I have been very lucky. The hardest fighting we have had was on October 29. We advanced, and there was only a road between us and the Germans, we on one bank and they on the other, but they had the advantage, as they were behind the brow. We started firing at one another, and a chum of mine got shot in the neck. As he fell his bayonet just caught me in the neck. I got down and started bandaging him up, but did not notice a gap in the hedge, and they took a pot shot at me.

The bullet passed under my arm and tore my pocket as it went across my chest. Previous to that the Germans said they wanted to surrender, so our captain said, "All right! Come in one at a time without your arms." But instead of surrendering they opened fire on us. They are a cowardly lot as regards that sort of thing, for I have seen them fire on the stretcher bearers and shell the hospitals.

Our unlucky day, however, was on the 31st when my regiment got left "on their own" and got properly surrounded at dawn. We had artillery, machine guns, and rifle fire playing on us all round. Our men were being mowed down in groups. We tried to hold our own, but they outnumbered us and it was awful to see. Those who did not get killed or wounded got captured, and at night we mustered only a few, with three officers. How I escaped I do not know. I seemed to have a charmed life. A bullet just nipped my little finger and killed an officer behind me. Some shrapnel burst and tore down my valise and back, smashing my razors. Then a bullet tore through my water bottle.

We were taken out of the firing line to rest a bit as we were so weak up till three days ago.

10 February 1915

HAIG'S TERRIFIC BATTLE.

robbed of the dash and obstinacy that marked the fresh troops, especially those newest to fighting.

HUN LIES TO CLAIM

DESPERATE GERMAN ATTACKS.

NAVY

A Naval Lieutenant. —It is simply a matter of luck that we are not with the other three ships who were sunk by submarines. Had it not been for damage to our wireless gear during last week's gale we should have been out in place of Aboukir and there would have been the end of us.

I have heard that some ships did cast their pianos and chairs overboard. I'll bet they regret it now. So far from doing so we, on the other hand, have got a piano on board, since the war began, to make us happy and jovial when out at sea with no amusement. Also we have recovered our "Bumblejar" harmonium to the parson's delight. I got it going the other day and played ragtime on it to everyone's joy. We have also started a paper in the ward-room called the Every-class Eye-opener, a dreadful thing full of personal remarks and scurrilous articles. However, it makes for laughter and we haven't much to laugh at these days.

A Naval Signalman, —"None but the brave deserve the fair," so the Germans will never gather many roses.

ARMY.

Driver F. Steward (Royal Engineers). —The weather was terrible (during the early days of the Battle of the Rivers), raining torrents, the constant artillery firing bringing it down. Up went the Uhlans' white flag. The order was to take no notice. We had the same trick played on us before. Most of the Germans threw down their arms and refused to fight.

An Officer at the Base. —A wounded R.A.M.C. man told me they go right up to the trenches and pull the wounded out, as fast as they are hit, and I have heard several of the patients say that the R.A.M.C. almost catch the wounded as they fall and take them away.

AIRMAN'S GREAT "EFFORT."

An Officer in the Royal Field Artillery. —The best effort of the lot is that performed by one of the Royal Flying Corps. He had engine trouble and had to land in the German lines. Near his landing spot he found five German officers in a car. He kept 'em away with a rifle while his pilot repaired the engine. They then escaped by air.

WATCHING OVER WOUNDED COLONEL.

Pte. Ludlow (Loyal North Lancashire Regiment). —I was Lieut.-Colonel G. C. Knight's manservant. The colonel got shot in leading his battalion into action on September 10. I saw the colonel's horse dashing away loose on the battlefield. I could see there was something wrong. I caught the horse with the assistance of a comrade, and I could see that it was shot in the neck.

Then I knew that there was something wrong with the colonel, so I went to look for him. I found him lying on a bridge not 800 yards from the enemy. I could see that he had been shot, so I looked after him under terrible difficulty; the shells were bursting all around us, and there was no sign of a stretcher coming up. But I could see his groom in the distance, and I told him to mount the horse and get a stretcher which he soon did, and with assistance we carried him to the medical officer. I stayed with him until he was sent to the village hospital.

The next day when the battalion turned out they heard that the colonel was dead, and the whole battalion was very downhearted about it.

SAVING NO. 3 GUN

A Member of the Royal Field Artillery. —We were in a fearful position practically in the open exposed to the enfilade fire of three German batteries. Our battery stuck it till our ammunition ran out, and then we had to take cover.

Then it was a fine sight. Our drivers brought up more ammunition under a terrific storm of shell, lyddite and shrapnel (I began to write this on the road and am now finishing it while we are in action during a lull), and then we returned the compliments. No. 3 gun was quite exposed, and as the detachment were out of action the drivers took the gun and wagon complete, with the wounded and dead, out of fire in fine style.

It was hard for us to forbear cheering. Presently the cavalry fell back upon us and retired behind us at a gallop. We stuck to our guns for five awful hours, and eventually got them away by hand. That night we buried our dead in the rain, beside a barn, a rather disconsolate but not beaten battery.

1 October 1914

REGIMENT STOPPED BY A FEW IRISH.

Private A. McGillivray, a Highlander writes to his mother:

"Of my company only ten were unhit. I saw a handful of Irishmen throw themselves in front of a regiment of cavalry who were trying to cut off a battery of Horse Artillery. It was one of the finest deeds I ever saw. Not one of the poor lads got away alive, but they made the German devils pay in kind, and, anyhow, the Artillery got away to account for many more Germans.

"Every man of us made a vow to avenge the fallen Irishmen, and if the German cavalrymen concerned were made the targets of every British rifleman and gunner they had themselves to thank. Later they were finely avenged by their own comrades, who lay in wait for the German cavalrymen. The Irish lads went at them with the bayonet when they least expected it, and the Germans were a sorry sight."

DEAD MAN'S CHARGE.

Trooper S. Cargill writes:

"I saw a ghastly affair on Tuesday. A German cavalry division was pursuing our retiring infantry when we were let loose on them. When they saw us coming they turned and fled, at least all but one, who came rushing straight at us with his lance at the charge. I caught hold of his horse, which was half mad with terror, and my chum was just going to run the rider through when he noticed the awful glaze in his eyes and we saw that the poor devil was dead."

SAVING THE GUNS.

A wounded non-commissioned officer of a Highland regiment describing the four days' fighting, writes: "The heaviest losses occurred in covering the retreat on the Monday and following days, for it was then that the Germans fought all they knew in a desperate effort to transform our retirement into a rout. It was here that our guns were lost. Halted, out in the open with weak infantry supports, and doing their best to stay the onward rush of the bluish-grey clouds of Germans, the artillerymen suffered terribly. German marksmen picked off the horses one by one, and then, when the German cavalrymen swooped down the men could not get the guns away.

"So long as possible they stuck to their posts; but the officers realised that it was a useless sacrifice attempting to save the guns, and they ordered their abandonment. I only saw one battery lost in this way. In another case where the German lancers swooped down and killed the last men of one battery the situation was saved by a couple of companies of an Irish Fusilier battalion—the Munsters, I think— who rushed at the Germans with fixed bayonets and put them to flight, while the enemy's artillery poured a merciless fire on them.

"Many of the Germans around that battery were killed, and of course the losses of our men were not light. The Fusiliers were furious when orders came that they were to abandon the guns as no horses were available. You could see them casting loving eyes on those guns all the rest of the day and at night, when the time came to fall back, the poor devils were dragging the guns with them, having captured a few German horses and supplemented them by men who were willing to become beasts of burden for the time.

1 September 1914

[Letter from Private G. Sims, 1st Battalion South Wales Borderers, now in hospital in London.]

I was put out of action at the battle of the Aisne, where the enemy, as I expect you have read, are very strong. After having a heavy day's fighting on September 14, under cover of darkness we advanced to within a few hundred yards of their trenches and dug ourselves in all right.

Our men were thoroughly exhausted, but we were told the position had to be held at all costs. We were not interfered with much during the night. Occasionally miles of countryside could be seen by the glare of distant fires, and a weird scene it was to see the dead being buried and the wounded being helped back.

We could plainly see the Germans strengthening up their position. Storms of bullets came over our heads a few times during the night, but otherwise we were free to continue our work till dawn.

The enemy started firing heavily as soon as it was daybreak, and commenced to advance in large bodies, but, as usual, only to receive a severe check. Our chaps, few as they were, bowled them over like ninepins. If they are the cream of the Germans, I don't know what the others must be like.

It was about six o'clock in the morning when I received my souvenir. It was almost impossible for a wounded man to get back from the firing line without being riddled. I stayed in the trench until five in the evening. The noise was deafening, shrapnel bursting all over the place and raining bullets.

I determined to try and get back to have my wound dressed, and I crawled back somehow, rolled down on to a road, crawled along again for a few hundred yards, and presently got in touch with some stretcher-bearers, who carried me to a doctor.

I with many others laid in a barn for two days, and the shells from the enemy's big guns burst unpleasantly near the hospital throughout the whole time. After a two days' ride in cattle trucks we reached a good hospital, where we were made comfortable.

12 October 1914

Opposite above: **Troops negotiate frozen ponds of muddy water in December 1916. The weather caused military operations to be temporarily suspended; men concentrated on survival in the freezing, wet conditions.**

Opposite below: **Exhausted soldiers enjoy a brief respite leaning against a shattered wooden barrier.**

Below: **Prior to the attack on Arras in 1917, the Royal Engineers spent six months constructing a network of tunnels so the troops could arrive safely and in secret.**

FIVE WOUNDS AND STILL SERVING.

To the Editor of The Daily Mail.

Sir,—May I hope that *The Daily Mail* will champion the cause of men who, though having been wounded five or six times, are still sent over-seas while there are thousands of young men in this country in safe jobs? I know of a young man who joined up in the early days of the war and has been sent home five times. He is entitled to wear five gold stripes, and, his sick leave being almost up, he expects to be sent to France when he returns to his depot. Is this fair or just?

3, Green-park, Bath.   ARTHUR C. INNES.

6 May 1918

BATTLE NEAR RHEIMS.

MR. THOMAS HARDY ON RHEIMS.

THE NIETZCHE BLIGHT.

We are able to publish the following extracts from a letter by Mr. Thomas Hardy, the famous novelist, who began life as an architect, on the bombardment of Rheims Cathedral: —

"Everybody is able to feel in a general way the loss to the world that has resulted from this mutilation of a noble building, which was almost the finest specimen of mediæval architecture in France. The late M. Viollet-le-Duc—who probably knew more about French architecture than any man of his time—considered it to unite in itself in a unique degree the charms of beauty and dignity. But the majority of people have found comfort in a second thought—that the demolished parts can be renewed, even if not without vast expense.

"Only those who, for professional or other reasons, have studied in close detail the architecture of the thirteenth and fourteenth centuries are aware that to do this in its entirety is impossible. Gothic architecture has been a dead art for the last three hundred years, in spite of the imitations thrown broadcast over the land, and much of what is gone from this fine structure is gone forever. The magnificent stained-glass of the cathedral will probably be found to have suffered the most. How is that to be renewed? Some of it dated from the thirteenth century, and is inimitable by any handiworkers in the craft nowadays. Its wreck is all the more to be regretted in that, if I remember rightly, many of the windows in the past lost their original glass....then the sculpture, and the mouldings and other details. Moreover, their antique history was a part of them, and how can that history be imparted to a renewal?

"When I was young French architecture of the best period was much investigated, and selections from such traceries and mouldings as those at Rheims were delineated with the greatest accuracy and copied by architects' pupils—myself among the rest. It seems strange indeed now that the curves we used to draw with such care should have been broken as ruthlessly as if they were cast iron railing replaceable from a mould.

CAN THERE BE AN EXCUSE?

"If I had been told three months ago that any inhabitants of Europe would wilfully damage such a masterpiece as Rheims in any circumstances whatever, I should have thought it an incredible statement. Is there any remote chance of the devastation being accidental, or partly accidental, or contrary to the orders of a superior officer? This ought to be irrefutably established and settled, since upon it depends the question whether German civilisation shall become a byword forever, or no.

"Should it turn out to be a predetermined destruction—as an object lesson of the German ruling caste's Will to Power—it will strongly suggest what a disastrous blight upon the glory and nobility of that great nation has been wrought by the writings of Nietzsche, with his followers, Treitschke, Bernhardi, etc. I should think there is no instance since history began of a country being so demoralised by a single writer, the irony being that he was a megalomaniac, and not truly a philosopher at all.

"What puzzles one is to understand how the profounder thinkers in Germany and to some extent elsewhere, can have been so dazzled by this writer's bombastic poetry—for it is a sort of prose-poetry—as to be blinded to the fallacy of his arguments—if they can be called arguments which are off-hand assumptions. His postulates as to what life is on this earth have no resemblance to reality. Yet he and his school seem to have eclipsed for the time in Germany the close-reasoned philosophies of such men as Kant and Schopanhauer. It is rather rough on the latter that their views of life should be swept into one net with those of Nietzshe, Treitschke, and the rest, as 'German philosophy' (as has been done by some English writers to the papers), when they really differ further in ethics than the humane philosophers mentioned differ in that respect from Christianity."

7 October 1914

CATHEDRAL REPRISALS.
To the Editor of *The Daily Mail*.

Sir,—I do not think the Allies would be justified in destroying German cathedrals by way of reprisal.

Would it not be better to make it one of the peace conditions that Germans should rebuild all cathedrals, churches, and other buildings of interest destroyed by them, finding labour, material, and money? Let German hands make good what German hands defaced, and let it be done under the supervision of French and Belgian officials, to be paid by Germany. This course would be so much more humiliating than payment of the cost that it would act as a powerful deterrent in future wars. W. A. SANDERS. Middleton House, Brownhills, nr. Walsall.

1 May 1917

It seems strange indeed now that the curves we used to draw with such care should have been broken as ruthlessly as if they were cast iron railing replaceable from a mould.

THOMAS HARDY

THE CONTRASTS OF WAR.

OLD WOMAN'S FATE.

(An Army Service Corps man writes to a friend in Dublin of his visits to many battlefields.)

I think my last letter was written at the battle of the Aisne, since which I have been prowling around from place to place, in the course of which I reached the coast. To see the lights of England was cheering in the extreme.

I saw several towns which have become "famous" on account of being destroyed by the enemy.

Rheims was one, where I saw the cathedral a day or two after the bombardment. It was a painful sight, but did not present the scene of absolute desolation which I anticipated. Of course, the place was a hopeless wreck, the glorious stained windows being completely eliminated. The beautiful carvings, the belfry, towers, flying buttresses were swept away as cleanly as by a knife.

The floor was a mass of molten metal, powdered slate, and masonry, with here and there the grim relics of the German prisoners trapped in the furnace. The altar alone remained practically intact and some oil paintings. I am glad Antwerp has been spared such a visitation.

Outside of Rheims is a statue of Joan of Arc, mounted on a horse and leading troops on with uplifted sword. Standing unscathed amid the general ruin, it seemed a portent. To the people it was no doubt an omen, and they had marked the fact by smothering the pedestal with flowers and fastening a tricolour to the sword.

Then I saw Senlis under solemn circumstances. I had been motoring most of the night, and about 3 a.m. entered its silent street. What a scene of desolation, and how unreal it seemed in the light of the moon, which shone with a splendour rarely seen except in the East. It seemed like a dream, except for the "tuff tuff" of the exhaust as the passing car alone woke the echoes. My chauffeur didn't like it at all, frankly desiring to "let her out."

"I don't 'arf like the look of this here, I don't mind telling yer." So he let her out. We slid through the vast forest, scattering the rabbits, who were startled beyond measure by the glare and noise.

My duties now take me around to the different Mairies, where I settle up accounts for fodder, etc., requisitioned by the troops. For this I have an interpreter and a clerk, so travel with my staff in semi-state. It is very hard to get business done with despatch, as my interpreter blathers away for hours before getting to business.

We see many things grave and (almost) gay. The most striking feature of war is the sudden change from profound peace to all the evidences of death.

Here is a small boy, not more than five playing in the road with a dog which he is trying to push about in a toy wheelbarrow. Not two hundred yards away a house collapses as a shell drops through the roof.

In this beautiful sylvan glade the only evidence of recent conflict is an unexploded shell half buried in a tree. A little further on to the river, and we see that the bridge is destroyed, while the far bank is topped by a blackened tower. Two days ago it was a glorious church, the pride of the ruined village which surrounds it.

Further on we find some dead soldiers, still lying where they fell, waiting till sufficient calm reigns among the distracted villagers to enable them to be buried.

In the house over the way lies an old woman, who, running blindly away from her house in the night was accidently bayoneted by one of her own countrymen. What a home-coming for her husband who is at the front!

Just outside the village, two men and forty-two horses are lying dead, the result of a bomb dropped from an aeroplane. Our way is hindered by the stream of refugees, which ebbs and flows as the tide of fortune changes. A sight which would move the stoniest is that of old women and adolescent girls scrambling for some broken bread lying in the mud, indifferent to its condition, which can be imagined when we know much has passed over it during the day. It is hard to realise how the army "eats up" a country. The people here are trebly unfortunate since three armies have passed through. We, of course, pay for everything we purchase, but the enemy simply ransacks the places.

I came across the Indian contingent, who look very picturesque, but serviceable. They look singularly fierce, and I cannot picture the enemy waiting for them to attack. Personally I should funk terribly if I met them; their very appearance causes misgivings. I should imagine it will be very hard to keep them in the trenches, as they are more used to brilliant charging, cutting, and thrusting.

The other evening a mysterious form in a ditch behind the house in which we were billeted provoked a frenzied rush of my enthusiastic servant and chauffeur, and I was just in time to save the farmer's boy from a speedy death.

5 November 1914

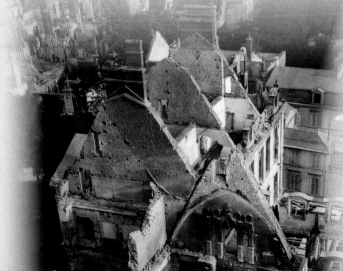

This page and opposite: **The city of Rheims and the Cathédrale Notre Dame de Rheims were systematically destroyed during the war. The German Army initially occupied the city in 1914 but withdrew to higher ground, from** **where they regularly attacked with artillery shells. The cathedral was the victim of over 300 direct hits. It was restored after the conflict ended under the guidance of the architect Henri Deneux, eventually reopening in 1937.**

BIG BEN OR THE TIME GUN.

*(Extracts from a letter from Sergeant Davis
(1st Lincs. Regt.) to his mother.)*

Charlie got hit once in his ammunition pouch, which turned the bullet off. A lucky escape; but we take lucky escapes as a matter of form now. The worst of it is that the women and children are getting it very nearly as badly as us. There was a continuous cannonade for four days and nights on the bridge, which the engineers built, and we crossed at night and still held the opposite side. The proper bridge was destroyed by them.

They had one big siege gun laid on it, which fired every ten minutes as regularly as clockwork day and night, generally having a rest between 3 a.m. and daybreak. This gun we have dubbed "Big Ben' or "the time gun." It has fired thousands of rounds, destroyed the village, killed plenty of horses and men, and, unfortunately, children, but has not hit the bridge once yet. The village is one mass of ruins.

The church was shelled once when full of wounded, included Germans. But I think this was an accident, as they could easily have blown it to pieces had they so wished. I think they killed three wounded when they shelled it. The others we got out in time.

It is getting very cold now at night. We have had several frosts. We have no blankets, but to-day all men who had no top-coats got issued a blanket or rug which the people at home presented. Fine rugs they are, some of them. If the people who gave them could have heard the blessings the troops poured on them they would send them for evermore. Some of them have been without top-coats since Mons. I did not get one as I still have my top-coat.

31 October 1914

FATEFUL FRIDAY.

FATHER KILLED AND 13TH CHILD BORN THE SAME DAY.

News reached Bromley, Kent, yesterday that on Friday, December 18, the same day that his thirteenth child was born, Private J. Waldron, of the Scots Guards, was killed in action. Only a few days ago the relatives at Bromley were discussing the superstition attached to a Friday and the number 13.

Private Waldron served throughout the South African War.

12 November 1914

They had one big siege gun laid on it, which fired every ten minutes as regularly as clockwork, day and night, generally having a rest between 3 a.m. and daybreak.

HOW LONG WILL IT LAST?

By LOVAT FRASER.

As this inquiry is constantly being made, I should like to say why I venture to differ from the "high French military authority" whose views have been published in *The Daily Mail*. He estimates that the war will last nearly three years. I do not think so, simply because I doubt whether this question can be looked at solely from the military point of view. If the war proceeded in accordance with the principles laid down in the military text-books undoubtedly it would take three years to finish. The probability is that factors which have nothing whatever to do with military principles will eventually determine its duration. Those determining factors will be, first, the attitude of the German people, and, secondly, the desires of the Allies.

THE RUSSIAN TRIUMPH.

The overwhelming repulse of the Austro-German forces in the east, at the hands of the Russian armies, has narrowed the area in which a decision has still to be obtained. Russia has definitely thrown back her assailants, and henceforth in the east the Germans must be on the defensive. We must not expect too much help from Russia, who has given her western Allies priceless help already, and may now elect to devote her chief attention to Austria-Hungary and to Turkey. But the failure of the German attack upon Russia means that if the Germans cannot now succeed in Belgium they will have failed everywhere. Immense issues therefore hang upon the terrific conflict still proceeding around Ypres and around La Bassée, for it represents Germany's last hope. Those valiant lines of British troops, those gallant French, those cheery and indomitable Belgians are fighting to destroy the last chance remaining to the Germans of attaining any single one of their objects. If the Allies win, if we can send enough men across the Channel to help them, if they can convert their magnificent stand into an irresistible advance, then every separate purpose for which Germany fought will have been decided against her. That is why it is of such

28 December 1914

TWO SOLDIERS AT BAY.

STIRRING BRITISH DEFENCE OF A MILL.

The following vivid letter of the defence of a mill at Mons by two British soldiers against the Germans was written by a regimental clerk to a friend in Newcastle:-

After we had been in the trenches for hours rumours were passed along that the others had retired. We could not see them as they were in an orchard over to the left. Our captain got on a "bike" and went off in a hail of bullets. He fell off several times and we thought he had been hit, but he got up and disappeared. About an hour afterwards he came back and said the other troops had retired over an hour before and we were told to prepare to retire, which we did as soon as the shells stopped visiting us. We went along a street in Mons and barricaded it, but returned to the trenches about 11 p.m.

I took my boots off, also my pack, to get a little rest. At four o'clock in the morning the captain came and woke us up. He had just got to the end of our platoon when the artillery gave us a vivid impression of Dante's Seven Pits of Hell. They had the exact range to an inch and dropped their message of death right into the trench. We retired at once. I didn't have time to put my pack or boots on and had to run up the cobbly streets in my stockinged feet.

"NO SIGN OF OUR MEN."

My feet were beginning to hurt, so I sat down and wrapped my putties round. When I got to the end of the street the company was nowhere to be seen. After about a quarter of an hour I saw a big mill. There was no one in. So I went up to the loft to see if there were any signs of our men. There was no sign of them, so I came down and met a woman, who gave me a cake and said there was a wounded soldier in a haystack near her house. I went there and found one of the Royal Scots wounded in the knee, so stayed with him. The woman came about an hour afterwards and said the Germans were crossing the river and would find us. I carried this chap to the mill and barricaded the door.

We then got to the top of the loft and saw thousands of Germans marching from the river they had crossed on a bridge of barrels. Thousands marched past and we thought it was all right, but about fifty came back and went straight up to the door of the mill and started to beat it, so I thought it was all up. One of them spotted Scotty's rifle against the window, and we exchanged cards. That kept me in as I did not want to be poisoned with lead, so the other chap sat at the window the other side and we had a little sport. They broke a few rifles trying to break the door down and moved up the street out of sight.

Just after that a motor-car came tearing down the street and threw something at the door. There was an explosion that shook the whole place, but did not do any damage, except blow the door in. After that a farmer drove a cartful of straw up the street, but as he was too old to be a soldier we did not fire. Then we found our mistake.

WHAT THE STRAW COVERED.

It was only straw laid over a shade and was full of them. They jumped in the door as it passed and we didn't get a chance to fire. They climbed up to the trap door and someone asked us in English to come down. I said, "No," and they fired a few rounds through the door and said if we came down and told them where the others were they would let us go. We told them to wait and held a council of war. The Scot said he wasn't particular what happened, so we said we didn't know where they had gone. Then they started. They riddled the door. We also helped, but the bolt still stood. The Scot rolled a big cog-wheel over the door and we piled everything er could on it, which was mostly oil cans. There was a little barrel of white lime, and we went to the window to empty it over any who were below and found all straw piled up in the doorway.

We saw their ways then. Someone lit it from the inside and three of them made a bolt for shelter, but only one reached it. The straw made a lot of smoke, but burned out, and everything was quiet. We didn't venture out until the next morning, and there wasn't a sign of anyone. Later we reached our own lines.

30 September 1914

FATE OF TWO BROTHERS.

ONE SHOT WHILE TRYING TO RESCUE THE OTHER.

A correspondent related to the victims narrates the following unusual incident:—

"In South Africa, at the commencement of the war, two brothers named Winslow, descendants of the intrepid and resolute member of the band of Pilgrim Fathers, were killed on the same day in fighting. The elder, who was on horseback in the front line, was shot down at the first volley of firing. His brother, stationed behind some rocks, at once rushed out to give him a drink. While doing so he, too, was shot by the German force.

"A fellow-soldier afterwards came across the sad sight of two dead brothers. The brave would-be rescuer had one arm around his elder brother's neck, and he still held the cup in his other hand. A hero's death, indeed!"

8 December 1914

SOLDIER'S SWEETHEART.

PARENTS' SEARCH FOR GIRL CALLED "WINNIE."

The story of a sad little romance comes from Crewe. On October 29 Private Percy Moffitt, 1st Battalion Grenadier Guards, was wounded at Ypres, was taken prisoner, and died in Hanover Camp, Germany, on November 26.

The German officials sent home Private Moffitt's belongings to his parents, and among them was the photograph of a girl called Winnie. She is unknown to the parents, but they believe she lives in London.

They have written to *The Daily Mail* in the hope that they may get to know their boy's sweetheart. "He must have thought much of her to carry her photograph with him," writes the father. If "Winnie" should happen to see this she is asked to write to Mr. R. H. Moffitt, 28, Edward-street, Crewe.

20 April 1915

Above: **A morning stroll in Picardy along a road covered in thick, soup-like mud.**

Opposite: **Infantrymen wait in the safety of the trenches.**

113

TERRORS OF THE FLANDERS QUAGMIRE.

Left: **Stretcher-bearers rescue a wounded soldier. Their challenge was to negotiate the mud without jogging the stretcher, which would cause additional pain and shock to the injured**

Below: **Men of the 16th Canadian Machine Gun Company hold the line at Passchendaele.**

Opposite above: **Troops and mules cross safely using a "corduroy road". These temporary tracks, designed to produce a safe crossing place on an impassable road.**

Opposite below: **Horses and limbers are caked in mud as they transport ammunition to the front-line.**

SWAMP OF DEATH AND PAIN

9 SONS FIGHTING.

THE KING'S CONGRATULATIONS.

Mrs. Bailey, a widow, of Gladstone-road, Ashtead, Surrey, has nine sons and two sons-in-law serving with the forces. The sons are:

GEORGE, Pioneer, Royal Engineers.
WALTER, Private, Devonshire Regiment.
FRANK, Driver, R.F.A.
FRED, Sapper, Royal Engineers.
CHARLES, Sergt. Queen's Royal West Surreys.
WILLIAM, 1st Class Seaman Gunner, R.N.
JACK, Able Seaman, R.N.
ARTHUR, Private, Queen's Royal West Surreys.
LEONARD, Lance-Corporal, Middlesex Regt.

The sons-in-law are Private Wilfred Pritchard, A.S.C., M.T., and Private Harold Quickenden, Anti-Aircraft Service.

Of three other sons one is working on munitions and two more are ineligible, one being 17.

The King has written expressing appreciation of the family's patriotic spirit and saying how gratified he is to hear of the manner in which they have so readily responded to the call of their Sovereign and country.

26 July 1917

Every inch we gained in Friday's battle is worth a mile as common distance is reckoned. Some troops went forward 1,700 yards or even more, fighting all the way; and when their relic came back some part of that heroic journey no enemy dared follow them, so foul and cruel was their track.

They left behind them a Golgotha, a no man's land, a dead man's land. Five or six miles separate our troops from any place where you can step firm, where you can find any break in the swamp. It is a nightmare journey to traverse it, in spite of the ceaseless labour of pioneers.

Our soldiers coming out of this swamp of death and pain maintain incredible serenity. If we could advance so far in such conditions we could go anywhere in fine weather. We were nowhere beaten by the enemy, though more defensive wire was left round shell-holes and pill-boxes and fewer machine gunners knocked out than in any recent attack. We were beaten by the rain that began to fall in torrents at midnight before the attack, so they all say and feel, and so it was.

One of them, still full of humour, said he considered Friday an unlucky day for him. "You see," he argued, "I was first hit in the shoulder by a machine-gun bullet, and as I stumbled was hit in the foot, and as I lay another hit me in the foot and another hit me in the side. Decidedly Friday is an unlucky day." It was a terrible day for wounded men, and alternate advance and retreat now always leave a wide, indeterminable no man's land from which escape to the mercy of either side is hard. But the best is being done, and the immortal heroism of the stretcher-bearers was backed by both the daring and skilful work of doctors at advance dressing stations and ambulance drivers a little farther back.

The trouble was how to find people or places. Wounded men, runners, contact officers, and even whole platoons had amazing journeys among shells and bullets searching for dressing-station headquarters, objective or what not, and, as we know, even Germans on the pure defensive had similar trouble and their units were inextricably confused. It was all due, as one of them said, to the sump, or morass.

All that can be said of the battle is that we are a little higher up the slope than we were and a little further along the crest road to Passchendaele. How we succeeded in capturing over 700 prisoners is one of the marvels of the day. A marvel, too, is the pile of German machine guns. They are some small concrete proof of the superhuman efforts of our infantry. If the world has supermen they were the men who waded forward up to their hips astride the Ravelbeck and stormed concrete and iron with flesh and blood. They were at least the peers of the men who fought "upon their stumps" at Chevy Chase.

To-day the artillery fire has died down, the sun is bright, though the cold west wind threatens showers.

15 October 1917

DISCOMFORTS AND TERRORS.

Rain in war-time. It is a punishment of which you can form no idea. For three days and nights we have been able to do nothing but shiver and whimper, and yet we must carry on. To sleep in a trench full of water has no equivalent in Dante, but what of the awakening when you have to watch for the moment to kill or be killed!

You must never know what man can do to man. For five days my boots have been foul with human brains. I have been treading on throats and stepping on entrails. Two dear friends, one of whom made a charming model for my last portrait, have been killed. It was one of the terrible discoveries of the night. His body lay, white, magnificent in the moon. I lay down close by him. Beauty of things woke within me.

Our condition as infantrymen is rather like that of rabbits which are being shot. We have acquired—or at least the more timid of us have—a perpetual inclination to look for a hole.

25 October 1917

SHOT WHILE HELPING WOUNDED.
(From Corporal W. St. John, 7th Cavalry Field Ambulance, to his father-in-law.)

It is not the bullets we have to fear so much, it is the shells, because it means death to be within fifty yards of one bursting. I had an awful experience a few days ago. One of our soldiers got shot in the leg and two of his comrades brought him to me to attend to. So I was on my knees dressing his wound when the Germans opened fire and shot the two chaps who were looking at me dressing the other one, dead; both shot right through the heart. I tell you it shook me up a bit, but we have to get used to it.

12 November 1914

SNIPING SECRET.
From an eyewitness.

Success in this somewhat murderous form of warfare is largely a matter of position and luck; but it is remarkable what can be done by pains and skill. At some points where we are fortunate in having some exceptionally good shots who are also keen on this work, we have established a mastery over the German sharpshooters which enables our men to leave their trenches while the occupants of the German front line dare not show a head above the parapet. It would be interesting to explain exactly how this result has been achieved; but the time for such disclosures has not yet arrived.

On the lighter side—that of camp yarns—the following story of Gallic humour is causing much amusement, and is, at any rate, ben trovato. At one point not far from our own line, where the French and German trenches are sufficiently close together for the occupants to converse, the French recently asked the "Boches" where the Emperor was. The answer was that the Germans did not know, whereupon the French replied that their President was actually going to visit them in the trenches.

"When?" was the eager enquiry.

"Oh! to-morrow, somewhere about mid-day," was the equally innocent answer.

About the appointed time, to the strains of the "Marseillaise" played on a gramophone, a top-hat on a stick was slowly marched down the trench so as occasionally to show above the parapet. The waste of German ammunition which took place is described as colossal.

17 December 1914

OUR GUNNERS.

YARD SQUARE TARGETS HIT AT 4 MILES.

WHAT MONCHY MEANS.

From W. Beach Thomas, War Correspondents' Headquarters. France, Wednesday.

I walked forward early this morning to see what could be seen of the capture of Monchy (south-east of Arras), a dominating hill which was to crown our advance. The hill smoked with shell-fire as I reached the top of Telegraph Hill and thence walked over the German trenches forming the famous Harp Redoubt.

The only line for smooth walking was over one stretch, the track of a tank which made a journey of 6,000 yards and did excellent work beyond this and Tilloy Village, now vanished. I met a mixed stream of our lightly wounded making for an advanced dressing station and German prisoners moving sheep-like in front of a single East Anglian shepherd. One of them was the only person who showed obvious nervousness when a high velocity shell, making a noise like a scratchy slate pencil, squeaked just overhead.

Our wounded struggled most gamely and stretcher-bearers were gentle as ever. A fine young English soldier, who asked me for a hand round a very slippery shell-hole, had taken his Lewis gun section clean through Monchy in spite of hidden snipers, made a temporary emplacement (foundation for the gun) on the far side, and had the satisfaction of loosing off a drum of bullets at some flying Boches. He was finally hit in the leg by a bit of shell from heavy fire directed on the place by the enemy after we took possession. He had fought hard for three days at first in support and then in the charge.

12 April 1917

GREAT ADVANCE.

ON THE BATTLEFIELD.

WONDERFUL SCENES AND INCIDENTS.

From W. Beach Thomas.

WITH THE BRITISH, FRIDAY AFTERNOON.

The moment which crowned yesterday's rapid victory was when the cavalry, hand in hand with the lighter and faster tanks, went through the infantry, who opened to let them pass.

I saw them yesterday from the other side of the Somme swing across the open at about 10 o'clock and disappear over a crest. Today I walked for several hours, from dawn onwards, along and across their tracks, over all the central part of the battlefield.

In an improvised wire cage close to where I started was collected part of the booty of this tank-and-cavalry dash in the form of 500 soldier prisoners and 37 officers, who tumbled ludicrously into this new offensive trap. They were sent forward by train on the orders of a German Staff officer, who had only allowed for the pace of the infantry advance and wished to reinforce a village garrison.

When the Germans began to detrain they found, to their complete amazement, the station in full possession of the British, and their surrender was a matter of course. They did not fire a shot. Some among them looked weak and boyish and were pathetically docile.

"They are just like sheep," said one of their guards, but the German officers kept a very stiff upper lip. "We shall win because we must win, and shall go on till we get what we want, " one of them said.

The battlefield itself was an incredible spectacle at first sight by reason of its mere emptiness and silence. Artillery fire had almost ceased. The guns of both sides were moving, ours forwards, the enemy's back. Acre after acre of ground had no sort of trench or pit, and shell-holes were sparse. The dead lay singly and inconspicuously at rare intervals, as if fallen from some plague. Even the enemy's abandoned field guns were often single, not in Latteries.

I saw one fallen aeroplane and at wide distances two broken tanks, but, walking on, one came to rough roadways, little groves, spinneys, and at last villages, in all of which were crowded signs enough of a vivid yesterday—indeed, of a present battle.

In a thick wood along the main road several miles south of Villers-Bretonneux were hidden some 6in guns, and close by a single field gun in the open was being cleaned. When our men appeared it had fired 11 rounds, to judge by the empty cases behind the gun, and the gunner was engaged in attaching instantaneous fuses to the shells, taking them one by one from a neat wooden box forwarded to him personally from Hamburg. A dump of unfused shells outside had been missed by inches by a British shell.

I saw during the morning more German guns than dead soldiers, but the battlefield was being cleaned up. With astonishing speed salvage parties and burial parties had begun work even during the battle.

The most interesting of the villages was Morcourt, tucked neatly into a hollow which had saved a house or two from wreck. The cellars here were full of German stores, especially of bombs. Just beyond the village along the southern wall of the Somme is a shack village of huts and roofed scoops and dug-outs. From one of the best a German officer must have bolted with unseemly speed for so obvious a dandy; he had left his cosmetics uncorked and his two special soaps unpacked. He had even forgotten to take away his shot-gun cartridges, some of them Eley's No. 7 made in England.

Signs of a quick bolt were everywhere, but scrambling down the slope of the chalk cliff or shrinking in the shallow holes were some who had run too late. Such sights were not good to dwell on, and I turned back to walk to Cérisy, where the heaviest fighting had been. The village is quite overlooked by Chipilly, on the opposite side of the Somme, as I described yesterday. But it was a surprise to find how complete this domination was—so complete that the German guns there had fired point-blank with open sights at one of our field batteries, which had pushed too boldly forward and was charging almost with the infantry.

It cannot have happened often in war on land that hostile batteries should have come thus face to face and blazed straight at each other like riflemen. It was a little disconcerting to find that the check from the northern bank was not overcome. Indeed, German eyes were looking straight down on us from certain points.

The quietness of the day had broken. The air activity was beyond all experience. Forty planes were in sight at one time, according to one keen-sighted officer. Two German planes slipped past and over a swarm of our fighting planes and were engaged by "Archies," and flew back to their own lines at exceptional speed.

Soon afterwards, well over the German lines, a sudden gleam high in the air caught the eye. It grew to a flame and a doomed plane, burning brighter every second, dived steeply down and fell vertical.

I trust it was a German, but the worst of many stirring things seen in battle is that the nature and ending of the story are unknown to the observer.

This phenomenon was succeeded by another yet more portentous to watch. A shell struck a large petrol dump, as I should guess, in the German lines, and the smoke, based on a furnace of red flame, rose an astounding height, looking like tiers of forest trees raised one on another.

A few minutes later a battle much nearer at hand was announced by the venomous rattle of machine guns in action among the trees north of Chipilly village. It meant that the Germans still held the base of this spur. They made their one heavy counter-attack yesterday a little north of this spot, where the enemy has as many as three divisions.

But rattling guns, falling planes, and the rest made no difference to the soldiers. Every man with a minute off duty of holding the line threw himself down and slept like a child.

When some hours later the tour of the battlefield was finished, it left a definite impression of the nature of the German defence. The battle support positions were wretched and the whole support area very thinly garrisoned. Small, isolated, shallow pits had been scooped out more or less at random, and the men manning them slept in wretched, evilly-smelling kennels, with sometimes a tin roof, sometimes shallow earth, sometimes just camouflage wire.

In the more southern area of the battlefield these were closer together. Very many still contained their machine guns and some trench mortars. A few of these, as well as field guns, were turned round and had been used both by the Australians and Canadians against the enemy. Indeed the German was so afraid of this that later today he tried hard to hit his own dumps with his howitzers. Not a great deal had been knocked out by our artillery, but in Bayonvillers a 4-ton lorry, still full of stores, had received a direct hit, and in the same neighbourhood is an 8-inch gun knocked out by a shell.

But rattling guns, falling planes, and the rest made no difference to the soldiers. Every man with a minute off duty of holding the line threw himself down and slept like a child.

The villages here are like those nearer the Somme, a mass of roofless houses. Here the Germans had made some neat offices, with comfortable berths in them.

AMAZING TANKS.

Abundant evidence is found at all centres of the amazing impudence and skill of tank crews. One large park of motor lorries coming up with supplies met our advancing tanks. Four mounted officers who could not believe their eyes rode forward to interrogate these poachers and were shot. The tanks then proceeded to deal with the transport, which began by upsetting itself in a vain effort to wheel and flee.

LATER.

Another amazing story of a tank was mentioned briefly yesterday. The full story is better. The tank crew found themselves among huts which they suddenly found to be a corps headquarters. After dealing with the chief officers and the occupants the crew saw some of the staff running and riding away, and started in hot pursuit.

In the direction of Péronne, far beyond our advanced posts, cavalry and tanks captured part of a Red Cross train, burnt another train meant for troops, and in the same village, Framvillers, charged down the street, shooting through windows at officers sitting down to a meal. Among smaller captures was the car of a flying officer who was shot as he drove away.

The alarm produced by this dash of the tanks was such that soldiers and transport fled helter skelter back in the direction of Nesle. Miles farther back bridges were seen to be jammed with troops, and a state of general confusion exercised every energy of the staffs.

A few men tried to organise local defences as at the village of Proyart, but such efforts were rare and spasmodic. Attempts to blow up dug-outs and burn manuscripts were observed, but for the most part, as I saw, little order was observed. Regimental books and accounts, as well as half-finished letters, lie scattered about scores of houses and dug-outs.

One officer in command of a unit had too little time to light a match, so stuffed his papers down his breeches leg. The lump was noticed as he walked into the "cage," but as he stoutly denied that anything was there which ought not to be, he was searched and the papers were found. He did not struggle, but cursed and swore vociferously at the people who presumed to search him.

Among other officers with him, and indeed elsewhere, are the largest number of artillery officers ever taken in this war. This is a greater compliment to the speed of the attack, as the guns were quite unusually far back, even the field guns. They were numerous, but were just being reinforced by an artillery column from Lille.

CAGE TOO SMALL.

One of the "cages" was interesting in itself. Our troops had to wait till the night of attack to fix it up, but had no sooner done it than a tank, not knowing the change, charged through it, and the work was re-done only just in time. Even so it was hardly large enough for the call on it. No fewer than 4,600 prisoners passed through it in the first 24 hours, and a thousand have come since. They include soldiers from the 117th Division, which had only just come into the line, as well as a few of the 109th, which was being relieved.

The corps concerned, whose headquarters received so rude a shock is the 11th, commanded by General Kühne. A tank flag was raised over his headquarters.

Fighting today has not been on a bigger scale, but one could see a certain amount of activity even while traversing yesterday's battlefield.

We are now elbowing the enemy off the Chipilly spur, and on the other side cavalry could be seen pushing out cautiously but continuously in the neighbourhood of Harbonnières and copses near Bayonvilliers. Machine-gunners and snipers of the outposts on the two sides kept one another busy at close range near Harbonnières Station.

The astounding experience of this battle is that there is no destroyed land or roads, no "No Man's Land," and one may, if one will, drive a motor car straight into the enemy's country without being stopped, and this very nearly happened this morning.

Prisoners are still coming back, and the depth of our advance is now at least 8 to 9 miles in the south. As to the total of prisoners I can give some figures but can only guess at the full total. Almost exactly 2,000 were taken yesterday north of the Somme. South of the Somme our various units have estimated their captures, which must bring the grand total to well over 10,000.

The guns taken must, in my opinion, exceed 200 field guns and a score or two of heavies.

As to casualties, the German dead were certainly five times as numerous as ours over the battlefield, and I believe ten times as numerous in the front trenches. Our total wounded is smaller by several thousands than was expected in the hospitals, and is absolutely, as well as relatively, small by comparison with the achievement. But a price is paid for every victory, nor can any arm of the Service be exempt.

10 August 1918

Right: **The 5th Australian Infantry Brigade, complete with tanks, advances towards the German lines near Lamotte-en-Santerre.**

In the farther corner a man sat on a box,
with his head resting on his hands. He was a
German, stone dead although I saw no wounds.

Below: **British and German casualties occupy a crater recently made by a mine. While many in the foreground lay waiting for help, the British soldiers are ordered to continue the advance.**

LANDSTURMMANN A LANGE.

Clearing up a battlefield after an attack is not a pleasant job. We had wrested a line of trenches from the Germans, and the fighting had been heavy.

I went into a German dug-out in the rubbish-filled gutter to which our "heavies" had reduced the original German front line. Three of our poor lads had crawled down there to die out of reach of the shells, and had spent their last pain-wracked hours in comparative safety. In the farther corner a man sat on a box, with his head resting on his hands. He was a German, stone dead although I saw no wounds. Then the match I had struck flickered out, and I turned to ascend the debris-strewn steps to the trench.

There was a twilight at the foot of the stairs, and I saw on a bench a photograph and a German soldiers' magazine. I took them from that cave of death, and examined them in the clear sunlight of the trench.

The magazine interested me little, as I cannot read German. The photograph portrayed "Landsturmmann (Reservist) A. Lange," according to "Meine Adresse," written on the reverse side, and his wife and child.

At my feet lay a dead German. From the position in which I had found the photograph I tried to reconstruct the story.

The Landsturmmann had been in the dug-out looking at the portrait, when the British barrage descended upon the trench with the abruptness of a thunderbolt. The Landsturmmann had placed the precious photograph on the bench, seized his rifle, and hurried into the trench to do his duty by the Fatherland.

Was the dead man A. Lange? Perhaps A. Lange, as so many of his comrades did that morning, emptied his rifle at the advancing British, threw his hands up and cried "Kamarad!" and is now in clover in Blighty. But if he had been captured I think he would have begged and obtained that photograph, for to a soldier the portrait of loved ones is dear and is the last possession he will part with.

Yes I think fate was stern with A. Lange.

I looked at the dead German at my feet. This man had died as becomes a soldier. He had been firing over the parapet when the shell splinter came that had smashed his head. He had collapsed into the trench. His right arm was raised as though to protect him from the fatal steel; still clenched in the dead fingers of his left hand was a clip of cartridges, half withdrawn from the leather ammunition pouch.

Not a pretty picture—but War!

There were too many of my comrades lying dead for me to sentimentalise over a German, who had, very possibly, accounted for some of them. But perhaps, after all, Landsturmmann A. Lange's tragedy is the greater.

My comrades gave their lives for the Great Truths of what one of A. Lange's compatriots called "the religion of all poor devils." And these truths are worth dying for.

A. Lange met his death defending not his wife and child but the abomination of German "Kultur." In one sense he is a victim of Germany's rotten philosophy as tragic as a Belgian child crucified on a barn door by A. Lange's compatriots.

The husband, wife, and child make a pleasing group in the photograph. They would have been happy enough if German war lords had not set the husband and father to the devil's work of slaying the husbands and fathers of his neighbours.

SIDNEY HOWARD.

2 July 1918

AFTER-THE-WAR SOLDIERS.

The number of officers and men who wish to remain in the Army after the war is quite amazing.

For four years the cry has been, "Give me my ticket." "When peace comes you won't see my heels for dust," has been another favourite expression.

The man desirous of remaining in the Army has hitherto been much in the shade. It has always been fashionable to regard the Army as an institution in which you have only one interest—to get out of it. Anyone seriously wishing to adopt it as a vocation has been regarded as a bit of a curiosity.

The "curiosity" still hides his candle beneath a bushel. Even though he knows much of the common talk about the Army to be mere cant, he does not like being looked upon as something between a hero and a fool.

But the prospect of early peace has served to throw the limelight on him. When conversation turns on civil life he does not say, "I am going to stop in the Army," but his eloquent silence makes you feel that this is what he means.

And when a rumour went round an officers' mess the other day that volunteers were to be asked for in the event of an Army of occupation in Germany being required, the great majority expressed themselves glad to volunteer.

When one recalls how ardently men have prayed to be released from the Army this seems not a little strange, but a few other considerations make the fact quite understandable.

Every soldier who has been where shells, bombs, bullets, "minnies," mines, and gas play a large part in life has said horrid things about the Army and has longed from his soul to be quit of it. But thousands of soldiers have survived these conditions or have never known them, and in the kindlier environment of home service or lines of communication they are more generally disposed towards the Army and in a mood to appreciate its advantages.

We have got so used to a mental attitude of sympathy towards the man in khaki that we forget that in peacetime the soldier's life is an astonishingly easy one. But many thousands of men to-day, having threaded themselves in the groove of Army ways and disinclined to change, do not forget this. They have learnt enough of the Army to know that for a quiet life, free from worry, they can do much worse than wear the King's uniform.

Thus there will be no lack of volunteers for the after-war Army.

L. S. M.

8 November 1918

Below: **A wounded soldier receives a welcome helping hand.**

Opposite: **Two British soldiers are buried on the battlefield while the Padre reads the solemn words of the burial service.**

You look at your watch; an hour and a half since it began! Five yards away is a lad with a broken leg. Another one is killed...

A BOMBARDMENT: WHAT IT FEELS LIKE.

By James Hodson.

You are in support, and you get into your little "cubby-holes"—shallow pits dug into the parapet just a couple of feet of earth above you. If you are lucky you are sharing the hole with a pal. It is comforting.

The hole is a close fit for two, and you are squeezed together as you sit, and your knees and feet are poking out in the trench. You light a cigarette and wait. You do not wait long. The whistle comes, and then the tearing, rending crash. Shrapnel, heavy and black and bursting low—you can tell by the crash of it. Bits patter like heavy hail on the trench outside and overhead. You nestle comfortably. Your tin hat is pressing into the earth above; your vision sees but the clayey side of the trench opposite. You feel rather safe. You know it is foolish and that any decent sized piece would come through the earth above you, but you do feel rather safe. You cannot help it.

The whistles are getting more frequent; now they are a chorus; now the whistles and bangs and kr-r-umps are hopelessly intermingled. The shrapnel is still tearing overhead, but the kr-r-umps and the crashes, with a peculiar metallic clan-n-g, and the rocking and trembling of the earth tell you that H. E.s are dropping all around. You venture a look at your pal, who grins at you in the gloom. You pull yourself together. You press your back into the soil and your tin hat into the roof. Doing that seems to help a bit.

The trench outside is full of smoke and fumes and they drift in and make you cough. Your knees and feet are covered with bits of dirt, and pieces of earth from the roof are beginning to drop on to you. The crashings, the earth-shakings, are still going on. How your little hole contrives to be missed you do not know. Shells are dropping all round, within yards. You speak, but you cannot hear your voice. There is a sort of splashing noise outside and you know part of the trench has fallen in.

The crashes are fewer; the smoke outside begins to blow away. The bombardment stops. It is as if weights were lifted from your head. You are fearfully thirsty and you drink from your bottle and pass it to your pal. Slowly, painfully, you crawl out. You are stiff and you ache. The quiet is profound, and you hesitate for a moment before breaking it with your speech. You look at your watch; an hour and a half since it began! Five yards away is a lad with a broken leg. Another one is killed...

You can get used to some extent to shell-fire for a few days, but not for a period that will include rests out of the line. Every turn "up" the line is like beginning all over again your apprenticeship to shells. But you take far less notice of shells on your journey out of trenches than on your journey in. Exhaustion kills fear.

11 April 1918

FALLEN.

Weary with battle and relieved from the positions we had won, we proceeded to bury the fallen. Sadly we gathered from the battlefield the men of our own beloved regiment.

When you do not know the dead the sight is grievous; but these! It is not that you knew their faces only. You knew the souls that the broken prisons have released.

Here, more tragic to you than any sight on this Aceldama, is he who was your chum.

Together you have marched and fought, halving sorrows and doubling joys. Together you crouched beneath the steel-throbbing sky; stumbled forward against the whistling storm of the belching machine guns; were watched for in the observed trench by the sniper with his trigger-finger of fate; were masked against the lung-rotting gas.

There was that bad day when you stood in a trench crumbling before the field-grey wave when all seemed lost. But he was by your side and you held, though the line alongside gave; though the hand-guard of your rifle blistered your hands; though the machine gunners were sick at the slaughter and the artillery grew weary of their targets. Held, until the might of the many shattered against the courage of the few and they withdrew.

But now he is dead.

It is not good to look upon the human body after high explosives have wreaked their wrath upon it, yet the sight of the torn clay has no terrors for you. You knew that to him the flame of the shell that smote him was but the light of the unveiled face of God.

The body is laid in a great shell crater with eleven others. The service is said by a chaplain who himself has fought in the ranks, and every word touches your aching heart. It is finished, and he marks the grave with a cross, made from a broken ammunition box; thus is Hope fashioned from the very refuse of war.

We turn to march from the battlefield. The sun is gone, but in the east rockets hiss into the darkening sky. The embers of battle glow again.

The earth throbs to the hammer-strokes of the howitzers, each convolution of the valley echoes the long flight of the spinning shells, the dark caverns of the gun-pits spout flamingly, the ridges behind are silhouetted as the darkening sky flushes.

Lucifer, fresh from the fiery pit, might pause in admiration, but we would forgo these splendours for one glimpse of an English lane under a sunny sky, for we have seen the dead fruit of these wonders.

The sodden earth is hallowed by the tread of our dead, the flooded craters are ruddy with their wounds.

But one day the tide of war will recede and the wilderness will blossom. Nature will remember so to enshrine their tomb that men shall wonder that the flowers here are so beautiful.

We who survive will not forget in the after years. The memory of the courage of our dead comrades shall inspire us as when God breathed into the nostrils of Adam.

SIDNEY HOWARD.

31 October 1918

GERMANY SURRENDERS.—OFFICIAL

The Prime Minister made the following announcement to-day:—
The Armistice was signed at Five o'clock this morning, and hostilities are to cease on all Fronts at 11 a.m. to-day.

LATEST NEWS.

CLEMENCEAU AND VICT◦
A TOUCHING INCIDENT.
PARIS, Mond◦
" Le Gaulois " relates the follo◦
incident :—
On Saturday M. Clemenceau pa◦
visit to the nursing home by ◦
Bizet, where some time ago ◦ ◦
went a severe operation.
On his arrival the Premier aske◦
the head sister, and handed her a ◦
nificent bouquet, with the words ◦
" Sister, on this day of victory ◦
you these flowers of France, for ◦
your devoted care I should nev◦
been allowed the honour of takin◦
in the victory of France."
The sister, who was deeply ◦to
thanked the Premier.
" Since then," adds the " Gaulois,"
the sisters of the home have bee◦
strongly ' Clemenciste ' as the Ch◦
of Deputies."—Reuter.

WHEN THE "BOYS" COME HOME.

What are you going to do about it, war-wives? Are your "boys" coming back to houses or are they coming back to homes?

I think it was Elizabeth who set me wondering about this when she came to see me the other day.

Elizabeth—we will call her that because it is not her name—was married some twelve months or so ago. Circumstances have so dealt with her that of housekeeping—except that it is something which someone else does for you—she knows nothing. Food and warmth have always happened to her at appropriate moments, have always happened to her in a comely manner.

She has, for instance, never had to stand for hours, one of a crowd, pushed and pushing, in a butcher's shop, with rigid, frigid dead beasts hanging all round her; milks, hot and cold, have always come at her call; butter too, and matches; gas, candles, and coal she has known only as things to be spent; about the saving of them she knows no more than she knows about, say, the nebular hypothesis or the construction of aero-engines.

So Elizabeth is, as you can see, a young woman of comprehensive ignorances. No, she is not—as you may be thinking her—either a fool or a knave (I wonder what the correct word is, if any, which one should use when one wishes to refer to a lady knave?) Simply, she has been, very strenuously and very faithfully, doing war work of a kind that has permitted no divided attention. She emerged from it for a brief while in order to get married. Then her Man of War went back to war and she went back to work.

Now her husband is invalided out. Soon he will be coming home.

"And I want to learn things before he comes, so as to be ready for him," said Elizabeth. "You see, I want him to come back to a home, not to just a house; and it's only I can make it home for him.

"I've met lots of war-wife girls who say they're going on with their work just the same when their 'boys' do come home. They say they like being free and independent, and that they couldn't be bothered with looking after a house—even if they knew how to, which they don't. Well, I don't know how to, either; but I'm going to learn. When my 'boy' comes home he's coming home—and it's only I can make it home for him."

MINNIE SHERRIFF MOTT.

29 October 1918

Below: **A lone soldier uses a temporary bridge to cross the waters just outside Peronne.**

Opposite: **The desolation of the Ancre Valley can be seen from these panoramic views taken from Hamel, looking toward Miramount.**

A HUGE WHITE FLAG.

By Percy Noel.

CHICAGO DAILY NEWS CO.

I have talked with officers and soldiers, eye-witnesses of different scenes of the momentous day and night, including a French major who was one of the party who received the envoys later at the headquarters of the corps in whose area they entered.

It was about eleven o'clock on Thursday morning when the orders were given to cease firing. Soon after enemy bugles sounded repeatedly. Soldiers in the French lines who came dubiously out of cover saw numerous white flags waving from positions on the edge of the Bois de Montreuil and at an outpost near Haudroy.

At noon a German major with an N.C.O. and a bugler appeared. The N.C.O. held as large a white flag as it was possible for one strong man to carry. The bugler blew frequent blasts. The sun was trying to break through low clouds that darkened the sky with threatening rain, but there was light enough for hundreds of poilus to witness it.

The French major whose battalion was occupying the line received the enemy major with military etiquette. The German said that he had come for instructions as to how parlementaires should proceed, and asked for confirmation of wireless messages that firing would be stopped until the passage had been safely made. The French major issued full instructions, in accordance with his orders from headquarters, and the Hun major returned to his lines.

HUNS BREAK THEIR RIFLES.

The German soldiers who saw the white flag go and come through the strip of level No man's Land drew their own conclusions. In the afternoon two or three hundred of them came forward in full sight of the French, convinced that the war was over, and broke their rifles by jamming the butt into the soft ground, holding the barrel tightly and stamping at the breech with heavily booted feet. They came over to the French empty-handed with a friendly air. They hailed their enemies as comrades, not the old familiar "Kamerad" of surrender but as men of the same métier coming in friendly fashion after years of bitter competition.

The French were cheerful but in no mood for fraternising. The Huns protested, "Armistice! The war is over!" The French compromised by accepting the lot of them as prisoners. The Germans did not seem to mind.

11 November 1918

They came over to the French empty-handed with a friendly air. They hailed their enemies as comrades.

WHAT THEY SAY IN THE TRENCHES.

Talk about "getting the old job back" arouses the greatest diversity of opinion. Many of the younger men want something bigger and better than their former occupation when they return to civil life. The "oldsters" are more anxious about a safe anchorage.

A few men openly express their reluctance to resume jobs which have been "held down" by women or girls during the war period. Many more are thinking seriously of the position of the lasses who will be ousted by the returning soldiers.

On one thing all are agreed: there must be no "barrel organ and monkey parade" for Service men in years to come. The man who has done his bit in the Great War should at least have an opportunity of doing his bit during the Great Peace.

If the war has taken from our womenfolk many of their bravest and best, it has also given back to many a mother her "boys" and to many a wife her "sweetheart." The petty things which in civilian life stood between so many men and their loved ones have been swept out of existence, and the old folk, the old home, and especially the "wife and children" have been idealised as a result.

W.H.N

17 October 1918

THE END OF THE WAR.

The Prime Minister made the following announcement to-day:—

LOST YEARS.

The problem of the "lost years" is an awkward one. A youth of 19 who enlisted in 1914 is now a young man of 23. Before the war he was a student or an apprentice; when peace is signed he will be past the age of study but without the equipment for a profession or a trade.

But the problem has its brighter side. Much has been written against our universities. It is claimed that they did not equip students for commerce or the professions and were inferior to Continental universities. This may have been so, but the war has shown that our 'varsities produced a type superior to the highly technical Hun—they produced men.

The war has swept universities out of existence temporarily, but there is a wider 'varsity where men learn the great truths of life—the university of the trenches.

It is a hard school. Men do not go in at one end as weaklings and emerge at the other as heroes, but I have never met a man who has not been affected by trench life. All are not improved, but each is altered for better or worse—almost invariably for the better. The misery of the conditions depresses—that is where the weaker nature is overwhelmed and embittered—but the incomparable comradeship of the spirit sustains.

War is of the devil, but the cheerfulness of the British "Tommy," the courage that laughs at unutterable horrors, the heroism of the soul that inspires the body to "carry on" despite the weariness of the flesh, the charity that men display in giving the last of their precious water to a man who has been hit—these are of God.

Never in the world's history has Christianity been practised on such a scale as in the trenches. Men fight and kill, it is true, but they fight for a great ideal and they kill what is vile. It is impossible to live for months acquainted with death and not to realise the pettiness of bickering over trifles. Perhaps to some the fighting man appears more callous in that for him death has lost much of its tragedy; but these fail to see the fighter's point—that the length of a man's span is of less import than what he did during it; that there is less tragedy in the death of a man killed while fighting for his ideals than in the longer years of one who shirks his duty and dies an old man.

The fighter has lost ground in the details of bread-and-butter grubbing—he cannot add up figures in a ledger as swiftly as before, he is not a skilled mechanic at the trade he left for the war, but his moral is higher. He has learned things that the stay-at-home has not, and his is the spirit of camaraderie that was once only the possession of the fortunate few who had enjoyed a public school or 'varsity training.

After the war wherever men may meet the question will be not "What was your school? " but "What was your regiment?"

SIDNEY HOWARD.

25 October 1918

I have never met a man who has not been affected by trench life. All are not improved, but each is altered for better or worse.

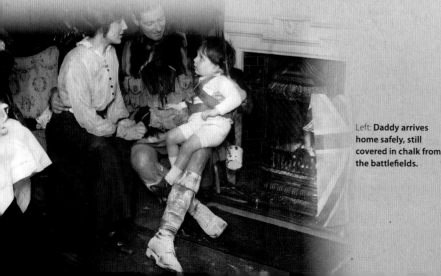

Left: **Daddy arrives home safely, still covered in chalk from the battlefields.**

SILVER-BADGE LONELINESS.

After a man is discharged from the Army and the first feeling of unwonted freedom has passed he begins to feel lonely. Often he is then more depressed than when he suffered in hospital the pain of a wound or an amputation. There he was with cheerful comrades in misfortune and a member of the great fraternity of khaki.

But when he put on civilian clothes and passed beyond the gates of the hospital or the depot he went out into a world that had changed since he left it. If he were middle aged and married things were not so strange, but with younger men it was different. The world to which they returned was empty of the faces they knew.

All the young men were away fighting and the discharged man could not easily fit into a place among his elders. In the country the loneliness was not felt so much; it was in the crowded cities and in the places of which he had pleasant pre-war memories that the ex-soldier felt lonely. There is no loneliness like the loneliness of a stranger in a crowd.

The silver-badged man missed two sets of chums—those he had known in civil life and those he had made in the Army. Somehow, he was not very quick in making a third set.

It used to be that school friendships were the most enduring, but in the future we ex-soldiers will cling also to those made in the Service.

Many men have told me of their first month out of the Army—of the bitter feeling of loneliness that assailed them, and how they wished themselves back. Some who were able did go back not because they liked the Army, but because they were used to the free-and-easy spirit of the men and their warm-hearted ways. Others frequented the headquarters of the old battalion. They were smuggled into barrack rooms and chaffed about their "ticket," and asked when were they "going to join up"? There were always men partly "crocked" at the headquarters who knew them and had news of the Service battalion—how Joe was killed or "Tubby" wounded and when Harry was due on leave.

The silver-badged man lived in the civilian world, but his heart was with his chums.

That is why no one is more eager for demobilisation. His are purely sentimental reasons. He wants those who joined first to be first back.

SIDNEY HOWARD.

30 December 1918

BACK TO THE ARMY AGAIN?

Three months have gone since the Army gave me my "ticket" and I'm still out of joint with things. I've tried hard to settle down; I'm still trying. It may be easier when the job "out there" is finished. At any rate, it can't be so bad when the others are home too.

Meanwhile I miss it all so much. I am keener on the regiment than ever I was. I get every detail of how the old company has done in the "push." I seem to have left my life behind when I handed in my kit. And I get little sympathy—probably I don't deserve any—for my folly.

It was all to have been so grand. How many times we talked of it in the platoon, especially after a "sticky" turn in the line! To get back home, to have a regular job, a weekly wage, a real bed, to know no more the horrors of 5.9's and mustard gas, to sleep at nights like a human being—it all seemed too good even for dreams.

Now that my dream has come true, I ought to be grateful. I'm not. Call me unreasonable, foolish, a silly sentimentalist—call me what you will, and I'll accept the reproach. But it doesn't alter the facts. I want to go back. I miss every hour the movement, the restlessness, the uncertainty, the expansiveness, the comradeship of the Army. And when I get fit to travel again I'll be off. Never till now did I appreciate how much Kipling really knew of the soldier when he wrote, "Back to the Army Again."

It was different four years ago. I was satisfied, in a way, with the normal life of a civilian. I never found it difficult to breathe in a city and I didn't regard as trivial so many of the things in the daily round.

But now! Four years of Army discipline and a taste of what war is have revolutionised both me and my outlook. I've succumbed to the magic of movement, of days when every hour is full of the uncertain and the unknown. I want elbow room, breathing space; I find civilian conditions too circumscribed. Above all, there is the wonderful, mysterious freemasonry "over there" that calls to me always.

My old mother knows; she understands. I catch her watching me when I put down the book or "fidget" about the house. In a quiet way she tells me that I'll get used to things at home just as I got used to life in the Army; that all the others will be the same way when they come back; that a comfortable home is infinitely better than a shell-hole bivouac; that I must settle somewhere; that I'll probably find a wife, and all will be well; that I'm suffering from the glamour of the last four years. Glamour! Shall I ever forget the counter-attack at Cambrai?

I hope that the others take it better than I am doing when their turn comes for "Blighty." Some of them are older and were not quite so impressionable when they joined up. But for the younger men it is hard, believe me, to cast aside all that the Army and the war have meant. It is doubly hard in these days when the victory drums are rolling.

23 October 1918

Left: **Crowds celebrate in London. The Armistice was signed at 5.10 am but it was agreed the ceasefire would begin at 11.00 am to allow the news to travel across the Western Front. Due to increasing technology people at home knew by 5.40 am but soldiers on the frontline carried on fighting, unaware of what had happened.**

Below: **Citizens cheer the troops after the liberation of Lille.**

THE KING'S CERTIFICATE ON DISCHARGE.

RANK..NAME.....
AND..REGIMENT..ETC......
Served with honour and was disabled in the Great War.
Honourably discharged on ......
George R.I.

THE KING'S CERTIFICATE FOR DISCHARGED SOLDIERS. - The special certificate of honour which is to be awarded to soldiers discharged through wounds or disabilities incurred on active service, including injuries in air or naval raids. A similar certificate portraying features applicable to the Royal Navy is to be issued to the Naval and Marine Forces. The certificate measures 21½ inches by 15 inches.

"PREVIOUS EXPERIENCE ESSENTIAL."

With certain exceptions, no soldier is demobilised unless he returns to his pre-war employment. Thousands of the men who have been released and hundreds of thousands of those who are soldiers still have determined not to remain in the jobs to which they have "officially" returned. They want better ones.

Coincident with demobilisation is the re-appearance in the "Situations Vacant" columns of the newspapers of the legend which war time exigencies had temporarily quashed—"Previous experience essential." In a highly technical trade experience is essential, but in commercial life there is no reason why the enthusiastic returned soldier should not be given the same sporting chance to make good that was afforded the war-time "substitute."

Which attitude is more helpful to national prosperity—"I cannot employ you because you are not accustomed to this business," or "You have not done this work before, but as you are so keen I will give you a trial"?

Before the war a young man of my acquaintance was destined by his father to be a clerk in a timber merchant's office; it was a "safe job." Unfortunately the young man did not like clerical work, although he gave satisfaction to his employer. In vain his father pointed out that if he stuck to his work he might become cashier, or even secretary. The son did not want to be either—he wanted to be a commercial traveller.

When he was old enough to assert himself he resigned his post in the timber merchant's office and tried to realise his ambition. Wherever he applied he received the same refusal, "You have neither a trade connection nor experience as a commercial traveller." In vain he pleaded "Give me a sample-case, pay my travelling expenses and a commission on all orders I take, and leave it to me to make good." He returned to clerical work, and his father said "I told you so!"

Later he left to go into the Army. He will probably return to a clerk's desk and then try again for the work he wants to do. Will he encounter the old prejudice?

His case is only one of thousands. To the soldier the fine-sounding promises of the politician means but one thing—a better job. Therefore "Previous experience essential" bars the way for the man who wishes to exchange uncongenial for congenial work.

British employers will help themselves and the returning soldier by applying to business the fact that the war was won by inexperienced but audaciously vigorous youth directed by ripe experience.

The policy of turning a man down because he "had never done the work before" helped to endanger our pre-war grip on the world's commerce. We can only recover it by fostering enterprise instead of turning it adrift with the rebuff "Previous experience essential."

SIDNEY HOWARD.

31 January 1919

This is a most wonderful April. It is the first we have had since 1914, for although in the intervening years the month was called by the same name, though the sun was as bright and the buds as green, spring brought not joy but only an "offensive."

SPRING COMES TO TOWN.

"When that Aprille with his shoures sote
The drought of March hath perced to the rote,
Than longen folk to gon on pilgrimages
And palmers for to seken strange strondes."
—Prologue: The Canterbury Tales.

The Englishman of 1919 is the Englishman of whom Chaucer wrote more than five centuries ago: April still sets him a-fret.

This is a most wonderful April. It is the first we have had since 1914, for although in the intervening years the month was called by the same name, though the sun was as bright and the buds as green, spring brought not joy but only an "offensive."

But hope has come back this April. Never was there such a furbishing of motor cars, such a "tuning-up" of motor-bicycles, such a venturing out of cyclists, such a cry for cheaper fares by those who depend on railways.

Country folk may criticise the enthusiasm of townsfolk, but spring means much to those who gain their bread in cities. It is the time of exodus. Weary workers long for the open country, the spell of the streets is broken, the theatre no longer lures, the kinema that was so brilliant on winter nights stands revealed as shabby by the lingering sun.

Nature sends her messenger April into the city to wake up folk who might have forgotten her. Trees in even the dreariest squares poke buds under the noses of passers by to remind them.

The cuckoo calls in the country and is recorded in the newspapers as news. The crusty suburbanite declares that he "doesn't believe it," but talks inconsequently of "getting a house with a larger garden," although he knows such talk is folly.

Shopkeepers catch the infection. Their shop windows fill with such ravishing feminine things that pretty girls with appallingly empty purses talk of new frocks and bewail more piteously than at any other season the fact that the most adorably marriageable bachelors are as hard up as themselves, and that therefore marriage would bring not gorgeous "creations" but sterner efforts in the art of making old frocks "do."

Clerks look up from the ledgers at the sunshine that floods the office and say that the weeks "drag" but week-ends "fly." The meekest of them grows bold, approaches the director as he walks through the office, and asks, "What about our holidays, please? We should like to know so that we can arrange." The other clerks echo,"Yes, what about them? Please!"

"Bolshevism!" growls the director.

But it is really only Spring.

SIDNEY HOWARD.

4 April 1919

Opposite above left: **The 1st Battalion of the Scots Guard parade along Oxford Street on their return from Germany in March 1919.**

Opposite above right: **The first permanent war shrine was erected in Cirencester Street, West London.**

Opposite below: **Determined sightseers swarm up the gates of Green Park to watch the Victory Parade in July 1919.**

Top: **This US contingent are just some of the 15,000 troops who took part in the Victory Parade through the capital on 19 July 1919. It was part of a planned four-day celebration including Thanksgiving Services and festivals.**

Upper middle: **The first Armistice Day commemoration was held on 11 November 1919. As crowds gathered in London these passengers watch from a bus at Bank.**

Lower middle: **The Armistice Silence is observed at Piccadilly Circus.**

Right: **Memorials to unknown British soldiers. On Armistice Day in 1920, the body of an unknown soldier, exhumed from a French battlefield, was carried in a procession through London to the Cenotaph, where a two-minute silence was observed. It was then taken into Westminster Abbey, passing through a guard of honour of 100 Victoria Cross recipients and buried in the Abbey using soil from the battlefields and given a Belgian black marble memorial stone. Over one million people visited the grave in the first week.**

Published by Atlantic Publishing in 2014

Atlantic Publishing
38 Copthorne Road, Croxley Green
Hertfordshire, WD3 4AQ, UK

Photographs and Newspaper facsmilies
© Daily Mail Historical Archive, Associated Newspapers Ltd.

Volume copyright © Atlantic Publishing

A catalogue record for this book is available
from the British Library.

ISBN 978-1-909242-70-8 (HB)
ISBN 978-1-909242-60-9 (PB)

Printed in China

Acknowledgements:

Newspaper photography: Harry Chambers
Editorial production: Alison Gauntlett

Thanks to: Morag McFarland and all at Solo Syndication
Thanks also to: John Dunne, Sarah Rickayzen, Lyn Mellor, Mel Cox and Alan Pinnock

Daily Mail Historical Archive produced by Cengage Learning

For further information please visit:
http://gale.cengage.co.uk/daily-mail-historical-archive.aspx.